Social Care Management, Strategy and Business Planning

of related interest

Enhancing Social Work Management
Theory and Best Practice from the UK and USA
Edited by Jane Aldgate, Lynne Healy, Barris Malcolm, Barbara Pine, Wendy Rose and Janet Seden
ISBN 978 1 84310 515 2

Leadership in Social Care
Edited by Zoë van Zwanenberg
ISBN 978 1 84310 969 3
Research Highlights in Social Work

Handbook for Practice Learning in Social Work and Social Care
Knowledge and Theory
2nd edition
Edited by Joyce Lishman
ISBN 978 1 84310 186 4

Professional Risk and Working with People
Decision-making in Health, Social Care and Criminal Justice
David Carson and Andy Bain
ISBN 978 1 84310 389 9

Partnerships in Social Care
A Handbook for Developing Effective Services
Keith Fletcher
ISBN 978 1 84310 380 6

Competence in Social Work Practice
A Practical Guide for Students and Professionals
2nd edition
Edited by Kieron O'Hagan
ISBN 978 1 84310 485 8

The Post-Qualifying Handbook for Social Workers
Edited by Wade Tovey
ISBN 978 1 84310 428 5

Managing Children's Homes
Developing Effective Leadership in Small Organisations
Leslie Hicks, Ian Gibbs, Helen Weatherly and Sarah Byford
ISBN 978 1 84310 542 8
Costs and Effectiveness of Services for Children in Need

Social Care Management, Strategy and Business Planning

Trish Hafford-Letchfield

Jessica Kingsley *Publishers*
London and Philadelphia

First published in 2010
by Jessica Kingsley Publishers
116 Pentonville Road
London N1 9JB, UK
and
400 Market Street, Suite 400
Philadelphia, PA 19106, USA

www.jkp.com

Copyright © Trish Hafford-Letchfield 2010

Library of Congress Cataloging in Publication Data
Hafford-Letchfield, Trish.
  Social care management, strategy and business planning / Trish Hafford-Letchfield.
    p. cm.
  Includes bibliographical references and index.
  ISBN 978-1-84310-986-0 (alk. paper)
  1. Social work administration. 2. Strategic planning. I. Title.
  HV41.H244 2010
  361.3068--dc22
                          2010006371

British Library Cataloguing in Publication Data
A CIP catalogue record for this book is available from the British Library

ISBN 978 1 84310 986 0

Printed and bound in Great Britain by
MPG Books Group

Dedication

For Ted, Katie, Mum, Dad, Anne and Uncle Albert

Contents

Acknowledgements

Having worked with a number of inspiring people throughout my career, most of what I have learnt or achieved is due to them. A special mention is given to just some of my colleagues for their unrelenting support and encouragement: Kate Leonard, Paul Dugmore, Priscilla Dunk, Steve Trevillion, Sharon Lambley, Jacky Grant, Jill Yates, Ann Flynn, Wendy Couchman, Justin McDermott, Diana Bourn and all my wonderful colleagues at Middlesex University. Apologies to those of you who I have inevitably but unwittingly left out. Thanks to Steve Jones at Jessica Kingsley for his patience and humour whilst writing this book.

I am grateful to those who have granted permission to reprint valuable materials. Every effort has been made to acknowledge the sources of this work. Any notifications of omissions or errors in acknowledgement are gratefully received. With thanks for permissions from:

Department of Health
Figure 2.1 The process for assessing need in the community
Figure 6.1 Institute of Public Care joint commissioning model for public care
Table 7.1 Contradictions in performance measurement

Improvement and Development Agency
Figure 3.2 Building a business case
Figure 3.3 'Top tips' in undertaking equality impact assessments
Table 6.1 Commissioning at different levels

Charities Evaluation services
Figure 6.3 Charities Evaluation Services planning triangle

Professor Lyn Macdonald for allowing me to reprint information from her website for Chapter 10:
Families and Schools Together: A social intervention programme evaluated using RCTs

Introduction

The title and contents of this book reflect a number of current key debates going on in social work and social care. They acknowledge the many tensions between 'management' and 'professionals' where the deployment of business sector principles within the environment of care are already well engrained. Over the last few years, I have had the privilege of teaching on a number of leadership and management programmes. Leadership and management education in social work and social care inevitably involves looking at the knowledge and skills that managers need in order to be effective in their organisations, and to become what Thompson (2003) refers to as an 'effective organisational operator' (p.198). The introduction of market and, subsequently, business principles into care environments since the 1980s has meant that its associated language and terminology has deeply permeated current management 'speak'. Even in my own experience as a manager I have found myself talking uncritically about quality and performance management issues and getting 'value for money' or working 'in a sustainable way'. Managers and staff I have worked with, however, have struggled with some of these concepts. This also reflects the lack of appropriate literature in this area, or a knowledge base about the strategic and business planning aspects of a social care manager's role that speaks directly to her or his own experiences and learning needs. Whilst there needs to be a degree of ownership of managers of such 'speak' in relation to strategy and business planning, we still have a long way to go to ease relations between government and local leadership, which enables managers really to engage comfortably with what they are being asked to implement on the ground.

Management is essentially a practical activity and particular aspects of social care make this role unique, setting it apart from other more traditional roles or other sectors. Managers continue to be dynamic in engaging with the debates about how best to manage services in what is a very challenging environment. This is the essence of professionalism and points to the need for a multi-layered approach to service development. Most managers do not become managers in a planned way and it would not be uncommon for even experienced managers to be reading more closely in hindsight about some of the issues outlined in this book for the first time. Recognising that preparation for management begins much earlier in an individual's life emphasises the need to recognise the value of the manager's knowledge, skills and value base emerging from their prior experience of direct practice. This expertise should be valued as it can be shared across the networks we work within as well as sharing up and down the hierarchies in our organisations and provides a powerful means of building organisational knowledge and capital. No one would probably dispute that we need to get better at developing strategies in care services in a way that helps us plan for getting the most out of what we have to work with. This move is inevitable in the face of increasing demands and rising expectations for quality services.

There are already a growing number of well-written texts which offer a comprehensive analysis of social work and social care management. These provide robust critiques of the managerialist approaches that have subsequently developed with the advent of neoliberalism in public services (Clarke and Newman 1997). This book does not aim to reiterate or indeed challenge these important analyses. The specific aim of this book is to try to make the whole issue of business planning a more accessible and friendly process, and to acknowledge the values and ethics inherent to managing it in the care sector. In covering some of the theoretical concepts underpinning the effective management of care services, it also incorporates a 'how to' approach around a range of different but, it is hoped, relevant topics. Therefore, I hope you find that it reflects some of the key critical debates and issues in social care, as well as offering very practical and helpful advice on how to tackle some of the everyday tasks involved in managing your team, service or organisation.

The first three chapters provide an overall introduction to the concepts of strategy and business planning in social care. Chapter 1 examines the evolving policy environment in which integration of services are being promoted at both the vertical and horizontal levels. Chapter 2 looks at the notion of developing strategic planning where principles of strategising are explored within the context of devolvement versus central government control. To provide a meaningful strategy, one needs to focus not only on the outcomes specified in government legislation and policy but also on those outcomes which meet the needs of the local community and are determined by their involvement in defining these. Working with stakeholders to redesign and develop services to meet the needs of the local community begins with the process of 'business' development, which is the subject of Chapter 3. In turn, the process of developing a business plan will draw on a wide spectrum of skills including resource and financial management, as covered in Chapter 4, and project management skills in Chapter 5.

The central role that commissioning plays in strategy and business planning has only relatively recently been properly recognised within mainstream management. Whilst not many managers would view themselves as commissioners, Chapter 6 aims to illuminate the different roles that operational managers have to play in the commissioning cycle alongside others within a strategic partnership. The latter chapters then go on to focus on some of the more detailed aspects of business planning. Chapter 7 examines the development of quality assurance, and indicators and methods for performance measurement to inform decision-making. Chapter 8 looks at decision-making as probably one of the most important functions of management overall, as at whatever level the decision is required, there are certain fundamental considerations that have to be made if the process is to be effective and successful.

It is often assumed that managers are supposed to act rationally, which fails to take into account the practical limitations of managerial decision-making; the impact of power and situational constraints as well as opportunities and best practice. Pulling some of these issues together under the heading of risk analysis and risk management is then covered in Chapter 9. Managers and professionals working in social care not only have to consider the needs, wants and rights of service users when making decisions; they also have to consider a range of issues, such as resource allocation, efficiency, values and equalities, legislation, policy and practice guidance and professional codes of practice (General Social Care Council 2002), to mention just a few. As a management activity, evaluation is an integral part of the cycle of strategising, business planning and decision-making and is therefore the subject of Chapter 10. Managers are likely to be at the interface between the many procedures and operations involved in making judgements about the value of alternative courses of action within a wide organisational context. The search for ways to improve the performance of care services is reflected in many different initiatives to measure performance or to set standards.

Finally, I am grateful to those individual managers who have read the different chapters in the drafting of this book and took time to offer their comments and advice from the 'coalface' so to speak. You will find 'Manager's comments' at the end of all chapters, where practising managers offer their perspective on the different topics and give examples from their own organisations.

CHAPTER 1

Thinking about the Legislative and Policy Environment for Social Care

By the end of this chapter, you should be able to:

- appreciate the legislative and policy context within which strategising and business planning takes place
- identify the current strategic goals driving care environments
- identify the range of contentious issues and debates between the state, care organisations and the social work and social care profession in taking the government's agenda forward.

Introduction

This chapter sets out the legislative and policy context for developing strategy and business plans in social care. It focuses particularly on social policy and its interaction with other key public policies such as education, health, social inclusion, public regeneration and crime. A fast-changing and indeed turbulent legislative and policy environment poses a number of complex challenges, particularly with regard to the importance of establishing strategic goals. Legislation and policy documents, which address individuals and groups in the community using care services, have stressed the need to improve outcomes for service users through shared assessment, joint resourcing and joint financing and the appropriate targeting of services (Cabinet Office 2000; Department for Education and Skills 2005; Department of Health 2008a).

It is an understatement to say that all organisations in health and social care are affected by their political, economic, legal and social contexts. Changing demands from stakeholders, and service user and carers' expectations of social care services are a significant driver of the way in which services are now commissioned and provided (Beresford and Croft 2003). At a government level, the impact of the national comprehensive spending review and the increasing regulatory environment heavily influences the core business of social care, necessitating constant dialogue between the state, care organisations and the social work and social care profession in taking this agenda forward (Department for Education and Skills 2005; Department of Health 2008a, 2008b; HM Treasury 2007). The development of care trusts and the emphasis on partnerships and planning between statutory, third and private sectors have directed social care and its partner organisations towards a greater focus on the autonomy and independence of service users within a social inclusion framework (Department of Health 2008a, 2008b). The modernisation of health and social care services (Department of Health 1998) sought to use a particular process of bringing public services into alignment with changes. This is based on the view that services were of insufficient quality, inflexible, overly bureaucratic and unresponsive, based on institutional needs rather than those of the individual (Clarke 2004). The subsequent restructuring of care services has largely displaced large-scale social services hierarchies, shifting the balance towards far greater integration of traditional organisations as we previously knew them. Further, government policy seeks to exploit the potential of empowering a wider range of people with support needs through increasing community involvement to develop approaches to care in which people themselves become genuinely part of their own caring communities (Means, Richards and Smith 2008). Such philosophy fits with its strategy for regeneration, neighbourhood renewal and social cohesion.

Discernable trends in approaches can therefore be seen in how services have been led and managed. This is not without controversy, however. Tensions have arisen where these policy ideals conflict with the reality of practice and its ongoing developments. The most significant of these have been the impact of increasing marketisation and managerialism, particularly since the introduction of the neoliberalist policies of the Conservative government during the 1990s and the subsequent discourse of Labour's 'modernisation' (Cabinet Office 2000; Department of Health 1998).

This chapter gives a brief contextual overview of these issues. It explores the current environment in which social care strategy and business planning is taking place and the simultaneous proliferation of terms and concepts which have consequently been drawn from the business sector. Throughout this book we will be critically examining these terms and concepts and seeking to identify to what extent they can be ethically and meaningfully applied to social care particularly from the perspective of managers and their organisations. Needless to say, managers have to deal with a range of conflicts and constraints operating at the level of practice where approaches to strategy and business planning have unquestioningly utilised business sector principles. This is a contested area and, as we shall see, remains open to considerable debate. At a strategic level, according to Needham (2009), the relationship between central and local government in the UK has been adversarial for several decades as the centre has stripped powers away and enforced tighter control in the name of decentralisation.

> A range of new institutional forms have been created or expanded: quangos, foundation hospitals, academy schools, housing associations, business improvement districts in which Local Authorities are sidelined. At the same time, an elaborate apparatus of quality assurance and performance management has closely controlled resource allocation, management practice and policy priorities at the local level. Interest in 'localism' and decentred policy solutions from across the political spectrum, more recently may be suggestive of a counter-trend, a willingness to delink centre/local narratives and prioritise. (Needham 2009, p.39)

Such trends indicate the need to develop critical management practice in the face of political, professional and organisational environments that have the potential to enable as well as disable progress.

Marketisation and the modernisation of social care services

Managing in care settings is qualitatively different from managing in other contexts. Managers do, however, find themselves addressing real tensions and issues such as how to manage the cost effectiveness, quality and performance of their service in line with government policy and its prescribed outcomes for care. These have to be delivered within tight political timescales balanced with ethical and practice dilemmas. Managers are also vital keepers and shapers of the modern welfare state where regardless of the socio-political and economic framework, they remain committed to bringing the highest quality of life to those who face multiple inequalities or experience complex needs (Weiner 1994). One of the fundamental issues facing care services is the need to adjust to a climate which promotes fundamental human rights and citizenship. This is exemplified by the growing power of service users challenging the attitudes of those providing services alongside the growth of the consumer movement brought about by new public sector management (NPM) reforms and managerialism (Aldgate and Dimmock 2003).

The term 'managerialism' is generally viewed in social care as a negative or derogatory one indicating a blinkered approach to applying straightforward business management to care environments. NPM, on the other hand, implies that modernisation of public services embodies something of greater value. It cites public sector values within its role of developing society where public sector bodies need to behave in a more consultative and transparent way to get the greatest benefit from resources available (Waine and Henderson 2003). Research examining the differences between public and private management has attempted to investigate the notion of 'publicness' (Greener 2009). Boyne (2002) also cites differences in factors between these two sectors such as the environment, its goals, structures and values but finds convincing support limited to only a few of these. One aspect of public organisations discussed in more policy-oriented research is the impact of professionalism, given that public sector organisations often have strong, established professionals working within them. This expert knowledge and professional power presents a number of tensions within organisational dynamics:

> The difference is that public managers have moved from a focus and concern with the process of their jobs, particularly in relation to their conduct and their ability to follow rules and normative standards of behaviour, towards one concerned with results; whereas private managers have moved from a focus upon results towards one increasingly concerned with conduct. There is a movement towards a meeting in the middle; but from different directions. (Greener 2009, p.18)

Within those public services with responsibility for care, two concerns, financial and organisational, informed the radical changes brought about by the Conservative government in the 1980s: first, criticism of welfare professionals and concern about rising costs of care and second, concerns about the 'disciplinary' state and the recognition of service users' voices in shaping services via the user movement. The Conservative government's concern to control growing public expenditure on health and social care meant that they took a critical view of waste and inappropriate targeting of resources identified in various reports (Audit Commission 1986; Griffiths 1988). Organisational bureaucracies were seen as inefficient and unresponsive to consumers (Clarke and Newman 1997). The idea that market efficiency rather than collective planning was the best way of ensuring efficiency, accountability and choice, was at the heart of government policy objectives.

Major structural changes epitomised in the Children Act 1989 and the National Health Service and Community Care Act 1990 separated purchasing and providing functions in the National Health Service and social services departments (SSDs) and established different business units.

It defined the role of SSDs as 'enabling' authorities, as purchasers and contractors, and worked to secure delivery of services away from their traditional role of direct provision. Key management themes identified during this period were an emphasis on the 'three Es' (economy, efficiency and effectiveness); the establishment of market conditions and the desire to redesign organisational processes around the needs of service users and other stakeholders. Significant relationships were reframed with users becoming 'customers' within customer relationship management approaches. Kirkpatrick (2007) has questioned whether these changes have been as thorough as we are often led to believe. In his view, management practices themselves have not been transformed, as there remains a significant gap between the theory and practice of strategic management in social services. The drive to externalise services to the private sector were seen as offering better services for the same or reduced costs. Applications of businesslike approaches to welfare provision raised issues about the quality of care and safeguards where partners from the private sector were principally concerned with profit-making (Hafford-Letchfield 2009).

Following the election of New Labour in 1997, far from reversing the direction of the Conservatives, the government moved on to a new level on a similar theme citing modernisation or the 'Third Way' as the means of updating services to match expectations of modern-day consumers (McLaughlin 2009). This involved setting explicit targets for public services with the emphasis on more effective means of improving standards but with less emphasis on competition. Democratic renewal through enhanced public participation has been a key concern of the Labour government. A focus has been placed on greater 'joining up' across central government, and between local government and other stakeholders, including local communities themselves, to develop better and more responsive processes of governance and service delivery, especially in the most deprived areas (Cabinet Office 2000; Pemberton and Mason 2008). In conceptual terms it has been argued that the role of the state should increasingly be viewed as one of 'steering and regulating' rather than 'rowing and providing' (Rose 2000). Professional 'tribalism' was portrayed as a key barrier to organisational effectiveness and efficiency (Flynn 1999). The continuing attack on the dominance of providers whilst seeking to sharpen accountability and looking for business solutions to social policy problems was noted by Newman (2001). He observes that this move from tight centralised control to a greater use of scrutiny, inspection, evaluation and audit has resulted in greater delegated authority for local managers who, at the same time, became more constrained by performance targets.

The New Labour government's programme of social and economic reconstruction is connected to the idea of user choice, equality, citizenship and empowerment, but at the same time there has been continuing privatisation of welfare and promotion of managerialism. Transforming the provision of passive support to one that is more active in supporting people to promote their independence has led to a range of initiatives designed to address inequality, poverty and social exclusion. The benefits of interprofessional arrangements found within youth justice, community safety and the formation of care trusts have also led to a significant reorientation of social work and social care with particular implications for the management and development of its workforce (Department for Education and Skills 2006; Department of Health 2009a).

There has been great criticism of managerialism as a set of beliefs and practices that assume better management will resolve a range of economic and social problems and reflects the dominance of market capitalism in the world (Dominelli 2002). The salient features of managerialism include:

- defining users as customers and consumers
- the central importance of 'management' as a mechanism to drive quality, efficiency and effectiveness
- the dominance of management knowledge and expertise which supersedes expertise in professional practice and professional specialisms. Professionals are likewise expected to undertake management tasks within the organisation
- the use of managerial skills to improve quality of services and performance in human services and the concern with inefficiencies produced by political interference
- the influence of the market economy on decision-making over other organisational or community interests
- The belief that setting standards, redesigning accountability and incentive systems, will improve lead to improved quality and performance.

Excessive proceduralism has emerged from the government's characterisation of professionals as paternalistic and self-interested and the drive to protect users' interests via audit, quality monitoring and other techniques (Gilbert 2005; Holmes *et al.* 2009). We shall look at this debate in later chapters, for example in the way that some technological developments in social care have led to the diversion of professional responsibilities to meeting organisational needs above those of service users (Burton and Van den Broek 2009).

Whole-systems approaches – service specialisms and horizontal integration

> Ultimately, every locality should seek to have a single community-based support system focussed on the health and well-being of the local population. Binding together local government, primary care, community-based health provision, public health, social care and the wider issues of housing, employment, benefits advice and education/training. (Department of Health 2008b, p.2)

Further reforms in the twenty-first century aim to connect services directly to people and shape the services around their personal needs. Long-term transformation of social care services and its partners is evidenced in the policy and legislation for children's and adults' services, both of which have 10- to 15-year implementation programmes. These transformations were initially spelt out in the following documents: *Every Child Matters* (HM Government 2003), the Children Act 2004, *Independence, Wellbeing and Choice* (Department of Health 2005a), *Youth Matters* (Department for Children, Schools and Families 2005b) amongst many others, such as those in the field of housing, substance misuse and crime. These documents provide a parallel focus in political, structural and managerial terms. First, in local government, was the appointment of directors of children's services across education, health and social services by integrating services across these domains to coordinate the approach to meeting the needs of all children and young people. This built on many initiatives already in place such as Sure Start, Connexions and Headstart. For example the Sure Start approach, launched in 1999, placed a strong emphasis on joining up and improving mainstream services in the most deprived areas of the country, in order to better prepare young children for school by enhancing their health, wellbeing and education. It involved parents and carers in the co-delivery of professionally designed services (Pemberton and Mason 2008). Current transformation of children's services is characterised by a tight and ambitious implementation timetable over ten years with the following five key outcomes for children and their families:

- being healthy
- staying safe
- enjoying and achieving
- making a positive contribution
- achieving economic wellbeing.

Second, the White Paper, *Our Health, Our Care, Our Say* (Department of Health 2006a), and the local authority circular, *Transforming Social Care* (Department of Health 2008a) and concordat, *Working to Put People First* (Department of Health 2008b) have set in motion radical changes to personalise services. These papers stimulated debate and encourage stakeholders to engage in a process that transforms the way social care is viewed. Social care has increasingly been delivered by a range of providers, many of which now lie outside the direct line-management structure of social services. The statutory function of the director of social services as defined in the Local Authority Social Services Act 1970 was amended to reflect structural changes in social care and the need to influence a range of service providers beyond the immediate scope of SSDs to deliver the government's vision. Joint appointments of directors with other organisations, such as primary care trusts, have since promoted strategic responsibilities for the planning, commissioning and delivery of services to all adult groups. The outcomes for adult services are:

1. improved health and emotional wellbeing

2. improved quality of life

3. making a positive contribution

4. increased choice and control

5. freedom from discrimination or harassment. (Department of Health 2006a)

According to Hudson (2005b) reform of organisational strategies and structures in social care uncritically endorses the concepts of 'choice' and 'autonomy', which sits uncomfortably with parallel concerns about ensuring cost effectiveness. Implementation strategies to make these ideas a reality have to ensure that the identified outcomes are underpinned by the means by which a coherent integrated approach is required. This starts with inter-agency governance at a national level, moving down through integrated strategy and process to the front line where delivery of services takes place through social care and its partners.

Some pieces of legislation exhort or command authorities to work together, but without changing the organisational structures through which they should do so. An example of a more forceful approach is exemplified in the Community Care (Delayed Discharges) Act 2003, where delays in moving people ready for discharge from hospital back into the community with care provision can result in a local fine for local authorities. These legislative and policy moves have attempted to break down the barriers which have unhelpfully fragmented and often frustrated the way in which people's needs are met. However, barriers to improved coordination and collaboration remain and are reflected in occupational cultures, lack of clarity about roles and disputes over responsibility. Whilst a coordinated approach to working with community need is required, collaborative working arrangements have been undermined by, and remain vulnerable to, divergent ideologies or priorities, separate training, blurred roles and responsibilities, financial constraints, competitiveness and different views and approaches to service users (Preston-Shoot 2009). Recurring themes from public enquiries into system failures (Laming 2009; Stanley and Manthorpe 2004) suggest, therefore, that law and guidance are insufficient in themselves.

Similarly, a range of policy guidance emphasises corporate responsibility for children requiring protection and support (Department for Education and Skills 2006; Department of Health 2000) and in relation to safeguarding adults, where an appropriate balance between safeguarding and personalisation needs to be established (Department of Health 2009a). Interprofessional knowledge and skills are seen as essential to good quality decision-making and an inter-agency collaborative model has been promoted to ensure an effective service response. The role and responsibilities of different stakeholders promoted through inter-agency training and protocols are seen as the means by which working collaboratively will be valued, tasks and responsibilities appreciated, communication improved and intervention integrated at strategic and individual case levels (Preston-Shoot 2009).

In summary, the government regards integration as a remedy for the fragmentation of services, which has been identified as a barrier to more effective care. A simpler, more user-friendly system is required, with a greater continuity of services and a single point of access wherever possible. Integration is seen as the means to this end. In this vein, the National Health Service Plan in 2000 called for a radical redesign of the whole care system announcing its vision to integrate key services within a single organisational focus (Department of Health 2005a). Government requirements in relation to integration, however, are now much more specific: 'By 2008 we expect all PCTs and local authorities to have established joint health and social care managed networks and/or teams to support those people with long-term conditions who have the most complex needs' (Department of Health 2006a, p.116). The key feature of an integrated service is that it acts as a service hub for the community by bringing together a range of services, usually under one roof, whose practitioners then work in a multi-agency way to deliver integrated support. The integration of services and the work of professionals to deliver better outcomes for the public is therefore a long-established goal.

Expectations of improvement are clear, with an emphasis on early intervention, prevention and support in the community (Care Services Improvement Partnership 2009). Some of these reforms are driven by the demographic challenges presented by both an ageing society and the rising expectations of those depending on social work and social care for their capacity to lead more full and purposeful lives. This has included the need to explore options for the long-term funding of a care and support system, to ensure that it is fair, sustainable and unambiguous about the respective responsibilities of the state, family and individual (HM Government 2007a). Personalising services in a way that can respond to the circumstances, strengths and aspirations for particular children, adults and families requires joint strategic needs assessment by the relevant statutory bodies, which actively engages other stakeholders in a local area agreement and supports social enterprise and sustainable community development. This sort of transformation involves working across boundaries in social care, such as housing, benefits, leisure, transport and health. In organisational terms, every area is expected to create forums, networks and task groups to involve staff across the sectors, and service users and carers as active participants in the design and change process.

The role of leadership and management

The above section has provided a brief overview of the current environment in which the need for strategy and business planning in social care has emerged and developed. As we shall see, throughout this book, the notion of a 'market' in care remains problematic, and strategic goals driving care environments have also given rise to a range of contentious issues and debates. The principles of market competition, for example, have affected traditional voluntary sector organisations (since known as the third sector) and radically altered their traditional relationships with statutory services from grant support to one of contracting and service specification. According to many critics, this has substantially reduced their campaigning and impartial role in representing the community at a grass roots level (Jones and Novak 1999). From a postmodernist viewpoint (Lawler and Bilson 2010) the intensification of some modern ways of thinking and their translation into organisational and management practices have challenged traditionally accepted orthodoxies in previous social care delivery through more rational examination and explanation.

Despite the above context, there has been a general limitation in the capacity to plan in social care, particularly one which is based on robust evidence. This is related not only to resource constraints but to the level of expertise in social services departments. A rapidly changing environment tends to lend itself to a much more incremental approach rather than any long-term planning on the achievement of outcomes for both adults and children's services. The complex role of management in taking strategic goals forward is recognised in the relatively recent development of leadership and management national standards in UK social care (National Skills Academy for Social Care 2009; Skills for Care 2008). Functional areas of management described as 'managing self' and 'personal skills'; 'providing direction'; 'facilitating change'; 'working with people'; 'using resources' and 'achieving results' provide a framework in which a unique mix of learning opportunities, qualifications and work-based learning can be provided. Any leadership and management development framework within the 'business' of care also has to emphasise social and moral practice over the technical, specialised activities of managers. This was identified in the final report of the Social Work Taskforce:

> We have heard about excellent practice in management and supervision. However, we are also concerned about the overall quality and consistency of frontline management, and the pressures under which managers and supervisors are working, on a number of counts. Professional supervision is often inadequate because line managers do not have access to training and development to help them to carry it out well. Even where training is available, managers are often too busy once in post to take it up. It is rare for the training offered to frontline managers to focus on how they support practitioners in becoming resilient in dealing with the emotional impact of the work, or on how they manage the performance of staff. In both areas, managers report feeling inadequately prepared. Time pressures on managers, and high numbers of staff reporting to them without any method for mitigating this, result in a need to focus narrowly on tasks and processes, and on meeting indicators, at the expense of concentrating on outcomes for service users and the quality of service. (Department for Children, Schools and Families and Department of Health 2009a, p.32)

The skills we might expect to see people developing in social care are more likely to be social, political, cultural and rhetorical skills (Hafford-Letchfield et al. 2008). In Chapter 2, we will look more closely at the use of political skills, which gives managers the ability to effectively understand others at work, and to use such knowledge to influence others to act in ways that enhance personal and organisational objectives (Mintzberg 1985). By working with and through others, managers can become more effective at networking, coalition-building and creating social capital. These are not skills that are necessarily or specifically taught on a management development programme but emerge through the development of tacit knowledge and its application to management practice (Hafford-Letchfield *et al.* 2008).

Managers have to deal with a range of conflicts and constraints operating at the level of practice. Professional discretion can be used in the form of 'quiet challenges' (White 2009, p.129) to resist managerialist expectations not considered in the interest of service users. Relationships between professionals and their managers are often described as antagonistic, obscuring the extent to which local managers might resist the prevailing business culture through the ways in which they interpret policy and co-operate with practitioners in structuring day-to-day practice (Department of Children, Schools and Families and Department of Health 2009b; Harris and White 2009). Proposed changes in leadership and management development have acknowledged, within the national standards and frameworks, the need for new structures to respond to shifting boundaries and shifting dependency, as well as those where managers have to take on some entrepreneurial roles and a 'customer'-orientated focus.

Following this introductory chapter, the remaining chapters in this book are going to pick up on some of these issues by moving you through the different aspects of developing a strategy and business plan in a reflective and critical way, as well as assisting you with the more practical aspects. Before moving on to these, however, we turn to address one specific issue which, whilst integral to the book as a whole, merits special attention. It is an important contextual issue that underpins all areas of strategy and business planning, as well as its critiques.

Co-production and changing roles for service users

Managers and professionals' relationships with the state have been well documented in the social work and social care literature. Less but growing attention is being given to the everyday experience of this relationship and how we should understand and improve it (Mayo 2009). A number of academics have examined the nature of the relationship we have with service users and the different terms used to describe and articulate that relationship, for example 'service user', 'consumer', 'customer', 'client' or 'expert by experience'. Analysis of these different terms and the political and social circumstances behind their adoption highlight the hierarchical power positions involved (Carr 2004, 2007; McLaughlin 2009; Simmons, Powell and Greener 2009). These different terminologies extend from genuine moves towards user participation and involvement to more consumerist discourses within social care. A corresponding development of mechanisms to facilitate consumer-type choices by service users has been energetically advocated by successive governments as well as service users themselves (Beresford and Croft 2003; Carr 2007; Glendinning 2009). Pressures for innovation have come from service users' experiences and increasing expectations. The model of 'co-production' attempts to steer this middle path between professionals and users.

> The current state of consumerism within social care rests upon an uneasy synergy between highly influential, articulate 'bottom-up' user movement and the 'top-down' ambitions of successive governments to increase the penetration of market-related mechanisms into the public sector. (Glendinning 2009, p.178)

Rather than separating out the consumption and production of government services, co-production emphasises the role that service users play in both the consumption and production of public services by highlighting the interdependence of consumer-producer relationships (Needham 2007a). Co-production moves beyond 'engagement' and 'participation' in that it can involve service users and their communities being actively involved in first, shaping service planning and decision-making processes and second, being involved in the shaping of the actual service outcomes and how to deliver them. Co-production aims to move beyond simply being invited by professional and managerial staff from contributing ideas towards taking a more active lead in determining how services develop (Pemberton and Mason 2008). A range of recent policy initiatives can be seen as co-productive in nature, bringing service users more fully into the production of service outcomes, such as in the use of direct payments and individualised budgets. Other examples include expert patient programmes in the National Health Service, home–school contracts in education and a greater emphasis on community justice in policing. Needham (2007) identifies three distinct advantages of co-production over traditional bureau-professional models of service provision:

1. the recognition of front-line staff expertise and voice as a result of their regular interaction with service users

2. the potential relationship between citizens' attitudes and quality improvement through emphasis on users' agency and empowerment rather than dependence which enables individuals to become more civically minded and encourages them to develop other horizontal relationships and social capital

3. the emphasis of user input into the productive process which improves allocative efficiency, making front-line providers and their managers more sensitive to user needs and preferences. This forms the basis for more constructive interactions, and a focus on public values thus ending cycles of hostility.

When thinking about the changing role of service users it is important to recognise the differences in goals, structures and purposes of the different stakeholders within the process of strategy and business planning. Co-production takes place in a more intimate setting where professionals consult with service users about their support needs on an individual basis in partnership. The growing interest in co-production, therefore, is not only about resisting passive accounts of service users but has potential for more cost-effective service provision whilst giving more autonomy to service users. The role of managers in creating forums in which common ground can be articulated and services improved, emphasises the importance of dialogue, interaction and negotiation.

A review of the impact of user participation in England and Wales (Carr 2004) demonstrated that change and improvement of social care services is yet to be properly monitored and evaluated. The lack of organisational responsiveness and political commitment to service user participation is a critical issue where exclusionary structures, institutional practices and professional attitudes can affect the extent to which service users can influence change (Carr 2007). Throughout the planning process, user participation initiatives should be integral to decision-making within a supported partnership, as the issue is not one of representativeness but of inclusion (Postle and Beresford 2007). In conclusion, whatever discourse or language we use in relation to service users, it inevitably acts as a signifier of the power dimension in our relationships with them. It is thus essential to develop a continuous critical dialogue concerning the language we use by deconstructing it and unearthing any assumptions made (McLaughlin 2009, p.1114).

Users have many of the characteristics and qualities that we associate with good leaders, given that user and carer movements evolved through the initiative, determination, foresight, direction and vision of individuals coming together to bring about change (Hafford-Letchfield *et al.* 2008). Within business planning activities, leaders and managers have a responsibility to draw upon the expertise and experiences of users, including putting in place structures and support to enable participation. Setting this context is therefore very relevant, as co-production is a complex concept with a range of implications for the different issues we shall subsequently go on to examine in this book. From a strategic point of view, many of the limitations of co-production include institutional resistance and there is a need to overcome resource-based and cultural constraints. The provision of social care is an iterative and negotiated process and, as we saw earlier, it also recognises the importance of collaborative relationships in delivering the service outcomes central to government policy.

> If co-production is to improve outcomes in social care, it will be at the 'transformative' level, avoiding versions of co-production that simply cut costs, demand compliance or reproduce power relations. (Needham and Carr 2009, p.17)

Chapter summary

This chapter has set out the legislative and policy context for developing strategy and business planning in social care. It has outlined the various strands of dominant thinking about what is unique or different about social care and thus the inherent tensions involved in incorporating private sector managerial techniques into customer-focused organisation run by professional managers. The coexistence of administration and professionalism within the development of care services has become increasingly uneasy with the move towards neoliberalist management and the role of the market in undermining the position of public sector professionals, which is sometimes seen as secondary to management (Harris and White 2009). The different moral foundations and differences can be difficult to establish empirically at times but the quality of leadership and management within social work and social care services is crucial for ensuring social justice and equality, as well as for economic and social reasons. It is hoped these issues will become more apparent as we work through the different elements of the planning process.

Manager's comment

As discussed in this chapter, managers in social care play a significant role in shaping and leading on the quality of practice within a performance-managed and target-driven culture. This presents challenges and opportunities for front-line managers, many of whom seek to underpin developments within an ethical framework, which ensures that the needs of all stakeholders are considered in planning processes, especially those most vulnerable – that is, the service users.

Part of the process of making work meaningful and ethical depends on incorporating the views of stakeholders in strategic and business planning. Pressures will exist regarding time and resource constraints; however, having a balanced planning system which incorporates the views of all stakeholders ensures a more coordinated approach. It enables workers delivering the service and service users receiving services to take part in the 'ownership' of the service; therefore they are more willing to engage and implement the developments.

In my role I needed to develop a strategy for domestic abuse services, with the remit of certain policy 'givens' relating to the nature of the organisation. To do this I began by considering the legal definition of the issue, and the available research evidence. I addressed the organisational policy drivers and the national government drivers which were present, then thought about seeking the views of service users and workers. Service users in this regard are not a homogeneous group, and included children and young people, adult victims and adult perpetrators, all of whom had divergent needs and expectations of services.

Front-line managers and workers assisted in this process, by identifying groups of service users who were willing to share their views and experiences in the participation events. This aspect of the planning was crucial; and key to its success was the involvement of participation workers who brought resources and skills to the project. They facilitated the focus groups and participation strands of work. They also produced a DVD resource of children's views of service provision.

This DVD has had a significant impact on all stakeholders, enabling them to focus on the needs of particularly vulnerable and marginalised service users. The use of such resources has enabled the 'voice' of the service user, in this instance, the child, to remain central to the planning process. The inclusion of service users in this way is vital to the successful development of outcome-focused strategy and subsequent planning, and places the needs and outcomes for service users at its core. This process enables mangers to ensure that social care values and quality of intervention remains at the heart of social care strategy and planning.

Gwynn Raynes is a manager within the National Society for Parental Cruelty to Children (NSPCC) and has a national lead for the area of domestic abuse.

CHAPTER 2

Strategic Planning

By the end of this chapter, you should be able to:

- understand the key management processes for developing a vision for the organisation

- understand the nature of partnership work and the importance of participation in developing and taking forward a more inclusive strategy

- identify different management tools commonly used to assess the external and internal environments affecting your strategic direction

- consider the significance of participatory leadership styles and political skills for managing effective strategic planning.

Introduction

All managers in social care, at every level, need to be able to engage with the long-term view and develop a much broader perspective on how to go about shaping future services. As we saw in the previous chapter, this will involve extensive collaborative and partnership working at many different levels. Strategic planning is the broad means of achieving overall objectives (Rees and Porter 2003). This not only takes place at the level of government and through strategic partnership boards in a local area but it must also be led at a senior management level within the organisation in a way that successfully engages middle and first-line management level within a specific service, department or team. Strategic planning can be a top-down or bottom-up process but should ideally incorporate both. Many traditional ideas associated with strategy and business planning occupy a privileged position within generic management theory and practice. These are often presented as the embodiment of rational thinking that incorporates logic, planning, monitoring and technique. The increasing pace of change in public services, however, has caused a reaction against detailed centralised planning which can become overly cumbersome or prevent services being able to react flexibly enough. A major challenge for managers in social work and social care environments is in determining the organisation's strategic direction and assessing the external and internal forces or influences, but in a way that facilitates continuous adjustment within highly turbulent conditions.

The changing nature of social care means that any strategy needs to respond to:

- legislative, policy and political drivers for working across a very wide range of partnerships

- increasing choice and control through greater involvement of people who use services within service design and which addresses users' own purchasing power

- significant developments in demography by taking into account the specific nature of the local population, for example ageing, migration and diversity (to mention just a few)

- a paradigmatic shift in the delivery of services from public to the third sector and private sector

- sustainability

- economic factors in terms of the significance of social care in the overall economy

- the impact of technologies

- changes in the regulation and accountability of care services

- attracting and retaining a quality workforce with the right knowledge and skills to meet new types of working

- developing ethical leadership, management and human resource practice.

This might seem a tall order perhaps. But there is growing recognition of the vital contribution that effective political leadership can make to social care. Later on in this chapter we will look specifically at political skills which can be used to foster participatory and distributed leadership styles (Ferris *et al.* 2005; Skills for Care 2008) and which are much needed to take the above agenda forward.

There are a number of limitations that confront managers in developing effective local strategies. Current developments in social care tend to concentrate on the business of making strategic arrangements themselves with less reflection upon the politics of organisational and professional change and their ideological imperatives (Carnwell and Buchanan 2005). This can result in inadequate coordination of joint working arrangements and lack of resources at the local level. As we saw in Chapter 1, the general strategic direction has to date been unable to overcome the uneven and fragmented process of previous quasi-market regimes within such a fast pace of change. In addition, some local authorities are increasingly attempting to narrowly define the 'core business' of care (Commission for Social Care Inspection 2008), which goes against current policy emphasis on the 'community' in shaping response to social, cultural, economic and political forces and provision. Concerns about accountability and representation within the way in which consultation and the communication of decisions are undertaken within strategic formulation and implementation therefore remain (Glasby and Peck 2004).

This chapter looks at the notion of developing strategic planning through the use of an evidence-based rationale, highly contested in the relevant professions. We will look at the challenge of building a shared vision and working through conflicting visions in complex settings where people often have very different ideas about which priorities need to be reconciled. This process of planning and implementing strategies in order to create interpersonal, group, inter-group and organisation-wide changes (Improvement and Development Agency 2008) is often described as 'organisational development' (OD) and is an important part of strategic planning alongside its business aspects. There are a number of tools described in the management and OD literature that managers can draw on, including more creative approaches, for example by techniques used in appreciative inquiry (AI) (Cooperrider, Whitney and Stavros 2003) which are perhaps more suited to care environments.

Following on from the previous chapter we will examine the multi-faceted nature of modern care work that poses a challenge to any rational strategy formulation. The joint strategic needs assessment (JSNA) (Department of Health 2007a) is a more recent tool devised to inform the priorities and targets set against both short- and long-term objectives. In itself, this is not sufficient in order to demonstrate extensive participation in strategic planning. Poverty, deprivation and health are continuing and increasing problems for individuals, families and communities in some areas, as a result of the rising expectations for the range and quality of services. Questions have been raised over the sustainability of some policy directives, specifically community-based support (Ferguson 2007). Developing strategies within the context of devolvement versus central government control are just one of the contextual dilemmas for social care managers. To provide a meaningful strategy, one needs to focus not only on the outcomes specified in government legislation and policy but also on those outcomes which meet the needs of the local community and are determined by their involvement in defining these. Substantial support for the legitimate involvement of people using services within a model of participatory democracy must acknowledge the potential of both managers and staff working in organisations to work in appropriately supportive ways (Postle and Beresford 2007).

The benefits and limitations of strategic planning

Strategic planning serves a variety of purposes by:

- clearly defining the purpose or high-level vision of the organisation and making explicit the way in which its objectives and goals are consistent with this mission and capability for implementation

- providing a means of communicating those objectives and goals to both the organisation's members and the community in order to foster a sense of ownership and consensus

- establishing the most effective use of the organisation's resources by focusing these on its key priorities

- establishing a base from which progress can be measured and evaluated

- providing a bridge between vision and practice which is sometimes referred to as the 'glue' which keeps the people involved together.

The main focus of a strategic plan is usually on the bigger picture, whereas the focus of a business plan, as we will see in the following chapter is usually on a particular product, service or programme of work. There are a number of theories, perspectives, models and approaches on strategic planning. The way in which a strategic plan is developed and implemented, however, very much depends on the nature of leadership within the organisation and on its culture and values. Seden (2003), for example, restates the importance of understanding how an employing organisation works in order to get things done and recognising the central importance of power and influence of managers in relation to the organisation's structure and culture. Leading strategically is also dependent on the complexity of the task required and the social, economic, political, legal and technological environment. These in turn are dependent on organisational aspects such as size and resources available.

Within the research community there has been growing debate about the relevance of strategic theory to current care service environments. Several researchers and practitioners have argued that the pace of technological change, globalisation and the informational revolution have determined that many structural approaches to strategy and, to some extent, the traditional concept of strategy itself may no longer be valid (Farjoun 2005). When environments change quickly, some organisations may not be able to adjust, develop and deploy their resources before their longer-term strategies become obsolete. A good example of this can be seen in the pace of change that has arisen from the impact of the transformation and personalisation agenda (Department of Health 2008a, 2008b) on local commissioning and contracting arrangements. Being aware of both the potential for developing new or more specialised ways of supporting local people and the anticipation of huge cultural change required from providers can provide a number of threats and opportunities on which strategy has to be built. Being able to analyse and plan responses to such a grand design is critical both to the survival of many stakeholders in the transformational agenda and whether they can play a key part in the relatively new system (Sawyer 2008).

The example of domiciliary care providers illustrates this. Providers have spent years trying to ensure that services are delivered to predefined service specification led by a profession-dominated system in which people's needs are assessed and commissioned (Sawyer 2008). The shift in purchasing power now given to individuals with their own personalised budgets or direct payments to buy the services they consider will best help them to achieve their own priorities and outcomes requires significant support for both providers and individuals using services to make such transitions. This has implications for managers in both commissioning and for provider services where resources are scarce and often focused on day-to-day priorities. Effort is required to explore the potential to develop new services necessary to support culture change and to ensure success. This requires attention to transition processes that are realistic and which include strategies to support capacity and continuing financial viability.

Building a shared vision and developing direction

A vision is usually defined as a set of key objectives, which trigger the process of strategic planning and change. Usually we make transitions towards change in stages or in parallel processes where change happens at different times in each of the different systems contributing to the overall plan (Martin and Henderson 2001). Choices have to be made about whom, how, when and where. Whilst vision establishes the overall direction, there should be capacity for flexibility to respond to any consultation and outcomes from this to shape a more detailed planning process. Developing direction is essentially about clarifying the purpose of change and agreeing how to make the transition. Clarity is important as it will provide some broad guidance about the direction of travel, the values that underpin the vision of how change will occur and the framework that will enable decisions to be made. This does not have to be a mechanistic linear process but can be more 'organic'. The appreciative inquiry approach, for example, utilises a self-organising approach where people are brought together for dialogue around values and to share reflections around the current systems processes in a more positive way. Storyboard techniques and facilitating dialogue that focuses more on learning and less on method may move one away from mechanistic linear plans and formats to portray its strategic plan to stakeholders, as the following case study demonstrates:

Case study – an inclusive approach to developing vision

In 2007, Croydon Council ran a series of workshops enabling staff and partner organisations to identify the values that define the 'lifeblood' of the council. The exercise used appreciative inquiry where participants were encouraged to look at problems from a positive perspective. The evaluation of this method was seen as life-changing for people and facilitated energy in the workshops, which was palpable with lots of high energy, music and colour – very 'non Croydon' in a sense. Rooms were created like playrooms rather than traditional council offices. The values identified were made central to performance appraisal and embedded in an approach using multi-source feedback where managers involve a range of people in their relationships such as staff they manage and their own manager and peers in assessing and measuring how these values are demonstrated in practice. (Improvement and Development Agency 2008, p.10)

Care organisations are often guided by values expressed at a national level in government policies. Usually there is an emphasis on standards and accountability, and values are expressed in the outcomes expected. Outcomes have to meet the needs of the individual concerned as well as furthering the wellbeing of the community. The different stakeholders involved in developing a vision can have varying values or there may be a big difference between an organisation's espoused values with those enacted or put into practice. It is essential to have a good understanding and awareness of the issues involved in partnership working at a strategic level in order to create and sustain vision. We will now discuss these issues in more detail.

The nature of partnership – working at different levels

Starting at the broadest level, the Local Government and Public Involvement in Health Act 2007, Section 116 placed a duty on local authorities (LAs) and primary care trusts (PCTs) to undertake joint strategic needs assessments (JSNA). JSNA is a process which enables the identification of current and predicted needs regarding the health and wellbeing of local populations and which informs the priorities and targets set by local area agreements (LAAs) from which commissioning priorities can arise (Department of Health 2007a). *Our Health, Our Care, Our Say* (Department of Health 2006a), for example, identified the need for directors of public health, adult social care and children's services to undertake regular strategic needs assessments which enable local services to plan both short- and medium-term objectives. LAAs have up to 35 national priority targets, which are subject to performance monitoring with local partners who are encouraged to agree additional targets to support improved local outcomes.

The *Commissioning Framework for Health and Wellbeing* (Department of Health 2007b, p.5) builds on recent reforms, aiming for:

- a shift towards services that are personal, sensitive to individual need and that maintain independence and dignity

- a strategic reorientation towards promoting health and wellbeing, for example investing now to reduce future ill-health costs

- a stronger focus on commissioning the services and interventions that will achieve better health, across health services and local government, with everyone working together to promote inclusion and tackle health inequalities.

A JSNA is defined as a process which identifies current and future needs for health and wellbeing in light of existing services and informs future service planning, taking into account evidence of effectiveness. It identifies the bigger picture, including any inequalities and aggregated needs, meaning that it is not really that useful for planning at an individual level. Whilst the process is coordinated by upper-tier management, contribution from a much wider range of stakeholders is vital, for example local public, private and third sectors and members of the community. An outline of the process for undertaking a JSNA is illustrated in the figure below.

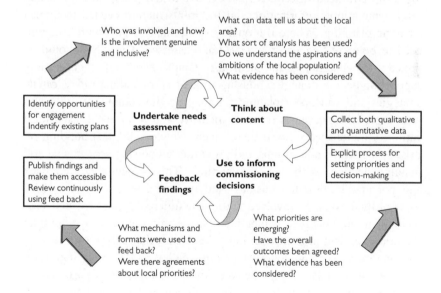

Figure 2.1 The process for assessing need in the community (adapted from D.H., 2007, p.8) Adapted with kind permission from Department of Health 2007a, p.8.

Community engagement is an essential element of JSNA and the process of engaging with people and communities to understand their needs will in itself have a positive impact on meeting these. Perhaps even more important, real engagement is essential if commissioners are to make any progress in the task of reducing inequalities. Effective community engagement results in a greater understanding of a community's needs and why and how local services need to change and develop, so that services are more appropriate to local areas. Communities are more likely to use services if they have had a stake in how they should be designed in the first place. Those whose voices are traditionally not heard are more likely to be socially isolated and experience poor outcomes (Kramer and Stafford 2008).

Partnership and participation in strategic planning

Local practitioners, including those from user-led organisations, often have detailed knowledge of community needs and are best informed about gaps in service provision. Their ability to facilitate exchange with local communities and groups is needed to identify those who may not have the capacity to make themselves known under their own steam. Establishing current and future needs (now and in the next few years), as well as predicting long-term needs (between the next five to ten years), should include local demographic information and the infrastructure needed to inform strategic planning. Where the quality of the data is uncertain, this will need to be more frequently reviewed and assessed. The JSNA should be linked to other strategies and plans, for example community regeneration; supporting people strategies; housing strategies; community safety; carers' strategies and workforce planning. Engaging the community fully and meaningfully, however, is resource intensive and from 2008, each local authority established a Local Involvement Network (LINks) building on existing networks and forums and providing a one-stop accountable and ongoing dialogue with local communities. This is inevitably a complex and potentially contested business and we will later go on to look at some of the challenges involved within the different levels at which such dialogue might take place. Sometimes partnership can be little more than rhetoric or an end in itself with limited evidence that partners (in theory) are genuinely working together (Preston-Shoot 2009). It is important to tease out the relationships between different concepts of partnerships when strategising and to identify the different philosophical and policy contexts as well as confronting the practical implications. The Scottish Community Development Centre (2005) has developed *National Standards for Community Engagement* which they define as:

Developing and sustaining a working relationship between one or more public body and one or more community group, to help them both to understand and act on the needs or issues that the community experiences. (Scottish Community Development Centre 2005, p.4)

They then set out key principles, behaviours and practical measures that underpin effective engagement. The national standards are based on principles such as fairness, equality and inclusion, which should underpin all aspects of community engagement policies and the importance of learning from the experience, and enabling all parties to be given the opportunity to build on their knowledge and skills.

The standards incorporate ten steps towards effective community engagement as follows:

• **involvement** – identify and involve the people and organisations who have an interest in the focus of the engagement.

• **support** – identify and overcome any barriers to involvement.

• **planning** – gather evidence of the needs and available resources and use this evidence to agree the purpose, scope and timescale of the engagement and the actions to be taken.

• **methods** – agree and use methods of engagement that are fit for purpose.

• **working together** – agree and use clear procedures that enable the participants to work with one another effectively and efficiently.

• **sharing information** – ensure that necessary information is communicated between the participants.

• **working with others** – work effectively with others with an interest in the engagement.

• **improvement** – actively develop the skills, knowledge and confidence of all the participants.

• **feedback** – feed back the results of the engagement to the wider community and the agencies affected.

• **monitoring and evaluation** – monitor and evaluate whether engagement achieves its purposes and meets the national standards. (cited in Kramer and Stafford 2008, p.372)

Public participation in strategic planning

There are three central questions posed in planning participation within the formulation of any strategy: What is the organisation or service for and why does it exist? To whom is it accountable? How will you know that it has been successful? A continuous and creative dialogue between managers and local citizens also involves sharing some of the dilemmas, seeking views and adapting decisions accordingly, taking into account the principles of equity and accessibility (Coates and Passmore 2008). There are a variety of methods for promoting and engaging the community which can involve:

- formal or statutory mechanisms such as formal consultation processes, public hearings or governance arrangements

- information and communication in the form of published newsletters, websites, leaflets or engagement with the media

- face-to-face interaction

- deliberative methods such as citizen panels or juries

- devolving responsibilities to user-led organisations to undertake consultation on your behalf.

Participation is traditionally modelled on a ladder starting with 'informing', moving through 'consulting' to 'involving', 'collaborating' and finally to 'empowerment' (Arnstein 1969; Kings Fund 1992). According to Coates and Passmore (2008), another way of thinking about the process is to envisage what participation looks like from both inside and outside and organisation. This is where managers and citizens may have different viewpoints about what is important or priority. Developing an 'outside-in' frame of reference means striking a balance between an organisation's internal priorities and the community's concern with particular issues. Postle and Beresford's study (2007) also suggests a more active role for front-line workers in supporting service users in initiatives such as self-help, campaigning and community action which offer an alternative interpretation of community-based work. By working through their front-line managers and staff, strategic managers can support professionals to support people to participate in emerging forms of active and inclusive citizenship to counteract any impact of more managerialist approaches to participation.

Integrating care within strategic planning

Models of integrated care are beginning to emerge for different service users and a greater concentration of strategic level partnership working is now firmly in place (McKimm and Phillips 2009). However, within integrated services, some issues remain politically contentious, for example a perceived loss of power and control experienced by the social care sector and the downplaying or compromising of some professional competences and expertise over others (McKimm 2009). The emerging legislative conditions and mechanisms to achieve partnership are capable of masking micropolitics. If not given explicit attention, face-to-face practical encounters between professionals from different organisational cultures working under different managerial styles may ultimately lead to a loss of focus on strategic objectives. This can give rise to considerable stress and loss of morale and productivity on behalf of the workforce (Parrott 2005). The complexity of interprofessional and integrated working is in itself a central characteristic which risks being ignored by policy makers in their haste to implement change and improve services:

> Managers and leaders need to keep a sharp focus on how policies, strategies and structures across society affect workforce patterns and the availability of appropriately skilled people to implement the vision. Issues such as how to involve service users, carers and volunteers in the delivery of care need to be addressed alongside professional development activities, education and training. A whole range of challenges underpins achieving an integrated public service agenda relating to values, power, status and control of resources: adding yet more layers of complexity to the integrated agenda. (McKimm 2009, p.140)

Integration (sometimes referred to as 'vertical integration') is a term used to describe a context where different components of a supply chain are brought together in a single organisation, such as those in a children's, mental health or learning disability trust. There are two main types of vertical integration, first, where agencies involved at different stages of the care pathway are part of a single organisation and second, where commissioning and provider agencies are part of a single organisation. Ramsay and Fulop (2008) reviewed the evidence base for integrated care and were able to identify the changes that integration brings about; the conditions that support successful integration; and gaps in the knowledge about what works well. Their summary provides the following helpful advice and recommendations for anyone considering integrating services within strategic development:

- Integrate for the right reasons; preferably build on opportunities where these grow organically. The objectives of integration need to be made explicit and top-down attempts have been shown to have less happy outcomes.

- Integration that focuses on bringing organisations together is unlikely to create improvements in care for service users unless they begin at the front line where they impact directly on users' experiences and where the most apt organisational supports for service provision can be identified.

- Several key contextual elements are important to successful integration at a local level including a culture of quality improvement; a history of trust between partner organisations; existent multi-disciplinary teams; local supportive leadership; staff who are open to collaboration, innovation and effective and complementary communications and IT systems.

- The significance of bringing together organisational cultures that have evolved separately over long periods is an obstacle that needs to be considered when planning future integration, and finding ways of working through these are imperative to success.

- Take account of how community-based services relate to the integrated organisation and address any power imbalances between front-line and community services.

- For front-line staff to recognise and buy into the integration process, a number of different incentives are required, including financial ones, and staff professional development.

- Whilst significant improvements in quality of care can follow better coordination of previously fragmented services, potential economies of scope and scale are likely to take time to achieve and there is little evidence to support efficiency. This is due to the resources needed to integrate different practices and the steep learning curve inherent in joining a new organisation.

- The time required to implement effective integration requires patience and it may take time to demonstrate changes in organisational structures and processes before they have a demonstrable impact on outcomes. (Adapted from Ramsey and Fulop 2008, pp.7–8)

Involving sector partners in the design and development of services – avoiding pitfalls

The ultimate goal of service user participation should be the promotion of health, quality of life or overall user satisfaction with services. However, these outcomes are often difficult to measure and can take a substantial amount of time to become evident. Many new initiatives springing up involving partnership are aimed towards eradicating bureaucratic and out-dated professional boundaries and establishing more 'seamless' services, improving service coordination and providing a more effective response across organisations.

It is easy to gloss over the fact that partnership work is actually very difficult, for example in working through the differences in organisational culture, terminology, practice, operational priorities and training, to say nothing of the lack of co-terminus service boundaries. Each partner may regard the other with a degree of professional scepticism and downright mistrust. Different interests, priorities and practices in multi-agency groups make collaborative working difficult, and trust can only be developed if based on an appreciation of divergent interests and views. Providing opportunities to explore different ideological perspectives is as important as establishing common ground. Researchers have noted that one way to overcome mistrust is to take small steps early on rather than immediately setting ambitious partnership goals (Webb 1991). This certainly reflects current thinking in regeneration and neighbourhood renewal where early wins have been found to be very important in new and distrusting partnerships. The sense of achievement gained by working together to achieve small goals can provide the momentum for tackling more difficult, longer-term problems.

The problem with strategic partnerships

Difficulties can arise in partnerships because of the multiple organisational structures that group members come from and the fact that each representative has a different reporting arrangement and a different level of decision-making power within their own organisation. Unless decision-making and reporting-back processes are clearly established, partnerships can be frustrated by their members' lack of authority and their inability to make the decisions and agreements necessary to move the work forward (Blyth 2005). Similarly, we need to recognise the limits of our own expertise and competence regardless of our experience. Having responsibility for leading partnerships, for example, may make us feel uncomfortable, ill at ease or unskilled. Striving for equality in partnerships raises structural conflicts related to historical and fixed differences between partners concerning terms and conditions of services, unfair stereotypes or prejudices. These issues need to be brought out into the open, and discussed to find constructive and practical ways of acknowledging and compensating for them.

Successful partnerships operate at one or more of three levels: strategic, operational and practice. At a strategic level, this includes reorientation and refocusing of existing services or extending services through alternative forms of provision. For example, the extended schools initiative is a key delivery element of the *Every Child Matters* HM Government (2003) agenda and is underpinned by the Children Act 2004. Remodelling puts schools in a position to shape the range and delivery of services:

> Extended services in and around schools bring together existing services and organisations to create a coherent offer for pupils and their families. Schools become the point of access to services but it is not expected that school staff will be responsible for its delivery... Extended services in a wider ECM context improve outcomes for children and young people by:

- tackling barriers to learning

- providing the basis for earlier intervention

- improving integration of children's services focused on the needs of the child and family

- giving pupils more opportunities through extended services. (Training and Development Agency for Schools 2006, pp.3–4)

This type of strategic partnership will be reflected in the different stakeholders involved, the development of the terms of reference, key strategic objectives and an action plan and comprehensive strategy document. Within the strategic level, there should be synergy between voluntary and statutory agencies and recognition of the need to understand and promote their differences rather than competing for resources. At an operational level, a key feature of successful partnerships may be the nature of agencies involved and the inclusion of the different voices of those being directly involved in order to keep service development relevant and meaningful. The critical role of coordination to operate across agency boundaries, build bridges between different interest groups, broker difference and build consensus cannot be underestimated. Here, work typically takes place within multi-disciplinary service teams and settings, broad inter-agency groupings and projects or integrated services such as in youth justice or community learning disability teams. At a practice level, early stages of the development of the team and emphasising how they can best work together by identifying the knowledge, skills and expertise within the group can provide more flexibility, particularly where members of the team struggle with operational issues at a practice level. Front-line teams in particular have a lot to offer regarding review and development of the service because of their direct interactions with service users and other staff from a range of agencies. Service users themselves may also be employed as consultants, particularly as many service user organisations have grown and become more established locally and nationally, through which they have a substantial amount of knowledge accumulated not only about the service but in 'what works' in effective user involvement (Connelly and Seden 2003).

No matter at what level you are working, partnerships within any strategy need to be fluid to enable those involved to respond better to the rapidly changing communities and the needs served. It is easy to develop parochial interests and drift towards serving the needs of employees and employers rather than responding to service users' needs. Sustaining partnerships over a long period of time requires energy and commitment. Their fluid nature can also make them susceptible to be dominated by powerful individuals or agencies and erode the diverse identities of different agencies as they blend and converge. Models of practice are best created at local levels to reflect the unique circumstances, such as rurality or cultural diversity, to avoid the risk of false parenthesis created merely to fulfil a legal, political or policy requirement which does not really benefit service users. Reviewing and evaluating the relevance and progress of partnerships, therefore, is imperative and we will be looking at how these can be considered within evaluation of services later on in Chapter 10.

Preparing your strategic plan – tools for analysis

Having discussed some of the contextual issues shaping strategy, we will now turn to consider some of the more practical tools in putting together your strategic plan. Strategic planning involves identifying what the potential influences are in both the external and internal environments. Changes may be imposed from the outside, as we saw earlier, but opportunities to shape the future through internal developments may also exist. It may be appropriate to establish what degrees of freedom are open to your team, service or organisation in planning the future and the consequences if no positive decisions are made. The lead time needed to plan activities must also be identified. It is useful to identify what an organisation's primary activity should be and to carry out an audit of its main strengths and weaknesses. You should pay attention to what options are being created by developments (in information technology in particular) as well as market changes. A further issue might consider what risks are likely and how these can be anticipated or minimised. One simple model that incorporates some of these key issues is the SWOT (Strengths, Weaknesses, Opportunities and Threats) analysis. The factors analysed within this model are:

Internal factors – the strengths and weaknesses

External factors – the opportunities and threats

At whatever level strategic planning is taking place, the process needs to be kept reasonably broadly based and try to avoid prescriptive approaches that are too detailed. One of the dangers in strategic planning is that unrealistic goals may be set. Whilst organisational capability can be developed, structures changed and cultures influenced, there are limits to the change that is achievable, and working towards incremental improvements may be the best option. In her discussion about new children's services partnerships, Dowler (2008) reminds us that

> Boards and their partnerships are often at an early stage of working together and just because a number of public services organisations have intersecting mandates does not mean that they are able to cooperate effectively… While governance arrangements have been signed by chief executives, front-line staff still have to assimilate the new concept of combining management by their employing agency with working in virtual teams across agencies. (Dowler 2008, p.78)

Tools for analysis

The SWOT analysis has become a popular analytical tool as it has the merits of being straightforward to apply. However, there are problems with its subjectivity. These can be counteracted if undertaken more rigorously using weighting mechanisms which facilitate discussion and debate the grounds for such weighting (Jacobs, Shepherd and Johnson 1998). SWOT provides an organising framework for intuitive information and as a means of summarising and integrating more formal analyses about the external operating environment and an organisation's current resources and capabilities. There are some downsides of SWOT, for example the analysis can result in a long list of observations which provide little overall insight or clarity about required action. As there are no formal mechanisms within SWOT to ensure that managers challenge their own frames of reference or their organisation's paradigm, indeed SWOT can be used to stick to what is seen as already known. Developing insight to challenge these, such as in the use of appreciative inquiry (AI), can be useful.

AI, as the term implies, is a methodology which focuses on appreciating and then giving leverage to an organisation's core strengths, rather than seeking to overcome or minimise its weaknesses. As we saw in the case example earlier, it focuses on exploration and discovery of moments of excellence in the organisation through deep inquiry, and openness to seeing new potentials and possibilities from that collective knowledge (Doel et al. 2007). AI suggests that treating organisations as mysteries to be embraced rather than problems to be solved represents a powerful shift in thinking (see www.aipractitioner.com for more information). Further, managers may conceive of strengths and weaknesses in terms of the strategy they aim to implement rather than that which currently exists. In this sense, it is important that the strengths and weaknesses are considered in terms of current realised strategy rather than just future intended strategy. There may also be a tendency for managers to see environmental changes as threats rather than opportunities. Such negative perceptions of change may hinder the identification of opportunities.

PESTL analysis

We have established that all care organisations are affected by their political, economic, legal and social contexts. Increasingly, technological developments are impacting too, as well as environmental and sustainability factors. All have to be appraised to respond effectively to these different forces and a more detailed analysis of these help managers not only to understand the complexities and interrelationships to be taken into account in predicting future trends but also to provide awareness of the key factors likely to impinge on the success or otherwise of any strategy being developed. The relationship between organisations and their environment is a symbiotic one. Consideration of these factors lends itself to a more complex environmental analytic tool commonly known as PESTL analysis (Political, Economic, Social, Technological and Legal). Farnham (2005) suggests that data gathered within these areas can be used for environmental analysis in two ways. First, as a 'macro' (outside-in) approach where organisations engage in scanning, monitoring, forecasting and assessing to identify and examine plausible alternative future environments that might confront them. The driving force is to ensure organisations understand the dynamics of change within each environment, before deriving organisational-specific implications. The second approach, Farnham terms 'micro' (inside-out) where the organisation is a starting point to examine its products, markets, technologies and so on.

Political

The political environment takes account of those issues driving strategy, such as those discussed in Chapter 1. Government decisions, resultant legislation, policy changes and regulations inevitably set the context, challenges and tasks requiring a response. Given the highly visible nature of care services, one needs an understanding of the formal political context and also how political officials interact with the organisations in order to achieve outcomes for public interests. The Warwick University school of management (Hartley and Branicki 2006) suggest that organisational political strategies are driven by three key pressures: political action at the individual, organisation and inter-organisational level; in procedural rules and external constraints and in the political resources or capital available, for example 'knowing who and knowing how'.

Strategic planning for children, for example, has put services into a vastly different policy arena and according to Hudson (2005a), constitutes a significant illustration of authoritative strategy, by which he means the deployment of power by an executive authority to secure coordination amongst a range of subordinate bodies. Hudson argues that this approach to coordination differs from the dominant discourse in the theoretical literature that sees coordination as a voluntary activity motivated by an appreciation of interdependence. He argues that this dominant exchange model does not apply when inter-organisational relationships are mandated by law or regulatory agencies. He sees the imposition of an authoritative integrating structure as enabling bureaucratic routines to be established. However, a process of interaction and negotiation between those seeking to put policy into effect depends on the way in which this tension is worked through in order to shape the future of integrated services (Hudson 2005a).

Economic

Economic forces are of vital concern, as the overall economic climate determines business opportunities and because an expanding or contracting economy stimulates demands for goods, services, investment and labour (Taylor 2009). Within social care, long-term and short-term trends need to be addressed proactively alongside a realistic appraisal of resources, such as finance, capital assets and the human resources available. It should be informed by taking account of messages from research and development studies around what helps to achieve outcomes in a cost-effective and efficient way. Techniques for costing or benchmarking services can be utilised and opportunities for pooling costs within partnerships need to be appraised. Estimation of future costs of care inevitably focuses on projected costs and on the assumptions that services will be provided in the future very much as they have been in the past. However, radical changes in legislative and policy directives depend on: developing useful information systems which describe the levels and types of need in the community; the supply of formal and informal care; unit costs of services and feedback mechanisms to inform your commissioning and contracting processes; and general familiarity with changes in the funding for care in order to bid for resources.

In going back to our earlier example of domiciliary care providers, we identified concerns about continuing financial viability whilst developing capacity to respond to self-directed care. This may have an untoward effect on instability in the labour market making staff retention more difficult, thus undermining gains in other workforce development areas. Managers will therefore need to satisfy themselves that models of service delivery and the resources available or allocated always proceed from a basis of equity.

Social

These include demographic and local performance information. Monitoring access to services by giving attention to diversity, mobility, income and geographic distribution levels will aid your analysis and thinking about these. Research and evaluation studies will also aid analysis. Patterns of service use and monitoring of unmet needs based on your current service information can be used to inform your commissioning and contracting activities and service or team development plans. For example, not only the needs of minority groups should be built into funding and development planning but this needs to be reflected in the involvement of the minority voluntary sector in the work of the commissioning organisation. The challenge of ageing requires age-proofing of mainstream and existing services as well as developing services to meet the specific needs of the wellbeing agenda for people in later life (Audit Commission 2008).

Technology

Technological change is one of the most visible and pervasive forms of change. The impact of new technologies in care enters every aspect of an organisation's management and delivery of services, as well as having an impact on the way we live and work (Weiner and Petrella 2007). Awareness of technological developments is essential for most organisations and impacts on the performance and quality of services and types of support provided. Examples might include those developments used to enable us to collect data from a large number of inter-disciplinary sources, such as information-processing systems as well as those impacting directly on service users, such as for self-assessment and administration of care (such as telecare and clinical interventions).

Legal

As well as the duties and powers derived from legislation and guidance, other types of areas affected by legislation include: the type of services developed and produced; the funding and resourcing of care, for example through integrated services or pooled budgets; workforce development; workplace design, for example health and safety; and accounting and budgeting practices. Given that working together remains a key theme in social policy for health and social care, legal and procedural approaches to system change mean that managers and practitioners have to work through challenging issues arising from operationalising the legal rules as expressed through agency policies (Preston-Shoot 2009).

In summary, the use of analytic tools such as SWOT and PESTL can assist managers and their stakeholders to question and examine specific areas in a more systematic way. Some critics argue, however, that they simplify reality, distort by simplification or offer a 'one size fits all' approach. This suggests that use of such tools are more likely to obscure than illuminate (Grandy and Mills 2004). In the face of these criticisms, combining these with a critical and evidence-based approach and taking account of the differing needs of stakeholders, particularly service users and staff, will help to problematise otherwise taken-for-granted assumptions for further questioning.

Leadership and political skills – working through resistance

No organisation operates in a vacuum and there is growing recognition of the vital contribution of political skills to delivering improved delivery of public services with diverse stakeholders (Hartley and Branicki 2006). This involves balancing the organisation's internal capabilities within a competitive environment. The acquisition of political skills are seen in this context and not as commonly perceived: as serving self-interest. Political skills refer instead to those which recognise one's power base when influencing and balancing competing interests, such as in the context of inter-organisational partnerships and coalitions or in developing integrated approaches to delivering care services. As we saw earlier, managers not only need to work with formal institutions and representatives of the state but with stakeholders lobbying on behalf of user groups as well as working within a complex and dynamic environment of legislation, policy and regulation. All of these will have repercussions that need to be addressed. Political skills in this sense include the soft skills of being able to read and respond to the context and to understand and act with political awareness in the interests of different stakeholders. This implies the need for 'leadership' and appeals to those theories that emphasise its more participatory and distributive styles.

Lawler (2007) traces the development of leadership in care services from its scientific management origins to the more humanistic theories. He highlights persistent themes in how to maximise the contributions of employees to the goals of their employing organisation. Lawler cites the common use of technology and work design as control mechanisms and recommends strategies to motivate staff to high performance aimed at encouraging more effective social relationships and re-engineering work processes. In the absence of clarity or certainty about events in social care, the concept of leadership, according to Lawler, is deployed as an interpretive device, something which enables people to make sense of events or as an organisational concept to ascribe some causality in their situation. Within the context of strategising, there is role for leadership in social work and social care, where roles are changing and becoming ever more complex resulting in further professional divisions and increased specialisation. Major changes affecting social work and social care professionals, as outlined above in the PESTL analytical framework, require leadership in the positioning and championing of social care to the outside world and within different partnerships.

Political skill has been described as the 'missing discipline' in management selection, training and development (Butcher and Clarke 1999, p.12). It incorporates an interpersonal style that combines social astuteness with the capacity to adjust to different and changing situational demands. This inspires trust and confidence, conveys sincerity and influences others to respond favourably (Ferris *et al.* 2005). It also includes an understanding of how interests, both of individuals and power blocs within the organisation, may operate to achieve outcomes through mechanisms of power rather than solely through apparently rational plans and purposes. Managing with political awareness means acquiring and using the skills, knowledge and competencies both to understand and influence politics. One needs to map the political terrain in order to achieve a balance of skills to get the most out of teams, partnerships, alliances, networks and coalitions. This helps towards overall improvement of what the organisation is trying to achieve (Hartley and Branicki 2006).

The complexity of partnerships involved in strategic planning, are often new territory for many managers and should reflect many different needs of stakeholders and staff they are working with. It helps to problematise otherwise taken-for-granted assumptions about why change is necessary and to establish a more open dialogue between managers and their staff when leading change. There are many negative consequences of politically charged change environments, such as increased turnover of staff and reduced performance (Department for Children, Schools and Families and Department of Health 2009b). Negative politicking can also be a major source of work discontent but the manager's political skills can help people to cope with stress more effectively. There is limited research on the potential links between politics and overall positive organisational performance. Whilst most research has focused on the influence of change within the organisation, the external environment is increasingly important, involving both formal institutions and inter-organisational relationships more generally. Elmore (1979–1980) specifically argues against any top-down implementation approaches to strategy development and its implementation. He argues that human beings are not just links in a chain of command. Policy makers (or managers) should realise that policy is best implemented by what he terms 'backward mapping' of problems and policy.

Backward mapping begins with a concrete statement of the behaviour that creates the occasion for a policy intervention. One then identifies a set of organisational operations that can be expected to affect that behaviour, and then the expected effect of these operations. This helps each level of the implementation process by identifying which effect one would expect that level to have on the target behaviour as well as the resources required for that effect to occur (1979–1980, p.612). The imperative is to begin with the phase at which a strategy reaches its end point where analysis and strategies are derived from the patterns of behaviour and conflict that exist. It is essentially a process that involves negotiation and consensus building, utilising participatory and distributive management styles. It is generally recognised that the emergence of policy in the UK to transform care services is firmly rooted in the top-down tradition of policy making and implementation. This rational approach involves a sequential system of strategic response, that of analysis, planning, action and review.

A more inclusive and participatory approach would focus on individual actions as a starting point for analysis, depicting them as responses to problems or issues in the form of choices between alternatives, and hence to feasible policy objectives (Elmore 1979–1980). Therefore, the critical issues are not how managers should allocate resources among competing government objectives or how to achieve those objectives. Rather, it is the management of the welter of relationships at the front-line service delivery level, where staff and users as partners experience close proximity to the problems in the community and their ability to grasp resources required to work with them. According to Hudson (2005a) backward mapping aims to isolate one or two critical points in a complex multi-stakeholder relationship with the closest proximity to the problem, and identify what needs to happen at those points to solve it.

Chapter summary – making your strategy a reality

This chapter has looked at just some of the concepts associated with strategic planning and the key management processes involved in developing your local strategy for care services. Developing an inclusive vision, considering the role and issues around strategic partnerships and the pros and cons of particular management tools to undertake an environmental analysis are some of the key elements in managing this process. Participation in developing and implementing a strategy is not a single mechanism but involves a wide range of activities, such as quality management, organisational development, conflict management, team-building and workforce planning.

In the next chapter we are going to start to unpick some of these activities by looking at how strategy might be translated into a business plan. Business planning is used to communicate to everyone involved or affected, how the strategy is going to be implemented and be taken forward. Given the complexity and turbulent environment in which care services are developed, a key message in *this* chapter is not to get bogged down in navel gazing and detail when developing your strategy. Having a 50-page long organisational development strategy with a two- to three-year implementation plan and a whole series of change plans, whilst important, is secondary to being instinctive and politically savvy. There is great value in investing in the development of more effective relations between and among the people involved. There is potential through debating change and thinking about your own approach to leading change that promotes the values inherent in care services and which engages everybody involved. A study of best practice in organisational development found that running with instincts allows an organisation to evolve continuously, as future needs often turn out to be different to what was thought to be needed previously (Improvement and Development Agency 2008). It is helpful to have a series of initiatives that intertwine. 'Transformation is the golden web and OD is the thread that holds it together' (Crouch 2008 cited in Improvement and Development Agency 2008, p.11).

A central concern for those involved in practising organisational development is the planning and management of changes in belief, values, culture, social interaction and behaviour in order to achieve organisational effectiveness. Organisational development recognises the insufficiency of analysing an organisation's environment and then setting out the series of planned logical actions to achieve its goals. What actually happens does not depend on rational considerations alone – it depends just as much on behaviour factors. The Improvement and Development Agency offer six tips for successful strategising:

- Be bold, brave and be different. No one size fits all.

- Don't forget the opposition; focus on participation and buy in from them. They are important in terms of scrutiny and may hold power so it's important for them to buy into the changes proposed.

- Make sure you understand your organisation's business, vision and strategic imperatives. Outcomes are important.

- Don't get bogged down in restructuring; create a sense of urgency and push for pace and don't put things on hold.

- Be savvy and focus on initiatives that will make the most differences quickly which will help to win people over by enabling them to see results and achievements.

- Timing is crucial, start from where the organisation is at and pace change in a way that is challenging but achievable. (Improvement and Development Agency 2008, p.17)

Developing strategy should seek to re-engage with citizens, staff and service users who benefit from your organisation. It should draw on the important ethical principles and ethics underpinning social care services. It is essential to recognise that users of care services are citizens, rather than just consumers, and that unless staff are committed to service objectives then expectations will not be met (Coates and Passmore 2008). Most importantly, viewing staff as a critical source of intelligence about organisational performance and as a wellspring of innovation (as illustrated in the appreciative inquiry approach) demonstrates the realisation that those doing the job will know even more about the possibility of incremental improvement than those in the most senior management positions. These senior managers have different roles to play. Trust is a critical factor and if it is absent, or if staff are disaffected, alienated or disengaged, then there is very little likelihood that (rising) citizen expectations will be met. Coates and Passmore (2008) suggest motivating and incentivising employees to view their service from the 'outside in', or from the perspective of the service user or citizen. This can create a reflective frame of reference where those affected by strategic planning have both the capacity for constructive criticism and the capability to devise creative solutions to the problems that they confront.

Manager's comment

The President of the Family Division's guidance (2009) offers an example of strategic planning with a national lead but practised locally through strategic partnership working. The challenge has been how to interpret this within the Cafcass (Children and Family Court Advisory and Support Service) and also share responsibility in making it succeed with partners.

The children's social care environment is changing fast and the impact of many drivers, for example legal changes, significant critique of services (Lord Laming, 2003, 2009), all work to influence individual agencies adjusting and developing their resources.

This guidance created a vision to ensure each family received a timely and safe service. To achieve this it meant Cafcass practitioners and managers had to shift their focus significantly. The strategic direction in the president's guidance led to a focus on strategic objectives. This court-focused document created an integrated vision for legal and social care staff to work in tandem. It created a centrality for the children and their families whilst giving an accountable framework, forging new and direct lines of communication. In particular, there were new vertical reporting mechanisms across agencies, for example in court user and Family Justice Council meetings and between local senior judiciary and middle managers in Cafcass.

Alongside this guidance there has been an understanding for all agencies about the need to modernise their services and increase both choice and control for service users. This guidance has offered the strategic vehicle to achieve this with complementary procedures in all agencies to hear user direct feedback and comment through comment and complaint procedures. The strategic direction of this guidance is also being informed by front-line teams in review.

Ann Flynn is a service manager in Cafcass working in the area of early intervention.

CHAPTER 3

The Business Planning Process

When you have worked through this chapter you will be able to:

- identify the key steps towards developing your business plan
- develop strategies to involve service users and staff in the business planning process
- consider the importance of sustainability when developing new services.

Introduction

All managers have an active role to play in influencing and working with stakeholders to redesign and develop services to meet the needs of the local community. This begins with the process of 'business' development to make the organisation fit for purpose. In turn, the process of developing a business plan will draw on a wide spectrum of skills including strategic analysis, forecasting and planning, financial modelling, risk analysis and risk management, as well as developing quality assurance and indicators, and methods for performance measurement to inform decision-making. Unlike managers in traditional business settings, managers in social care need to achieve a balance between the 'hard tools' needed with the more 'soft' or democratising elements or tools which aim to harness empowerment of those involved and to help achieve cultural change. Tools and techniques used in developing the business planning process are not apolitical or merely technical in their application to practice. This chapter starts to identify the key management tasks and tools involved in developing your business plan, in preparation for a more detailed look at each area involved in the chapters that follow. We will also address key issues such as reflexivity and the inclusion of service users and providers in the business planning process. We will look at combining methods of analysis to enhance credibility and usefulness. Finally, issues around sustainability in business planning will be touched upon.

Characteristics of good business planning

In the previous chapter we discussed how you might develop the long-term vision of where your organisation wants to be and some of the dynamics involved in establishing your strategy within current dynamic environments. You were introduced to some of the tools commonly used to assess the strengths and weaknesses of your organisation and to identify specific opportunities and threats that could be capitalised on to take a particular strategy forward. It is from this strategic development framework that you will then go on to develop your business plan. A reminder of the strategic development framework is illustrated in Figure 3.1 below.

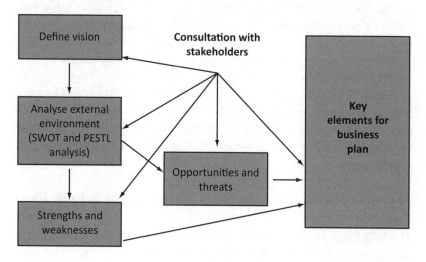

Figure 3.1 The strategic development framework

Like strategic development, the development of 'the business' should be a shared endeavour. A doable business plan is one where the high-level intents, desires and objectives of your organisation can be translated into specific and measurable actions and outcomes that are understood at organisational, directorate and personal levels, or wherever relevant. Each and every person in your organisation will then know what she or he should be doing to help your organisation achieve its strategic objectives. The active education and empowerment of staff within the organisation can encourage ownership of the strategic objectives and the indicators selected to demonstrate any achievements.

Structuring and developing your business plan

Developing a business plan involves the use of project management techniques to manage the programme of activity. You will need to think about the skills, capabilities and capacity of those who can be involved on the project team and make sure that the production of your business plan is given enough priority, resources and senior management support so that the iterative process of producing the plan can be properly managed. The initial data-gathering exercise is important to bring together information that will help you understand the current strategic and operational issues that affect your organisation, service or team's performance. This could include a mission statement; organisational charts; recent service evaluations; audits or survey reports; staff learning and development plans; minutes from important meetings; local information about demography or regional developments, amongst many other sources of relevant information.

Suggested below are nine focus areas considered central to every business plan. These areas are not mutually exclusive in that there will be some degree of overlap (Department of Health 2007a). Many of these areas will be addressed in much more detail in subsequent chapters of this book and so only a short summary is given at this stage as a means of providing an general overview.

Aspects of your business plan – what might it look like?

Executive summary

This tells the reader where the organisation, service or team wants to be in the future and spells out the benefits of any proposed changes. The summary should provide a brief history of the current context and sets out the specific characteristics that define your organisation, service or team from others. It will also include your vision statement and a summary of the strategic goals. These should be written in ways that are easily understood and accessible to a range of audiences such as service users, staff, the local community and stakeholders.

Organisational profile

This makes a clear statement about the current position of the organisation, service or team and how it currently operates. Include a description of *what* types of services are currently provided, *how* they are provided and a summary of the key achievements made so far. Details of any significant contracts or shared service agreements developed so far, as well as a description of the types of partnership arrangements or joint ventures your organisation is involved in, will add further illustration. Structural and organisational charts are helpful for showing the roles and responsibilities of key people in the organisation alongside brief details about current governance arrangements.

Strategic goals

This section will help the audience understand the overall vision and plans for future development with text that spells out the rationale behind these. Vision statements typically comprise a concise, high-level, inspirational summary of where you want to be at the end of the planning process. An example of a vision statement can be seen in the Crime, Disorder and Substance Misuse Reduction Strategy agreed by the Carlisle and Eden Crime and Disorder Reduction Partnership in Wales in 2005: 'To contribute to a high quality of life for all, across both urban and rural communities. To create an environment where people can feel secure and live without the threat or fear of Crime and Disorder' (Carlisle and Eden Crime and Disorder Reduction Strategy 2006, p.3).

The vision statement should be regarded as a unifying idea that is core to the values of the organisation and which links together each of its functional areas, as well as being geared towards meeting the needs of internal and external stakeholders who have an interest in it. You should give an indication of what success might look like in terms of the benefits for service users, the community, the staff and the organisation, service or team. You can also describe how the cultural environment will need to develop and change to reach the goals identified and what new partnerships or governance arrangements could be exploited to further develop and enhance service provision. The strategic goals will include a timeline for each objective and suggested indicators of success. This section should also describe the consultation process you have undertaken in more detail, for example the type of information provided to stakeholders and responses, with an outline of how this has influenced the outcome of the final strategy. Give details on any stakeholder analysis undertaken and an outline of how stakeholder relations are currently managed. This could, for example, involve the use of external advisors and a summary of how any special interest groups were represented and involved.

Market assessment

This provides a 'higher' level analysis of the current economy or market conditions in which your organisation, service or team operates in and any threats and opportunities in relation to the proposed new service developments or service provision. This might include a narrative with supporting graphics such as charts and tables showing what research has been done into changing demand and commissioning patterns. You will need to demonstrate how you have analysed, anticipated and responded to these patterns. You will also need to demonstrate how you have analysed, anticipated and responded to developments in the supply of services. Your PESTL analysis may come in handy here to demonstrate a more thorough understanding of the external environment in which you operate. As we saw in the previous chapter, the PESTL analysis enables you to articulate how future initiatives and service delivery plans are aligned with issues, trends and developments at both national and local levels.

The service development plan

This provides much more detail about the proposals for changing services aligned with your SWOT or PESTL analysis. The service development plan should set out how your services will develop over a set period of time. Essentially, you will be setting out each new initiative with sufficient detail for the audience to see where their actions fit within the activities needed. The service development plan will shortlist and document those key initiatives that are being suggested with indicators of the timescales and resources required. An example of a service development plan is illustrated in Table 3.1 (p.61).

Resources

This is where you start to put the meat on the bones and address the financial implications of your business plan, including any opportunities to bid for new funding or to restructure current funding arrangements. The main purpose of this section is to establish the overall viability of your service development plan and the resources required to translate this into action. As this will be based on a number of assumptions, it is critical that you acknowledge what assumptions are being made and document these clearly.

Financial resources will incorporate both capital and revenue expenditure and provide details about where there might be opportunities to bid for new resources. Bidding enables an organisation to prioritise with partners, corporately or at a service level, the resources to deliver measurable benefits or changes in funding. This will entail giving some background information on the performance of current budgets and historic financial performance. It is important to use your finance personnel to help you with the presentation of this information. If your financial modelling is built from the bottom up, and is driven by assumptions about activity levels, staff numbers, salary levels and inflation, then it should be relatively easy to assess your exposure to any new risks identified. Resource planning has two dimensions: money and time. Both constraints may be challenged by innovative exploration of possibilities for partnership and collaborative working in the provision of resources. Some breadth of appreciation as to

Table 3.1 Template for service development plan

Service Objective	Activity required	Person/s responsible	Expected outcomes	Timescales	Performance measurement
1. Establish 'drop-in' clinic for teenage sexual health.	• Identify two sites and negotiate use of existing clinics. • Recruit team from existing resources. • Develop promotional material and community outreach programme for young people. • Access local PALS young people's network for consultation.	**Mithran Bhatt,** PCT (sexual health). **Mary Connelly,** Secondary Schools Liaison Officer. **Katharine Letchfield,** Council Planning. **Adebola Adje,** commissioning team.	a) Two local clinics established providing 16 hours of sexual health advice each week. b) Local Teenage Sexual Health team established comprising one specialist nurse and one sexual counsellor.	Full service to be operational by November 2010.	No. of appointments offered. No. of young people seen. Reduction in teenage pregnancies. Reduction in STDs in young people between 15–21 years by 15% within two years. User satisfaction survey.
Continue to list your objectives here.					

the practicalities around these possibilities should therefore be examined and assessed in your resource section.

Risk assessment

The risk assessment section is vital to spell out what could potentially go wrong in the implementation of your business plan and the steps required to mitigate against these. Throughout the development of your strategy and action plans, you will need to have considered the key risks at each stage and whether or not you can manage these risks. Best practice business planning involves a continuing assessment of the key risks that impact on your organisation, service or team, and the development of plans to manage any risks. Your projections will need to assess how sensitive your plans are to changing circumstances and whether there are any difficulties that could arise which need contingency arrangements or corrective actions. The sort of assumptions made might relate to volume in demands, capacity to respond, efficiency and productivity information such as current user/staff ratios, administrative support, unit costs and whether these might be affected by inflation. Risk scenario analysis is the subject of Chapter 9.

Leadership and workforce development

This is a vital component of your business plan where the implications for the workforce of any new service developments or changes of direction are identified. These may involve new roles and responsibilities, training requirements and changes in staff pay and conditions. Consideration of leadership potential and the types of skills and knowledge within the organisation should go alongside an overview of the proposed management structure of the organisation, service or team and how management communicates and relates to the rest of the workforce. Your business plan may require its own structure for management and implementation combining the 'hard' (technical) and 'soft' (organisational) activities and benefits. On the hard side, specialist technical skills may be required to support the specification and delivery of projects. On the soft side, an understanding of the service context, as well as the organisational and cultural setting, is also needed.

When writing this section, there may be areas that need direct support from the human resource (HR) department (if you have one) in relation to any HR issues. Under employment law, you are required to demonstrate consultation and involvement of employees and other stakeholders in recruitment, training opportunities and new job role design or evaluation. These will also be in tune with the national occupational standards and guidelines from key workforce development organisations in social care and professional regulators in the UK, such as Skills for Care (SfC), the Children's Workforce Development Council (CWDC), the Social Care Skills Academy and social care councils within the four countries in the UK.

Governance

Governance arrangements describe how you will manage and control the new service or initiative and monitor and evaluate its implementation. There will be a significant overlap between the different governance, risk and financial sections in your business plan. It is also important that your organisation, service or team assesses themselves against any national performance frameworks for social care and other public sector services to identify the standards, guidelines and rules against existing or new systems which might be required to devolve and decentralise new activities. Your business plan will indicate how the performance management system and its indicators meet both national and local standards.

The business case

Until now we have been talking about what constitutes a business plan. It is worth making a distinction here between the two terms, often used simultaneously when talking about business planning, that of the 'business plan' and the 'business case'. A 'business plan' is a tangible written document, along the lines suggested above, the purpose of which is to present a rationale, analyses and recommendations for change. A 'business case', on the other hand, is where an argument or picture is developed to maximise financial returns or efficiency savings in order to help make decisions about whether or not to go ahead with a project. It also enables the reader to rank proposals alongside other initiatives within the strategic priorities in the organisation.

The nature of public sector organisations determines that a range of factors, particularly the generation of public value and social inclusion, must be considered in determining the most appropriate use of taxpayers' resources. Developing a business case is an overarching concept guiding the overall process of decision-making and project management. Business cases are therefore managed dynamically through the whole life cycle of business planning. Effective business case management is bound up with the decision-making process along the life cycle of a potential project, from judgements about its strategic value, through to decisions about procurement and implementation. During this process, a series of 'approvals' will be needed, as responsibilities are passed from one person or group to another, such as from a director of service down to an individual project manager and team. You may also draw on a range of tools and techniques, skills and competencies. Figure 3.2 demonstrates the process.

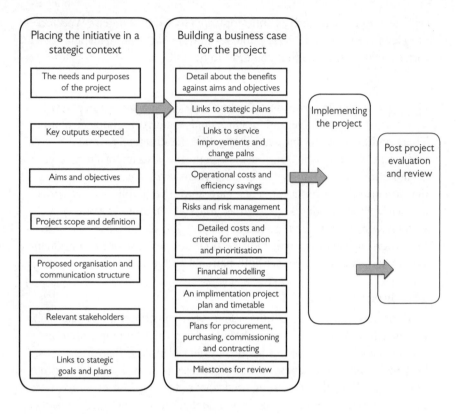

Figure 3.2 *Building a business case*
(Adapted from guidance provided by the Improvement and Development Agency, with the London Borough of Lambeth (2007))

Equality impact assessments

Since the implementation of the Race Relations (Amendment) Act 2000 and Equality Act 2006, it is essential that public services develop an equality scheme which actively promotes equality and human rights within the community. The equality impact assessment (EqIA) process requires initial screening for all new and revised policies, strategies, procedures and functions and is now a key element in business planning. This stage must be completed at the earliest opportunity and determines whether or not it is necessary to carry out a full equality impact assessment or EqIA for any new area of activity. Two key questions are assessed at this stage: first, what are the proposals looking to achieve and second, who in the main will benefit from these? Some developments in social care have the potential to cause adverse impact or discriminate against different groups in the community, as well as making positive contributions to achieving equality and diversity (Hafford-Letchfield 2009).

There are no standards procedures for EqIA, as the approach and process is determined locally, but it is helpful to make use of different perspectives, experiences and challenges when completing an EqIA. At least one of the team involved in the EqIA should be the manager responsible for the delivery of the service being assessed and it would be an asset to have at least one of the team who is able to offer an independent or different perspective, such as a service user (see www.idea.gov.uk). Involving technical experts or specialists is also appropriate. An impact assessment must be completed before the formal implementation of a policy, strategy, procedure or function can take place. Usually the sooner an impact assessment is completed the better. The time each assessment will take will vary depending on the nature and complexity of the service, but allowing time to complete a meaningful assessment is essential and should be considered when putting together your business plan. Top tips for improving your equality impact assessments are illustrated in Figure 3.3.

- Use the process as a 'health check', a way of consolidating knowledge of your service.

- Build capacity within your organisation, rather than promoting dependency on others for 'expert' advice.

- Satisfy stakeholders, both internally and externally, that the process has been sufficiently rigorous, in proportion to the importance of the issue and the policy.

- Be flexible in your approach; use a variety of methods such as group and one-to-one sessions, workshops and presentations to spread the message across departments.

- Focus on outcomes and tangible improvements.

- Think about the most appropriate and effective means to communicate the message and the outcomes of the EqIA, both within your service and to wider partners and the community. Be innovative!

- Establish the process within the council's wider review and decision-making processes

- Link the process, including the reviews, to service planning and risk management, so that it becomes embedded into the culture of your organisation.

(Reprinted from the Improvement and Development Agency website, www.idea.gov.uk)

Figure 3.3 'Top tips' in undertaking equality impact assessments

Consultation with appropriate stakeholders is a legal requirement of the EqIA process, as it gains their perspectives on the work that is being undertaken and the services proposed or delivered. There are legal duties towards race, gender, sexual identity, age and disability within the Equalities Act 2006, and its preceding legislation, to identify the range of groups that might be subject to discrimination in any service development or review. Sources of information will vary depending on the nature of the service but may be found in the following:

- any previous equality impact assessment
- service monitoring reports
- previous research and customer satisfaction surveys
- user feedback and satisfaction reports
- workforce monitoring
- staff surveys, opinions and information from trade unions
- contract monitoring reports
- complaints and comments
- press coverage
- outcome of consultation exercises
- feedback from focus groups
- feedback from individuals or organisations representing the interests of key target groups or similar
- the knowledge, technical advice, expertise and experience of the people assisting in the completion of the EqIA
- national and local statistics
- information from formal audits
- census data
- academic, qualitative and quantitative research
- demographics. (www.idea.gov.uk)

Where there is insufficient information available to provide a clear overview of how the activity is impacting on different communities and if it is practical, further research or consultation should be conducted. Where this is not practical, you should ensure that this is highlighted in the final action plan. Your organisation may be targeting services to a particular part of the population, historically referred to as 'seldom heard', 'hard-to-reach' or 'traditionally disadvantaged' and may require increasing involvement levels for that community or sector of the community. The real value of completing an EqIA comes from the resultant actions and the positive changes that emerge through conducting the assessment. Any actions or cost implications should be identified and fed directly into local service and team plans and, where appropriate, into the corporate annual equality action plan. A delegated person will need to report on actions in subsequent reviews. As all equality impact assessments are public documents, they should be published in an accessible format and signed off by a relevant senior manager. If the equality impact assessment is very long or complex, then an executive summary will help to make it more accessible to the wider community.

Involving service users in the business planning process

Earlier in Chapter 1 we established that the principles of involving users of care services in the development of policies and services is firmly incorporated into government legislation and guidance. A number of contextual factors and organisational practices may facilitate participation or serve as barriers to engagement, involvement and representation (Carr 2007). Beresford and Croft (2001) identify the desired outcomes of participation as a transfer of power from providers to users in a way that facilitates their participation at every level of decision-making, and to be in control of the services they receive. The status of participation in policy-making, as opposed to in everyday activities in social care, requires significant financial resources and a considerable number of service users with the capacity, time, skills and interest to participate in all of an organisation's decision-making situations (Campbell, Maynard and Winchcombe 2007; Hernandez, Robson and Sampson 2010). Enabling legislative frameworks and government guidance to become a practical reality for service users can be assisted by integrating everyday participation and practices in a way which recognises that different aspects of an organisation such as culture, structure, practice and review are addressed simultaneously.

Hernandez *et al.* (2010) found that in organisations where participation was positively promoted, user involvement was already embedded in policies and procedures. This created an organisation's ethos which recognised the value of participation and provided opportunities for this to be nurtured. It cannot be assumed that what policy makers, service planners, providers and purchasers would value and prioritise in their service developments necessarily coincides with what service users want. When developing effective partnerships within both strategy and business planning, this needs to go beyond considerations of organisations and professional groupings to involve service users fully as a key stakeholder

(Beresford and Branfield 2006). Studies done by Beresford and Branfield confirm that users are capable of offering a complex and sophisticated model of service development based on outcome measures where they have a more central role in its formulation. This represents a move away from more managerialist models underpinned by organisational, ideological and professional assumptions that are accompanied by voluminous bureaucratised, formalised criteria. Strong tensions exist in the consumerist impetus of mainstream user involvement. Carr (2007) suggests that participation challenges the very fabric of the institutions in which it is taking place, exposing problems with the political, strategic and structural elements of established non-user organisations:

> Exclusionary structures, institutional practices and professional attitudes can affect the extent to which service users can influence change. It appears that power sharing can be difficult within established mainstream structures, formal consultation mechanisms and traditional ideologies. (Carr 2007, p.267)

There are a number of things to take into account when involving service users in developing a business plan. Many organisations, particularly those which are user led, do not have secure or reliable funding and need financial support to network and get involved. This can however result in the outcomes of consultation becoming funding led rather than as a vehicle for service users to expressing their own genuine concerns. Involving user-led organisations themselves rather than some organisations who work closely with users will facilitate more democratic models within the partnership and ensure equity and diversity in the involvement strategy. You will need to consider any inequity within consultation strategies where some user-led organisations are competing with bigger charities.

Organisations that have a limited profile particularly with more marginalised groups highlight the merits of having a database of user resources that can be utlised and developed. Service user involvement in some aspects of business planning, particularly objective setting, enable these to be more focused on users' lives as opposed to the service system. Therefore holistic perspectives that take into account issues such as housing, transport, leisure, education, income and benefits are more likely to address wider issues around discrimination and diversity.

Beresford and Branfield (2006) identified the following barriers to user-controlled organisations fully participating in health and social care policy and provision:

- the devaluing of service user-led knowledge and the disempowering experience of not having their knowledge valued or taken seriously as a key source of information or evidence on which to base actions or decisions

- access and tokenism where more wider access needs to be promoted to ensure that all groups are included
- the 'culture' of health and social care organisations
- limited resources which restrict users' capacity to share and disseminate their knowledge. If user views are not consistent with what services want to hear, their funding might be then be put at risk.

Within the above study, service users identified four ways of making more impact on policy and provision:

1. training and education particularly together with managers/providers in order to shift culture and change attitude

2. commitment to change as a prerequisite for challenging barriers

3. recognising the full diversity of service users in order to engage and include with a range of knowledge

4. the importance of networking to strengthen user knowledge and increase its credibility and visibility in policy and services which are mutually dependent and closely linked.

This section on the participation of users in the business planning process concludes with the words of Turner, Brough and Findlay-Williams (2003): 'In an age of spin...there remains an urgent need for people to be honest, to be open enough to look at difficult issues and to use their experiences to help shape a better world' (p.57).

Building sustainability into care

Health and social care aims to help people live healthier and better lives striving towards 'a social care system that provides care equally for all, whilst enabling people to retain their independence, control and dignity' (Department of Health 2008a, p.1). Ensuring that your business plan promotes sustainable development is crucial on a number of points. Sustainable development is about ensuring a better quality of life for everyone, now and for future generations. Sustainability is not solely about protecting the environment. The Bruntland Report (1987) provides a widely used international definition of sustainability as a 'development which meets the needs of the present without compromising the ability of future generations to meet their own needs' (p.ix). This concept of sustainability goes hand in hand with many public policy imperatives, which impact on care in the way well planned and delivered care can contribute to developing social inclusion and local communities, away from a one size fits all approach. Sustainability literacy is also a necessary ingredient for engaging with stakeholders, meaning that everyone should have enough knowledge and skills to be able to contribute towards sustainable development no matter what role they play. For those you work with to be sustainability literate means enabling them to understand why we need to change to a sustainable way of doing things, at home, at work and in their community. It recognises, rewards and reinforces other people's decisions and the actions that contribute to sustainable development.

Sustainable development is a term used to describe both the process and the outcome. In Chapter 2 we discussed LAAs whose primary objective is to deliver genuinely sustainable communities through better outcomes for local people. This objective can be optimised when local aims are taken forward within partnerships which promote a more holistic approach and explicitly links tailored and cross-cutting outcomes across the local area agreement (LAA) for service users. One example might be how improvements to community safety can in turn deliver real benefits for older people. Older people may be more likely to engage in their local neighbourhood if they feel safe going about their daily lives, with the outcome that lower costs are incurred by health and community care providers in looking after sedentary older people. Other benefits occur through minimising duplication in the pursuit of common or aligned goals across programmes of service initiatives in the sector and by taking a more fully integrated approach to community development. This can also encourage more innovative practice where the outcome or performance indicators are holistic and cross cutting.

Thinking about social enterprise within your business objectives

Social enterprises play a vital role in targeting at grassroots level seldom heard and hard-to-reach groups and to stimulate local creativity in responding to social problems. Social enterprises are distinctive because their social or environmental purpose becomes central to what they do. Rather than maximising shareholder value, their main aim is to generate profit to further their social and environmental goals. Social enterprises account for 5 per cent of all businesses with employees, and contribute £8.4 billion per year to the UK economy and are highly relevant to developing health and social care services. Many social enterprises are already actively engaged in delivering and reforming public services particularly in health and social care. In 2002, the government pledged a £125 million investment fund to assist voluntary and community sector organisations and social enterprises (Department of Trade and Industry 2002). The social enterprise movement is inclusive and extremely diverse, encompassing organisations such as development trusts, community enterprises, cooperatives, housing associations, 'social firms' and leisure trusts, among others. These businesses are operating across an incredibly wide range of industries and sectors from health and social care, to renewable energy, recycling and fair trade. This offers a business model with the prospect of a greater equity of economic power and a more sustainable society, by combining market efficiency with social and environmental justice. Social enterprises are business-like entrepreneurial organisations with primarily social objectives. Their surpluses are mostly reinvested back into their business or the community to help achieve these objectives and change people's lives for the better. Social enterprises are not driven by the need to maximise profit for shareholders and owners.

In essence, social enterprises use business solutions to achieve public good. They tackle a wide range of social and environmental issues and operate in all parts of the economy, helping to make it stronger, more sustainable and socially inclusive. Social enterprises have the potential to spot and move into gaps where services are not being provided. They can add value by providing services in innovative ways which better reflect the needs of service users. In 2006, the government established a social enterprise action plan (Department of Trade and Industry 2006) which established commitment from 12 government departments and bodies such as the Department for Business, Enterprise and Regulatory Reform, the Department of Health, the Department for Children, Schools and Families, as well as the Office of the Third Sector. The intended actions of the government are divided into four themes, which aim to:

1. foster a culture of social enterprise, especially by inspiring the next generation to start thinking about the social impact of business

2. improve the business advice, information and support available to social enterprises

3. tackle the barriers to access to finance that restrict the growth of social enterprises

4. enable social enterprises to work effectively with government to develop policy in areas of expertise. (Department of Trade and Industry 2002, p.7)

We will return to the issue of sustainability in Chapter 6 on commissioning and contracting, as there are many different models of establishing social enterprise in your business plan.

Case study in sustainability – food for thought

The horticultural and catering course, From Greenhouse to the Kitchen, at Liverpool prison is an example of how the prison service, working with local organisations, including the National Health Service, can help offenders get jobs on their release. Prison staff transformed an underused classroom into an industry standard kitchen and built a greenhouse on a tiny patch of prison land. Funding came from the primary care trust (PCT) which believed that the training offered by the project would reduce the risk of ex-offenders suffering the mental health problems that arise from unemployment and social exclusion. It is also hoped that by learning how to cook healthy, nutritionally balanced meals, the men will take a more active role in family life. Offenders can get accreditation towards a City and Guilds certificate in catering or horticultural studies. The scheme has led to projects with different partners. A workshop has opened specialising in refurbishing small electrical appliances, training in shoe and watch repair and several men completing the course have been offered employment on discharge from prison (Jackson 2008).

Chapter summary

This chapter has provided a brief overview of the key components of a typical business plan and can be used as a checklist when starting to plan a review or improvement to an area of service. This is relevant whether on a more grand scale or at a very local level in your own team. The remaining chapters of this book will build on this framework to help develop the different aspects involved but will start to take a more critically reflective perspective when drilling down to the detail. Needless to say, business planning in social care is just not the same as business planning in the private industry, albeit there is often an expectation that the theories and principles can be directly transferred. The tensions that result from this have been the subject of many well written critiques (Harris 2003; Lawler and Bilson 2010; Means *et al.* 2008).

As a manager or professional practitioner, reconciling some of these demands is not easy as there may be many contradictions involved. Managers' concerns are now largely organisational with a focus on the implementation of policy and the expected commitment to efficiency and economic rationality, at the same time giving rise to antagonistic relations between managers and their staff (Harris and White 2009). Work done by Sennet (2006) reminds us that the public sector often follows the private sector in terms of organisational forum and culture. Lawler and Bilson (2010) suggest being mindful of ethical principles, such as respect and responsibility, which help to promote reflection on our management actions and increase 'capacity for compassionate concern' (p.167). The chapter has tried to combine these with a 'how to' approach to business planning that incorporates wider reflection on some of the ethical issues involved in planning for outcomes in social care which maximises the wellbeing of the whole community.

Manager's comment

As a service manager I am very aware that financially the vast majority of social care organisations are on an extremely tight budget. Adherence to financial requirements underpins the whole gamut of work that managers undertake. Conformance is a word that is now commonplace in financial briefings and bulletins. This is without doubt extra pressure within what is an already stressful environment. However, the business plan can be a useful tool with which to fight back, as it brings some clarity to what it is that managers are endeavouring to achieve.

This chapter has provided a useful guide as to what details are required in the plan. Before embarking on the plan, however, you may find that you need to run a project in order to clarify the financial position. To do this, you will need to identify the issue that you wish to explore. Then, draw up a project overview and write it down in the way that makes most sense to you. Remember, this is your support tool so use whichever method you find useful. I tend to use a table format, but you could equally use the format described in Chapter 4 of this book. You will need to name the issue, specify the expected outcome, list the objectives that will enable you to reach the outcome and describe the success criteria. It is also a good idea to highlight any assumptions. For example, I recently became concerned that people in receipt of direct payments for their social care support were accessing a block contract respite provision and still receiving their payments whilst they were there; in effect they were being funded twice (*the issue*). This meant that there was even less money available for everyone else. I needed to resolve this (*expected outcome*) so I appointed a project manager and social worker to establish who was affected, review all the cases, ensure that the current direct payments were at the appropriate level and arrange for any repayments (*objectives*). A database was also needed to ensure this didn't happen again with the budget adjusted as repayments were made (*success criteria*). The *assumptions* were that all workers involved would have a shared value base around requesting the return of any overpayments and that all involved would cooperate.

Finally, once the project overview is completed, write a business case to illustrate it, for example you could do as I did and write it up as a case study. Once you have these in place you will find the rest simply follows on.

Ali Burrow-Smith is a senior manager and registered social worker with the National Health Service in Peterborough.

CHAPTER 4

Managing Resources in Your Business Plan

When you have worked through this chapter you will be able to:

- understand the different funding streams used to support care services
- understand the key management processes in developing a budget framework and preparing for delegated budget responsibilities
- consider the significance of workforce development as a central resource in the strategic and business planning process.

Introduction

In previous chapters we referred to the importance of assigning costs to action plans in order to give the organisation as accurate a picture as possible of the resources needed to deliver the objectives of the business plan. This is both a top-down and bottom-up process done in parallel to ensure that there is the best match possible when allocating resources. It also facilitates the managers responsible for reconciliation and adjustment in order to make sure that any plan is achievable and workable. Poor financial planning and management of resources can adversely affect service users and can result in personal distress and the loss of crucial support to some of the most vulnerable people or groups in the community. Effective long-term financial planning and good budget management ensures that delivery of services to service users is protected by avoiding poor short-term decision-making. This implies the need for very sophisticated resource management systems and well-developed skills of the people responsible for managing and administrating finance for social care.

This chapter begins by looking at the different sources of funding for care services with reference to the complexity of political, social and economic factors that impinge upon decision-making about how resources are allocated. As we saw in Chapter 1, rapid changes have taken place in the way government policy directives have removed major legal barriers to the integration of funding. This has placed emphasis on joint commissioning and the pooling of resources between major stakeholders and the reshaping of care services to support integrated working within partnerships. There is also a general trend to bring funding closer to the individual service user (Department of Health 2008a, 2008b) and delegating more responsibility for budgetary matters in the process to front-line managers and staff. We will therefore address some of the practicalities of setting a budget and managing a budget. Within any strategic developments that aim to make services more responsive to individual users of services, there is a requirement on the statutory sectors to engage with the independent and third sector by agreeing shared outcomes and keeping any services commissioned under constant review. In the next chapter, we will go on to look at the types of issues that might arise in commissioning an appropriate mix of services from both the commissioners and providers' perspective.

It is widely acknowledged that people are the best asset of any organisation particularly as social care services are very labour intensive. The availability and quality of staff is critical in achieving the desired outcomes in your business plan or project. Therefore, this chapter will conclude by looking at the implications within business planning for workforce development. Here, you need to appraise the current position of the workforce and consider whether the labour force is in a position to meet the demands of the business plan and to consider what constraints or opportunities will affect future supply. Within any new developments in care services there are many opportunities afforded through cross-sectoral learning and development to ensure that the knowledge and skills of the workforce are able to deliver the outcomes required, and these need to be capitalised on.

The bigger picture – national funding for social care

Finance for social care comes from a number of different funding streams and a brief overview of the overall context is set out below.

The comprehensive spending review

The government sets the budget for public spending on a three-yearly cycle known as the comprehensive spending review. This provides a framework for medium-term financial planning and defines the key improvements that the public can expect from these resources. Spending reviews typically focus upon one or several aspects of public spending while comprehensive spending reviews focus upon each government department's spending requirements from a zero base.

At the time of writing (2010) the most recent review, in 2007, noted a marked extension in the length, breadth and depth of certainty that the

UK system now provides to managers about their future budgets. There was a major streamlining of the UK's public service performance management regime in which 110 largely departmental-based public service agreements were consolidated into 30 explicitly inter-departmental public service agreements articulating the government's top priorities for the coming period. £26 billion was pledged for personal social services (HM Treasury 2009) accompanied by a series of reforms to strengthen devolution and accountability in both the National Health Service and personal social services. This included the creation of two independent streamlined inspectorates, reporting annually to parliament on performance of how resources have been used.

Devolvement of resources and responsibility for delivery has also been strengthened by giving greater freedom and flexibilities to the best performing local organisation, with incentive systems of payments to health and care services that successfully tackle health inequalities. There were also significant policy developments, for example the consultation *Shaping the Future of Care Together* on funding for long-term care (HM Government 2009a) and through a number of reviews of the workforce in recognition of the pressures on front-line services due to increasing demand (Department for Education and Skills 2006; Department of Health 2009c).

Formula spending share

This is the system which translates the overall spending plans outlined in the comprehensive spending review into specific allocations for each council. The 'formula spending share' takes account of factors that will impact on children's and adult social care services locally, such as deprivation factors or age groups, and is informed by the national census. Within local authorities themselves, it is important to draw on local management data on the specific issues affecting the locality so that delegation of subsequent budgets reflects local needs. On average, children's services and adult social care services' expenditure accounts for nearly a quarter of a council's total budget and is the second largest after education.

Specific grants

These are intended to support targeted government priorities for improving areas of poor performance or to support new service development initiatives. These can cause some tensions in budget management where some priority areas receive increased funding whilst other mainstream budgets remain under severe pressure or suffer actual budget reductions. Specific grants are time limited with provision coming to an end, having to be absorbed into mainstream funding or their impact having to be considered within any ongoing financial plans, or to develop an exit strategy.

Fees and charges

Under Section 17 of the Health and Social Services and Social Security Adjudications Act 1983, local authorities are given discretionary powers to charge for non-residential social services. The local authorities decide on how to set charges for non-residential social services. These charges should be fair and no one should be asked to pay more than they can reasonably afford. The Department of Health issued statutory guidance on charging for home-based care and non-residential social services to all local councils in November 2001. (Department of Health 2001) The intention was to ensure that charging is based on fairer, well-designed charging policies. In particular, service users on low incomes are protected from charging, and any charges levied on disability benefits are subject to an assessment of disability costs, to ensure reasonableness. Charging policies have been revised to accommodate a single calculation of contribution system for individualised budgets. This aims to make them more transparent, easy to understand and cost effective to operate, and to clarify the best method for collecting a contribution from service users.

Pooled budgets

Under the Health Act 1999, Section 31, a discrete fund can be created in partnerships with key agencies to pay for an agreed set of services. Partners must establish formal written agreements stating the agreed aims and outcomes of pooling financial resources. This will identify the host partner who will take responsibility for the overall management of accounts and auditing. Further, the timescales need to be set in such a way that the internal processes of each of the agencies involved for agreeing their contributions can be met. Further support for budget pooling has been given in local authorities by the Children Act 2004 and local area agreements (LAAs) (see Chapter 2) which are geared towards achieving the *Every Child Matters* (HM Government 2003) outcomes. A national review of the effectiveness of pooled budgets conducted by the University of East Anglia and National Children's Bureau in 2006 found that most pooled budgets worked best in the following conditions:

- where partnerships were reinforced with jointly agreed governance arrangements which clarify lines of accountability

- with the establishment of a joint commissioning unit that has the support of all partners

- where an agreed model for joint commissioning clearly sets out the processes involved as a guide for partners, contractors and service users who are involved in the design and delivery of services

- which begins by working with targeted groups of children, for example, where health and social care needs and services will overlap. One example given was the early intervention in community adolescent and mental health services (CAHMS) or via parenting education groups which was seen to help to ameliorate very serious problems thus making them more manageable. These are the sorts of areas in which child care professionals led ultimately to efficiency savings

- where key staff involved in the joint commissioning of services had the expertise and skills to negotiate with senior professionals across sectors and felt that they had gained the confidence of all partners

- where legally binding partnership agreements were used to formalise pooled budget arrangements

- where there was a clearly devised workforce developments plan to improve the capacity of staff to improve services. (University of East Anglia and National Children's Bureau 2006, pp.3–4)

The business planning process requires you to identify the key risks that impact on your organisation and be able to put in place contingency arrangements or corrective actions to mitigate any risks that might occur (Department of Health 2006b). Many risks in developing new services or reviewing existing services revolve around the commitment and securing of resources which will be identified within your SWOT or PESTL analysis. For example, within your financial planning you will have made a host of assumptions within different areas such as:

- the demand for services and the organisation's capacity to meet them in the short and longer term

- efficiency and productivity which takes account of the resources available and the source or supply of these. This might include, for example, how quickly or efficiently your organisation's internal and external processes support the flow and throughput of work; information about the ratios of staff to numbers of referrals or casework; and the skills and competence of staff in delivering services and so on

- unit costs, which enable you to develop a basis for establishing confidence in pricing services and which will be used to inform your commissioning and contracting plans

- value for money including quality and performance management issues.

A business plan should clearly identify what pressures or changes could occur and might give rise to risk in relation to resources. For those risks identified, it is necessary to detail the steps required to reduce these and what contingency arrangements could be put in place.

Considerable pressures and responsibilities on budgets can make them especially volatile and difficult to control. These pressures include, amongst others:

- the rising costs of children-looked-after placements, as one placement can easily cost over £100,000 per year

- increased demand arising from the growing older population and their changing needs

- the increasing costs of proper support to adults with complex needs living in the community

- the use of agency staff within the context of recruitment and retention issues within the social care workforce

- volatility in demand for domiciliary and residential care resulting from market pressures

- the impact of self-directed care and personalisation of services. (Social Services Inspectorate and Audit Commision undated)

One of the principles of good budget management, particularly for front-line managers, is the role they play in providing information to local authority members, their management executive committee and senior managers about how well service policies and priorities are being delivered. This assists complex service change programmes to be conducted in a stable financial environment which minimises risk. It helps the organisation respond to changes in demands for services and ensures that resources are targeted more accurately to the community's needs.

Defining and managing your budget

The process of setting or being delegated a budget enables managers to communicate expectations in making a business plan operational. Budgets are detailed plans containing financial data presented in monetary terms and provide a practical expression of the aims of the organisation or service. A typical budget would include two key aspects: *income* – the resources available and *expenditure* - the uses to which these resources will be put (Martin and Henderson 2001). Martin and Henderson identify a number of important benefits for budgeting besides its use for detailed financial planning purposes. They refer to it as a 'collaborative effort' between different levels in an organisation or across organisations in a way that contributes towards improving communication about their future activities. Budgeting is also seen as a crucial tool in coordinating the right level of support by providing an overview, as well as incorporating all the detailed activities for senior management. In a slightly more optimistic fashion, they also cite budgets as 'a bit of a challenge' (Martin and Henderson 2001, p.289) to staff in order to do their best within the resources available.

A well-managed budget is thus an indicator of the manager's own performance which contributes to the overall picture of how they carry out their role and functions. Whilst controversial, this is supposed to encourage staff and managers to provide feedback on the activities they are responsible for and to identify and report on any limitations or restraints where resources are insufficient when good budget monitoring and communication is in place. Doing the groundwork, timetabling and good negotiation skills are all part of effectively designing and drawing up a budget. A good budget is one which is simple to understand, is clear about how the actual figures match with the stated aims and objectives and takes account of the overall financial climate under appropriate budget headings. Those to whom budget-holding responsibilities will be delegated should therefore be involved in all stages of setting and agreeing a budget.

Criteria for evaluating effective resource management in your business plan

There is an essential relationship between resources or inputs and the consequential quality, as well as quantity, of service provided. We shall address some of these aspects in two later chapters on performance management and evaluation, as both are concerned with quality measurement. It is important to distinguish between financial resources and other types of resources or assets such as human resources or physical assets such as buildings, furniture or equipment. Most managers will have delegated budgets and hence a degree of financial autonomy. There are four key criteria used to assess resource management. These are efficiency, effectiveness, value for money and equity:

Efficiency describes the relationship between the organisation's inputs and its outputs. Efficiency entails securing minimum inputs for a given quality and quantity of service provided. This is achieved when a given quantity of output is provided at minimum costs. Defining and measuring the outcomes of care is of course naturally problematic. The term 'output' is usually restricted to more measurable aspects of care such as the number of services provided and the number of people receiving support. Measures of this type of efficiency are frequently referred to as 'technical efficiency', that is, the relationship between the inputs used and the resulting quantity of output. 'Cost efficiency' is the combination of assessment and services within prevailing costs that produces a technically efficient output in the cheapest way.

Another aspect of care associated with efficiency is the concept of 'outcomes'. 'Outcomes' are generally much longer term and include less easy to measure benefits of care services such as an improved sense of wellbeing or the meeting of wider needs such as cultural and social. Definitions of efficiency, for example, all refer to the internal efficiency of the service or organisation and do not describe the social values to society, for example around the quality of life of older people living in residential or other types of care or the relevance of experiences of young people looked after in relation to their life chances. Managers need to remain critical about what signals efficiency in this respect. The cost implications of direct payments and individualised budgets have led to debates about cost and cost efficiency and incorporate a consideration of quality (Glasby and Littlechild 2009). A study by Zarb and Nadash (1994) suggests that direct payment schemes have met a wider range of needs than traditional services and led to fewer unmet needs. People receiving payments had more reliable support and experienced fewer problems with their care as well as higher levels of satisfaction than those using directly provided services. This indicates a need for other criteria than financial efficiency to judge the value of outputs of service provision.

Effectiveness is a concept that endeavours to bring together both the measurable and more subjective elements of care services relating to the objectives of the services as well as its outputs. It is a concept which embraces an implicit, if not always explicit, assumption about the social value of the output and moves nearer towards an assessment of the outputs of an organisation.

Value for money is something that is stated if an organisation or service is both efficient and effective and attempts to bring the measurable and immeasurable, the objective and subjective together. Value for money is used in two ways, first of all in terms of outputs compared to the inputs, as judged in terms of effectiveness and efficiency, as the above reference to direct payments illustrates. The second is more limited, where managing resources seek to attain best value by evaluating the services purchased against other criteria.

Equity involves further subjective judgements about the deployment and distributed resources. Service users are not a homogeneous group and each group merits consideration with informed decisions regarding the extent to which resources should be tailored or whether positive steps should be taken to combat untoward discrimination, as discussed in the previous chapter. Political factors and pressures are also relevant, for example where children's services are likely to be increasingly in the spot-light. The impact of cost decisions on informal carers is another example and requires a detailed knowledge of user and carer issues.

Horizontal equity is where users with similar needs receive the same amount of resources. Vertical equity uses criterion to argue that users with the greatest needs should receive more resources. This latter principle is enshrined in the development of access criteria now standardised in the distribution of resources in social care. These types of decisions around resource distribution involve value judgements which are not always made explicit.

The complexity of setting and managing a budget

Coleman and Earley (2005) suggest a systems framework for understand-ing the relationship between resource inputs and outcomes in service provision, given that this is also mediated by a myriad of other factors. The main elements of this model comprise the external environment from which resources are obtained as outlined earlier; the processes that take place within the organisation which they term 'the production technol-ogy' (p.170). It also includes the human relations system, which forms a bridge between the external environment and the organisation, affecting the way that services are provided. Whilst the budgets of a very small organisation may be delegated to specific people, within more complex organisations, leaders determine both the extent of decentralisation and nature of managerial responsibility which is either devolved or delegated in nature (Field 2007).

Costing analysis

Effective resource allocation is only possible if those taking decisions know just how much the various elements of staffing, building and other assets actually cost. The relevant costs that one should take into account when making decisions also depend in part on the time frame over which the resources will be used. Recurrent and capital costs should be distin-guished. Recurrent costs are those that will have to be met year on year. Capital costs are those resources that will last for a longer period and often represent a bigger and often one-off investment. Rational budgeting ap-proaches are typically plan-led where early on in the process, planning and budgeting are integrated and provide an estimate of the volume of physical resources required to support the plan. Other types of costings are:

DIRECT COSTS

These are costs that can be identified specifically with a particular sponsored project or can be directly assigned to an activity relatively easily and with a high degree of accuracy. These might be staff salaries, heating or travel.

INDIRECT COSTS

These represent the expenses of doing business not readily identified with a particular grant, contract, project function or activity, but are considered necessary for the general operation of the organisation and the conduct of activities it performs. Additional time for organising and managing project meetings in order to take an initiative forward is an example of an indirect cost. Costing this in monetary terms provides a mechanism for determining fairly and conveniently what proportions of the department administration each project should bear.

The emphasis on full economic costing for voluntary organisations when bidding for contracts and funding has been a very topical issue, particularly with the shift towards greater outsourcing services to external providers. The government and its sector representatives have issued comprehensive guidance in this area as understanding the organisation's full costs is critical in strategic decision-making, and ensuring sustainability (Finance Hub 2008). Full cost recovery is a method of cost allocation which ensures appropriate portions of overheads are allocated in projects and services when putting together bids and contracts.

Difficulties in securing funding for overhead costs lead to underinvestment in:

- management and leadership
- internal and external infrastructure
- strategic development and governance.

This difficulty is historically exacerbated by a trend on the part of the third sector's funders towards funding the direct costs of projects rather than overheads or 'core funding'. Failure to secure funding for overhead costs makes important services, including public services, and the organisations that deliver them, vulnerable and unsustainable. It is also useful to note that an indirect cost rate represents the ratio between the total indirect costs and direct costs mechanism.

FIXED COSTS

These are costs which have to be met irrespective of the number of services you provide, for example staffing, buildings and maintenance and administration.

VARIABLE COSTS

These are costs that increase or decrease as output rises or falls and constitute those expenses that change in proportion to the activity in the service. The break-even point is relevant here, as if the level of providing a service is exactly equal to the cost of delivering it, then one is able to stay in budget.

UNIT COSTS

Costs can increase year on year. But the process of costing individual units of services in the public sector is known as unit costing and is a fairly crude method where the total cost of a service is divided by the number of individual services provided to give an average cost (Hafford-Letchfield 2009). Without linking what we spend (input) to what we provide (output) cost effectiveness cannot be evaluated. Measuring the cost per unit produced is therefore one way that we can define value for money. Comparing the unit cost of the service over time facilitates tracking of progress on cost effectiveness. By comparing unit costs with other similar organisations, the relative efficiency can be assessed. The calculation of the unit cost is very simple. It is represented by taking the total cost of a service and dividing it by the number of service units provided.

$$\frac{\text{Total cost}}{\text{Number of cost units}} = \text{Unit Cost}$$

One of the main problems with this approach is that one can only determine an average cost which might mask a wide variety of variables not included.

When purchasing more than a single unit or service, the *total* cost will increase with the number of units. It is common however for the *unit* cost to decrease as quantity is increased as in bulk-purchasing or block contracting, as an assumed discount will be taken into account. This reduction in long run unit costs, which arise from an increase in production or purchasing, is due to the fixed costs being spread out over more products. This is what is referred to as economies of scale.

MARGINAL COSTS

When planning your budget, you should look at the marginal cost of producing an additional unit of output. The marginal cost is the cost of the additional inputs needed to produce that output. For example, if it costs £10,000 to assess 100 people on a training programme but £10,200 to assess 1001 people, the average cost of the assessment is £100 but the marginal cost of the 101st assessment is £200. More formally, the marginal cost is the derivative of total production costs with respect to the level of output and so, therefore, marginal costs and average costs can differ greatly.

OPPORTUNITY COSTS

Scarcity of resources necessitates trade-offs which in turn result in opportunity costs. Whilst the costs of goods or a service are often thought of in monetary terms, the opportunity costs of a decision are based on what must be given up or the next best alternative. Any costs that involve a choice between options have what we call an opportunity cost. The consideration of opportunity costs is one of the key differences between the concepts of economic cost and accounting costs. Assessing opportunity costs is fundamental to assessing the true cost of any course of action. In the case where there is no explicit accounting or monetary cost or price attached to a course of action, or the explicit accounting or monetary cost is low, then ignoring opportunity costs may produce the illusion that its benefits cost nothing at all. The unseen opportunity costs then become the implicit hidden costs of that course of action. Opportunity costs are useful when evaluating the costs and benefits of choices and are often expressed in non-monetary terms. The concept of opportunity costs has a wide range of applications including user choice, time management and analysis of comparative advantage.

It is certainly not easy to grasp some of the key concepts about different costings as illustrated above. They may appear quite complex and require support from an expert in economic or financial management. However, there are some underpinning principles which managers need to understand to be able to engage in planning and budgeting:

1. Develop a basis for the establishment of prices for the external market known as contracting.

2. Undertake a cost comparison with alternative service providers as in Best Value or with other services during the contracting process.

3. Set targets for productivity, number of hours, number of service users receiving services and so on.

4. Identify options for cost reduction.

5. Establish and justify whether the service appears to be good value for money and accountability.

6.   Create an internal market for services and to identify the level of charging.

Case study on costings – from Ruth Brown of Community First

As a development worker, I have introduced the template to two organisations, each with an income of between £120 and £160,000. One is a mental health charity, predominantly funded by social services departments but looking at sustainable and independently funded projects; the other is a women's support charity, funded predominantly by LSC [Learning and Skills Council], Sure Start and Community Fund, with some independent grants.

Costing up until I introduced the template was done on a 'gut' feel. It is quite extraordinary how very close a gut feel can be, and I wouldn't want to underestimate the skills these chief officers have. However, as we all acknowledge, gut feel does not always accurately reflect the contribution of central functions to delivering the service, or the role and importance of indirect costs.

Both organisations quickly absorbed the implications of government policy and the template, and were keen to understand their central functions and how they could allocate them proportionately.

Both groups are now using the template to review their costing processes. The women's support group plans to use the template before each new funding application is put together. They found the more rigorous approach allowed them to cost their service more accurately, and build reserves in a clear-cut manner, either through average costing or through putting in a reserves percentage with the confidence of being able to back up why it has to be that amount and why the funder should pay it.

Although the pressures of running an organisation limit the time chief officers can spend on changing processes, my colleagues and I are working hard to help chief officers overcome these pressures and work towards full cost recovery.

Both groups are increasingly confident in arguing their case, and I believe the model will give them the evidence they need to tip the balance towards full cost recovery. They are very positive about how it can allow them to cost more sustainable projects (e.g. training in the work place to pre-empt and prevent mental health issues). They both are committed to full cost recovery, and I believe that with support, will achieve it.

From: www.fullcostrecovery.org.uk/main/products.php?section=3 1&sid=56&content=ruth_brown_community_first

For more information about Community First visit their website at www.communityfirst.org.uk

Budget planning

As evident from the complexity of costing services above, efficiency is likely to be promoted by a rational approach to decision-making in which your professional judgement comes into play to evaluate alternative uses of resources in terms of their likely contribution to achieving your strategic and service objectives. A rational approach requires some form of planning in which objectives are set out and ways of achieving them indicated, as spelt out in the previous chapter. This will also be a political process, perhaps with limited potential for forward planning and may involve a number of interested stakeholder groups influencing the decision-making process. The more traditional approach to budgeting concentrates on incremental budgeting where planning is incremental and mainly involves making annual adjustments to established patterns of expenditure. This is done by reconsidering the current year's budget as the basis of planning for the next. Changes are then made in response to changes in income or the development of new services but generally the organisation continues as it has done before. There may be long-term stability with inherent historic tendencies around expenditure rather than more creative development.

Zero-based budgeting

This is a different technique, which enables you to start from scratch each year or at a specific time and requires those involved to state their intentions and justify their expenditure before spending is allowed.

In principle, the practice of rationally planning the budget is a cyclic process of:

- audit – to establish the present situation
- determining and defining aims and objectives
- identifying and costing alternative actions to achieve the objectives
- prioritising – establishing which alternatives actions could achieve the objectives
- linking and matching component parts to the development plan
- implementing and putting selected plans into operation
- evaluating and measuring progress towards aims as a result of implemented plans, and then back to
- audit, and so on in cyclic fashion.

Effective development planning with the data it produces paves the way for budget preparation. However, as one knows from experience, the interrelationship of plans and what is eventually budgeted for is not always as evident as it might appear in theory.

We started off this section on the complexity of setting and managing a budget by looking at the prediction of income and planning expenditure within income restraints.

Income

One of the fundamental problems in planning is that forward forecasting is a very inexact science. Some form of government grants are subject to change according to national and local policies and financial wellbeing.

Expenditure

In most organisations there will be basic costs that have to be met, year on year and have to be entered into the budget at an early stage to allow for changes that may affect figures. These will include administrative functions, buildings and use of facilities. A starting point could be the financial report for the past year or current year so that the costing of the total plan or proposal is known. There will be some costs that cannot be more than an 'educated guess', for example staffing costs. Staff will inevitably be on different pay scales or spinal points in the scale or be awarded additional payments for experience, duties and qualifications, or even in some areas for performance. Where new roles and responsibilities are being developed then job evaluation or re-evaluation can help to estimate the salary range for key posts in the new service. Management costs must be included as well as administrative, accounts or reception functions at service level or by purchasing functions such as payroll, legal, human resources, IT and marketing, which need to be allocated back to the service level and added to the costs incurred. Some other on-staff current costs (such as food and utilities) may be subject to strong inflationary pressures and need to be kept under regular review.

Weindling (1997) discusses the ideas of gap analysis, which is the difference between where you are and where you want to be. The importance of involving stakeholders in contributing to the long-term planning process will enhance their ownership of policy and practice around budgeting. The case below presupposes that budgetary evaluation enables the 'gap' to be identified but also illustrates the variety of internal and external influences that inhibits tight planning.

Case study – ensuring budgets are set to reflect operational realities within learning disability services

Day services for people with a learning disability are the subject of modernisation to meet the expectations identified in the government's strategy for people with a learning disability in both Valuing People (Department of Health 2001b) and Putting People First (Department of Health 2008b).

This means that there is ongoing change in the operational environment of providing day services away from 'centre-based' services, to services which make more use of community facilities and encourage more people into education and employment.

The budget-setting process needs to be well connected to service delivery to avoid continuation of budgets reflecting traditional centre activities and to reflect the new spending patterns. Some of these issues have been picked up in joint reviews as illustrated below:

- Transport budgets were not adjusted to reflect the fact that fewer service users need to be transported to the centres.

- Although expenditure levels on transport had fallen, this was not as great as the reduction in usage, thereby increasing unit costs, and yet no attempt was made to rationalise the transport arrangements.

- Other centre-based budgets such as consumable materials andprovisions were not reduced.

- New budgets were not created to reflect expenditure on accessto community.

- New budgets were not created to reflect the support costs to be borne by children's services and adult social care services relating to educational activities or work placements.

In these examples, the problems of finance staff setting budgets on the basis of the previous year without discussion with service managers resulted in problems for the manager in budget management and problems of budget accountability.

Quotes from Joint Review reports included:

'Finance set my budget...I would shape it differently...it would be more realistic', and 'Still have the allocated funds for non-staffing budgets that were handed over from [previous authority] four years ago...have struggled to get these aligned with reality'. (Adapted from Improvement and Development Agency 2006)

Monitoring your budget and financial control

As stated earlier, planning the budget is a forward-looking exercise and a statement of intent. Once the financial year starts, the budget is used as a record of the income and expenditure flows that have occurred or are committed up to the present time. This backward-looking form of the budget is an essential tool in implementation and is used for monitoring and evaluation. Monitoring is undertaking through regular checks between the intended expenditure at a stage in the year under any subjective heading and the actual expenditure at that time. When discrepancies occur they may, for example, be due to incorrect recording of payments or wrongly entered data or a mismatch between invoicing and payment. They may also be due to unforeseen changes in expenditure and income. Monitoring these types of activities on a regular basis is part of financial control. Evaluation is another important aspect in considering how resource use meets the overall objectives for the service or organisation. It is much more strategic in its viewpoint, concerned not so much with the detail but with the impact of the plans that the resource use has fulfilled. It also prompts thinking about the quality of the outcomes arising from resource use.

Operational financial management is concerned with ensuring that money allocated in the budget is properly spent for authorised purposes and that budget plans are adhered to or if not, changes are properly authorised. Financial control is present in the following areas of administration:

- purchasing of goods and contracting of services
- banking of funds received by the organisation
- management of the employee payroll
- security of assets
- maintenance of petty cash accounts
- maintenance of voluntary funds
- insurance matters
- data security to prevent the misuse of information. (Coleman and Earley 2005)

Mismanagement may be due to poor checks, the use of 'short cuts' or deliberate acts but problems are more likely to arise as a result of the complexity of arrangements within an organisation. In order to protect the interests and practices of those involved, the Audit Commission suggests a number of essential practices across four management dimensions: leadership; people; processes and stakeholders. They offer a toolkit which can be used to help the organisation to:

- establish a profile of its financial management
- test organisational leaders' skills in financial management
- compare this with where it wants financial management to be positioned, in order to maximise organisational effectiveness in the short or longer term

- build a team-based approach to improvement in financial management
- identify strengths and areas for improvement
- develop an action plan
- help prioritise improvement
- review and track its progress over time. (Audit Commission 2009)

Internal audit occurs when a specialist member of the organisation looks at the detail of operational management and undertakes financial checking. External auditing is undertaken by persons unconnected to the organisation. This may go beyond financial checks and may report on how the organisation is achieving its stated aims and making use of its resources. Often external auditing informs and then prompts policy development. The greater the degree of devolution of responsibility for resource management, the more important is financial probity and the achievement of value for money for both current expenditure and asset management.

Asset management

In order to secure value for money, an organisation must manage its assets well. Coleman and Early (2005) suggest that managing assets involves a number of processed which they identify as:

- Maintaining security and ensuring that public property is properly secured and protected.
- Maintaining existing assets by regular inspection of the property or equipment preferably with the expertise of professionally qualified people. Since some experts could have a pecuniary interest in recommending maintenance, the inspections should be independent of maintenance contracts. Maintenance also needs to be included in budget plans.
- Disposal of assets where they have reached the end of their life span or are no longer needed. Decision-making about disposal needs to be undertaken by more than one person so that there can be no accusation of fraudulent activity.
- Replacement of assets. Pressure on resources and the need to purchase for new developments may inhibit the planned replacement of equipment or routine repair to property or regular ground maintenance. This needs to be offset against the potential need for increased expenditure in the future and charted in an asset management plan.

- New assets could be identified as desirable if resources allow in the future and then incorporated into strategic planning. (Coleman and Earley 2005, pp.184–185).

If assets are an important aspect of your service, perhaps as a provider of care, then your budget plan should include evidence on three aspects of developing and maintaining assets such as the physical condition of premises to ensure safe and continuous operation within legislative requirement; sufficiency in relation to the needs and demand; and suitability with a focus on the way in which the provision meets the service needs.

In summary, managing resources and improving financial management is always going to be difficult in the context of public services. A number of common reasons are frequently identified such as 'it's the responsibility of the finance department', and the difficulties in planning when managers feel that they are fire-fighting against an uncertain backdrop of financial settlements from central government or local demand.

Some of the solutions lie in establishing clearer relationships and procedures about the respective roles and relationships between corporate and service departments and in turn with front-line managers and, crucially, with staff delivering the service. This latter group are sometimes left without updates on resource issues and their implications, or they are not encouraged to make links between performance and financial management despite providing lots of management information. The budget-setting period is sometimes the only time that service and front-line managers get involved in financial management issues in a culture that can also lay blame if managers are not sufficiently ambitious or properly trained. These are issues for both training and support within any management development programme. As Field (2007) points out, whether you are working in a small organisation or a large complex organisation, a degree of decentralisation, devolution and delegation of budget management is required and it is important that managers are clear about the extent to which financial responsibilities are given and this should also be clear in a manager's job description.

> The breadth of financial competence needed by managers depends on the approach to finance within the organisation, their managerial level, whether budget responsibility is devolved or delegated and the level of support received from accountants and administrative staff... At a more strategic level effective management may involve the use of specialist financial techniques and require a deeper understanding of financial management. Reassuringly perhaps, senior managers do not need to train to become accountants; as their roles become more onerous the level of technical support received from finance specialists

should increase. It is important however that the manager resists the temptation to transfer responsibility for finance to accounting staff and has a broad understanding of financial techniques, can participate in their use and sensitively interpret and act upon the outcomes. (Field 2007, p.55)

Workforce development

This chapter would not be complete if it did not consider development of the social care workforce or put more crudely, the 'labour' involved in social care as a major resource for meeting the population's support needs. At the time of writing (2010) the social care workforce is in a period of rapid transformation with a number of established bodies whose job it is to specifically support workforce development together with its stakeholders, as illustrated in the figure below.

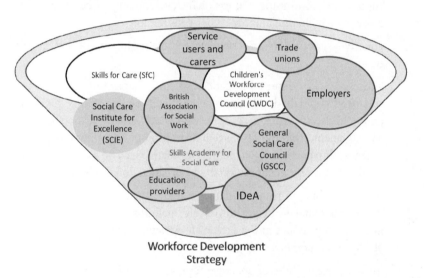

Figure 4.1 Just some of the partners involved in developing the workforce

The social care workforce is increasingly working in an integrated way with other services, particularly with education, health and housing, and this trend is expected to continue in the future. There have been a number of efforts to put some professions within the workforce on an equal footing with other professions. This has been achieved through the professional regulation and registration of social workers and the introduction of the social work degree and the post-qualifying framework. Two significant national reports have indicated the need for increased levels of funding for training. This has resulted in higher levels of qualifications for social care workers, and the need for proactive steps to improve the status of work in the sector to prove that the workforce can adjust and advance into the future. The first reports are *Interim Findings* published by the Department for Children, Schools and Families (2005) and its review in 2006. These set out a vision for 2020. Some of the challenges and key priorities for action are:

- appropriate support from supervisors, managers and leaders to ensure that staff feel valued and committed to their roles particularly new workers. A range of induction programmes have been developed including a newly qualified social workers' initiative to support staff in their first year of practice with reduced workloads and ongoing training

- workforce strategies with a focus on training and development and support for continuing professional development, to equip workers to deal with change and for career progression

- effective supervision and systems for managing workload as the norm

- addressing key issues in leadership and management, including the need to embed the approach offered by the Skills for Care and Children's Workforce Development Council Leadership and Management Strategy. This attempts to promote a common approach to leadership and management development based on a whole systems model that integrates individual and organisational needs

- improving human resource management which, if not effective, can contribute to delays in workforce reform, failure to tackle recruitment and retention issues and a lack of longer-term planning such as the ability of an employer to 'grow its own' employees

- drawing clear lines of management accountability and extending registration to develop the accountability and professionalism of the social care workforce

- using commissioning as a tool to raise quality in social care services, including a greater focus on improving outcomes and considering workforce quality as part of the commissioning process. (Department for Children, Schools and Families)

The second report for the adult social care workforce, the document *Working to Put People First* (Department of Health 2009c) identified six key themes as priority for the workforce in delivering future services:

1. leadership of local employers in workforce planning whether in the public, private or third sectors and of directors of adult social services in their strategic workforce commissioning role

2. ensuring the right steps are taken to promote recruitment, retention and career pathways to provide the many talents the workforce needs

3. workforce remodelling and commissioning to achieve service transformation

4. workforce development so we have the right people with the right skills

5. more joint and integrated working between social, health care and other sectors

6. regulation for quality in services as well as public assurance.

There are vast arrays of occupational groups that make up the social care workforce and at the time of writing (2010) it is estimated that there are 100 million employees, one of the biggest sectors in business and industry. Other substantive texts on this topic can provide more depth in relation to training and supporting the workforce in your management role (see Hafford-Letchfield *et al.* 2008). In relation to strategy and business planning, familiarisation with the National Minimum Data Set in Social Care (NMDS-SC) launched in 2007 to gather standardised workforce information for the social care sector should be part and parcel of the organisation's planning tools (Skills for Care 2007). The NMDS-SC aims to gather a minimum set of information about services and staff across all service user groups and sectors within the social care sector in England.

The projected increase in the need for social care over the next decade makes workforce strategies and policies for extending working life and improving recruitment and retention particularly important, especially in the face of the Employment Equality (Age) Regulations 2006 and the ageing workforce (Social Care Workforce Research Unit 2009). A report based on the NMDS-SC in 2009 demonstrated that some of these variations in age by sector are statistically significant in terms of planning services for the future. Information about the workforce, such as gender, sexual identity, disability, race, ethnicity and religion and patterns of employment, such as full-time, part-time, casual and permanent can also contribute to equality strategies in employment. The Association of Directors of Social Services unequivocally states:

social care as a profession works with the impact of discrimination, and whatever the individual understanding, everyone within the profession is charged with the responsibility to deal with inequality and injustice...equalities are therefore at the core of the social care value base and constitute a moral imperative... The business case for modernisation and reform of public services...covers opening up areas of recruitment in an intensely competitive labour market, financial savings on disciplinary, grievance and tribunal costs, tapping into a vibrant voluntary sector resource and, demonstrating that the (diversity) strategy, adopted results in sustained and recent progress. (Association of Directors of Social Services 2004, cited in Hafford-Letchfield *et al.* 2008, p.98)

Within the context of this chapter on resource management, leaders and managers have a pivotal role to play in ensuring that any planning of workforce development is integrated in a variety of ways within the culture, structure, practice and review mechanisms of the organisation.

Chapter summary

Managing finance and resources for care is a challenging task. The outputs and outcomes required are multiple and have both public and private benefits for the community. There are many different stakeholders with different interests in how resources are used. Ambiguities in relating inputs to service outcomes make it difficult to measure efficiency in care and support provision. This chapter has highlighted some of the key operational issues and knowledge needed to assess how aspects of your business plan might be funded and how this is scoped and evaluated within the area of your own delegated responsibility. Decentralised budgeting has been encouraged on the principle that local authorities and its managers are better informed about local needs and costs than those at the centre. The mixed economy of care also encourages many institutions to contract and compete for resources and to raise quality and performance standards. However, a number of tensions have arisen, as we have seen in the section on workforce development above, and as discussed in the next chapter where unreflective approaches to efficiency may also harm equity. Increased uncertainties about sources of funding and opportunities mean that some managers need to be able to cope both strategically with the impact of these policy tensions on their organisations as well as attend to the careful details of day-to-day budget management.

Manager's comment

As a workforce development professional I regularly hear about the concerns that managers and other employees have about the need to be fully equipped to deal with the challenges of administrating sometimes difficult devolved budgets, complicated funding streams and business planning in a changing environment, and taking into account the development needs of a diverse and eclectic workforce.

I have seen some of the most experienced and outwardly confident managers and leaders balk at the prospect of embarking on a finance management project as part of a leadership and management development programme. They even consider withdrawing at the thought of delivering a presentation on their finance and business planning project to their peers. On the other hand, both new and experienced employees alike will often complain that they are not given enough financial responsibility or control over the delivery of the service they directly provide in a profession that is increasingly espousing the importance of customer choice and control.

Managers and employees alike report to me that they often feel inadequate or unable to keep up in a profession that seems to demand constant change without enough time to assimilate or embed the previous change programme. Of course, many of these concerns or anxieties are not always unreasonable but neither are the catalysts new or insurmountable. The world of social care and social work is now, and in truth always has been, in a state of constant development and change and has always come under financial scrutiny and pressure.

The social and health care workforce has always been, and is always likely to be, at the vanguard of significant change at the same time as needing to keep an eye on resource pressures, because in reality customers, other taxpayers and changing technology have always presented challenges and opportunities for the workforce; it's the nature of providing people intensive and costly social and health care services in a society where people continue to live longer, with increasing expectations and complex health and social care needs.

As a local authority organisation development and learning manager who is responsible for managing my own budget and responding to the needs of a learning community that is constantly changing and growing, I have to identify and promote creative learning methods and resources that respond to the learning and development needs of people employed by local authorities, health care trusts and the third sector. This also includes volunteers, service users managing their own budgets, commissioning their own services and employing and managing their own staff and carers; and I also support the learning and development of the people and carers they employ or commission.

I recognise that responding to change, managing finance resources and business planning, whether as a new or experienced manager, will always be challenging; and if finances become difficult, as we expect they will, we will have to find creative ways to manage our resources, deliver our services and maintain our learning and development. It is worthwhile reflecting that as we aim to encourage service users to manage their own budgets and commission their own services, including pulling on support in their own families and communities, we will need to move away from relying on training courses and learning programmes. We need to explore how we can learn from practice and experience, from reading, sometimes getting it wrong and learn more actively from our peers and by sharing our knowledge and skills.

Neil Chick is an organisational learning and development manager in a London local authority.

CHAPTER 5

Project Management

When you have worked through this chapter you will be able to:

- describe a systematic approach to project management and the different phases and steps to enable the process of defining, planning, organising, controlling and closing a project
- identify the key skills and knowledge required in order to manage a project successfully.

Introduction

In Chapter 3 we looked at the process for developing an overall business plan. This may involve a number of projects, either small or large, that need to be actively managed in order to contribute to the overall success of the plan. Indeed, putting together a strategy or business plan is a project in itself. Creating an infrastructure for approving and monitoring the project in your business plan is very important. Project management provides an overall approach for managing a defined change process. It provides a set of tools to help bring structure and to impose discipline when managing change. Undertaking work that involves multiple priorities, complex and numerous tasks, deadlines, constant communication across organisational boundaries with limited resources, all make potential use of project management techniques. In other words, the more complex the change process anticipated, then the use of project management becomes more important. Rosenau (1992) describes a project as having four features:

1. the presence of three-dimensional objectives such as: performance specification, time and cost

2. a degree of uniqueness, that is, it is carried out once, is temporary, and usually involves a new group of people coming together to implement it

3. it involves resources, people and materials, but which are often only marginally under the control of a project manager

4.   it takes place within an organisation or setting which has a multiplicity of other purposes.

Thus, it is not the size or complexity of change that determines the conceptualisation of a project. Instead, it is about having a clear focus on both its beginning and end. Project management offers a systematic approach to managing the process using a number of logical phases and steps which enable you to define, plan, organise, control and close a project. If not personally responsible for its direction, this approach remains useful. It offers a means of seeing the bigger picture and in developing an appreciation of how each person's role and responsibilities fits within any project being worked on, particularly if it affects your area of work and responsibility.

As indicated above, a project can be very large and long term such as the transformation of services in line with a key government policy like *Every Child Matters* (HM Government 2003). It may also be small and short term such as implementing a specific staff training programme. To reiterate generally, a project is one which:

- involves numerous and complex activities
- occurs over a set period as a set or chain of unique events
- has a distinct beginning and end date, in that it is finite
- has defined or limited resources and an allocated budget
- has many people involved from different functional areas of the organisation or involves other organisations
- involves a set of sequenced activities
- has a clear aim or outcome and is orientated to achieving this
- results in an end service or change in service.

Examples of projects one might be involved in are:

- the development of a new service in response to new legislation
- establishing a quality assurance system for a team
- establishing an information system, for example an information system using information and communication technologies (ICT)
- training staff to implement a new role or responsibility
- setting up a user consultation forum or panel
- achieving a reduction in resource in a particular service area.

The project management process is generally seen to extend through five stages. This starts with defining the project's goals; ensuring that these are SMART (Specific, Measurable, Achievable, Realistic, Timescale); planning the work programme; leading its implementation; monitoring progress of the project and finally completing the project to ensure that it is embedded into mainstream activity. These stages are often iterative where the later stages of a project are being informed by knowledge gained from earlier ones. Adopting a project perspective for aspects of a business plan encourages managers to be more explicit about key aspects of the process and their role within it. These might include:

- **purpose** – an understanding of why change is needed
- **definition** – an outline of what the project seeks to achieve and defining the project in terms of scope and objectives. Definition would also include an analysis of the context, constraints, stakeholders and risk
- **plan** – a map of the sequence, duration and interdependencies of the specific steps required to achieve the project's objectives in terms of milestones (intermediate goals), activities (work to be undertaken) and resources (people, materials and budget required)
- **monitoring and control processes** – regular assessment of project progress compared to the project plan will highlight the need for corrective actions. Such actions may involve the provision of extra resources or time in order to achieve original objectives or may involve the redefinition of project objectives
- **evaluation** – upon completion, a determination of whether the project objectives and benefits have been achieved. Project evaluation is not seen as an optional add-on but as a crucial part of the project planned from the outset.

Managing a project – significant steps
In order to manage the complexity inherent in most projects, a number of tools have been developed which are reviewed below.

Work breakdown structure (WBS)
The WBS defines the scope of the project specifying the work that falls within its remit. A WBS is used to express real objectives through increasingly detailed elements of work where activities or tasks that can be undertaken by project team members are clearly defined. WBS is the first step in the production of the project's plan. If costed, these tasks can be used to identify the necessary budget. Common sense should prevail when thinking about how small each task should be. It is best to break down the work into smaller elements until you arrive at the smallest discrete piece of work that is significant within the project. Identifying a basic framework

to start working out your WBS is illustrated in Figure 5.1, which takes the example of planning for a staff development event.

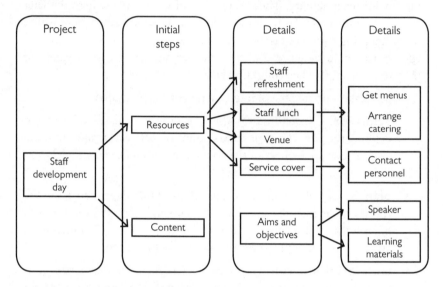

Figure 5.1 *Initial structure for planning a staff development day*

The characteristics of a successful WBS should enable the status of each activity to be assessed easily, and should demonstrate each activity's in-dependence from other activities with a definite beginning and end date to each. The sorts of issues that require consideration when deciding on activities needed to complete your project include: their dependence on the availability of resources and equipment and the availability of staff indicated in the plan. The latter would need to take into account any particular training or development needs that staff might have. If any of the activities are subcontracted, you will also need to consider how these impact on other project activities. Hence, you can see how quickly some activities become very complex and this is one of the positive aspects of developing a WBS.

Figure 5.2 (see p.104) illustrates a Gantt chart which enables these sequential and parallel activities to be visualised when constructing WBS. An essential concept behind project planning is the sequential nature of some activities (for example, some activities are dependent on other ac-tivities being completed first and these 'dependent' activities follow in a sequence with each stage being more or less completed before the next activity can begin). Of course, experience tells us that life isn't always like that in the social care environment but this is what is often called 'sequential' or 'linear' WBS. Similarly, other activities not dependent on completion of any other tasks may be done at any time before or after a particular stage is reached and these are referred to as non-dependent or 'parallel' tasks.

Milestones plan

This shows the deliverables that build towards the final objectives of the project. By linking dependent milestones together it shows the sequence of states a project will pass through. Milestones can provide the start point for a WBS.

Responsibility chart

This defines the responsibilities of various groups involved in the project, differentiating between those who execute the task; those who take decisions about it; those who need to be consulted or kept informed; and those who can provide advice and expert guidance.

Gantt chart or activity schedule

The Gantt chart is in effect a combination of the milestone plan and responsibility chart. It shows each task in terms of estimated duration, the activities on which it depends in order to be completed, and subsequent tasks that depend on its completion to proceed. Gantt charts have become a common technique for representing the phases and activities of a project WBS so that they can be understood by a wide audience. Gantt charts (named after Henry Gantt's ideas from more than 100 years ago) are helpful in representing the relationship between tasks and sub-tasks and provide flexibility in displaying information relating to each task. Many organisations use project management software which include Gantt charts or you can use a simple Excel spreadsheet and even a flip chart with Post-it notes. One of the advantages of using software (which come with their own tutorials, so we won't be looking at specifics here!) is that they enable you to carry out 'what if?' scenarios to try to understand the impact of proposed changes to aspects of the project, such as resources, specification and timing (Jones 2007).

A network diagram

This involves mapping of the dependencies between the tasks in the change process. This should enable the identification of a critical path of activities which need to be completed to time if the overall project is to meet its deadline.

Total project timetable

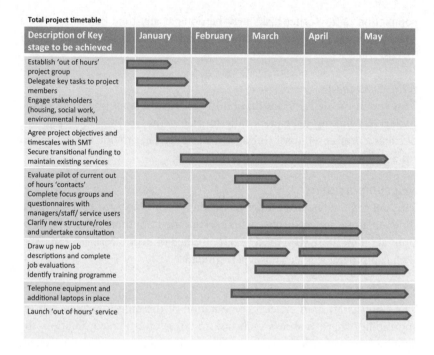

Figure 5.2 Gantt chart – using the example of implementing an out-of-hours contact service

Risk matrix

The risk matrix plots the likelihood of the occurrence of an adverse event against the impact on the project if it does occur. The development of a risk matrix encourages managers to look for the possible consequence of change. It facilitates the development of risk management strategies, either to reduce the likelihood of the unfavourable consequence or to develop contingency plans to deal with effects if the risk is realised.

Undertaking a stakeholder analysis is an essential aspect of project management. Identifying and listing all the key stakeholders facilitates an assessment of whether each stakeholder or group of stakeholders is an opinion former or has the power to block ideas, so that if the change is to be successful they must actively support it or will need to at least acquiesce in the change. The stakeholder analysis should take into account the extent of influence or power in relating to achieving the project outcomes. Such assessments then form the basis for the development of stakeholder management strategies to secure the support necessary to allow the project to proceed. A stakeholder analysis has more widespread uses and is by no means confined to project management.

Extremely complex projects, such as significant organisational change initiatives, often comprise a series of projects, grouped together in a programme. In these cases, discrete sets of activity and constituent parts of the overall project management process (for example, the process of defining objectives, and analysing context, constraints, stakeholders and risk, may be viewed as stand-alone projects).

Preparing a 'project overview statement'

We are now going to look at the various elements you need to think about in producing the initial project overview statement. This is an important step and serves as an initial brief for the management team or a senior manager responsible for giving the 'go-ahead' for the project. The project overview statement also has a number of other uses such as providing general information for other managers and staff, as keeping people informed is a routine and necessary activity in the successful management of projects. It also provides an early statement of the outcomes desired and the general direction needed to achieve these. It should state the problems and opportunities to be addressed by the project, so undertaking a SWOT analysis as described in Chapter 2 is a useful precursor to this stage. The project overview statement is a reference document, as well as a control point for reporting progress in the project and a simple audit tool for evaluating the effectiveness of the project in achieving its stated aims, objectives and outcomes. A statement which provides an overview of the project is really a statement of intent.

Writing your project overview statement
THE PROJECT OUTCOME

This may be a brief but specific statement such as 'Three social work staff trained and approved as approved mental health practitioners by April 2012'. This statement is not misleading and also uses terms that allow others to measure its completion. For example, 'train staff as approved mental health practitioners' doesn't tell us anything about how many and when this needs to be done by. It also does not measure the essential task of approval by the authorising body so that the requirements of Mental Health Act 2007 can be fulfilled. In summary then, your project overview statement is important for two reasons:

1. It is a clear statement of what is to be done.

2. It is an event whose completion can be measured.

Responsibility for the project

There is only one project manager even if your project involves a number of stakeholders. You may not necessarily be the project manager in your particular project but this does not stop you identifying your specific role within it.

Timing for completion of the project

This is critical information which communicates to others the priority that has been given to the project and also sets in motion a number of planning and resourcing activities. Having a completion date may initially be a 'guesstimate' but enables you to get the project moving and it may be that your final approved completion date is reviewed after the initial planning cycle of the project is completed.

Identifying project objectives

Your project has one major outcome to be accomplished and several objectives in support of this. The stated outcome provides the purpose and direction towards which all objectives, work activities and tasks will strive. Objectives can represent the major components of your project and can be seen as milestones which direct work activity. Writing your objectives should follow the SMART formula:

Specific: be specific in targeting an objective.

Measurable: establish a measurable indicator of progress.

Achievable: is it capable of being achieved and tangible?

Realistic: is it realistic in terms of resources available?

Timescale: have you timed it and specified the duration?

Returning to our staff training example above, one of the objectives might be to obtain cover for those staff attending the approved mental health practitioner training, or to find an appropriate training course, or to secure funding for both the course and staff cover. By specifying these objectives or steps, we are providing a road map that helps decision makers and other stakeholders to understand the scope of the project, the resources required and the timescales involved.

Establishing criteria to measure success

You can start by asking members of the project team or those involved or affected by your project to identify criteria to measure its success. These criteria might be revised as the project plan progresses.

Identify resources required

Resources include staffing, equipment as well as financial or budgetary ones. You will need to be specific about how much, how long and whether capital or revenue costs will be incurred.

Identifying assumptions and risks

Identifying assumptions and risks associated with each objective will help you think through the issues associated with executing the project. The sorts of questions one might ask are:

1. What resources are realistically required to complete this objective? What risks are associated with obtaining them?

2. What likely problems or delays could occur and what effects might this have on the overall project schedule and any resource availability?

3. What assumptions can be made to correct any delays in completion within the given resources and constraints and how realistic are they?

A proforma, such as the one in Figure 5.3 below, includes a checklist that you or your manager can use to assess your project overview statement.

Project overview	Project name	Project manager
Problem/opportunity		
Expected outcome		
Objectives 1. 2. 3		
Success criteria 1. 2. 3.		

Project overview	Project name	Project manager
Assumptions 1. 2.		
Prepared by Date Approved by Date		

Figure 5.3 *The project overview statement*

Controlling your project

Once you have written your project outline plan and thought about the sequence of activities required to plan your project from beginning to end, you may wish to use a tool such as a Gantt chart or another visual representation which incorporates the WBS described above. You will need to take measures to control and ensure progress against those critical activities identified.

Project plans and their implementation are only as successful as the manager and team who are responsible for implementing them. In building an effective team you must give consideration to the technical skills needed of its members and also to the degree of team-building and team-working. This might be the time to revisit what you know about leadership skills and team-building skills. The project manager is a leader who helps design, coordinate, control, and implements the project plan. The project leader will also need to stay the course until the project delivers its final product, to envision the bigger picture as well as all the phases of project planning and implementation whilst working on detail. Strategic expertise also involves the ability to ask guiding questions which direct people towards the ultimate goal and planned end result through the critical path. Leading a project is a way of assessing your skills and abilities as a 'starter-finisher' and to 'provide direction' and to 'achieve results' (Skills for Care 2008).

There are a number of skills involved in controlling your project.

Delegation

Developing criteria for judging what people can achieve themselves and what is appropriate to delegate is an important skill in project management. Managing a project usually means managing and juggling ongoing everyday work as well as the project itself. Delegation criteria might include looking at existing arrangements for the allocation of work; assessing the strengths and developmental needs of staff working on the project; the speed of response required and availability of people's time to undertake a particular task. Project managers must anticipate future commitments by thinking about the placement of people in the service in relation to the project as well as the rest of the service. Even when delegation has many advantages there still may be a number of barriers to effective delegation and, paradoxically, this may be time-consuming initially. Time may need to be spent in identifying what is to be delegated; establishing appropriate control procedures; and briefing and training those stepping up to new challenges. There may also be a number of factors which affect control of your project, such as your own lack of authority and lack of resources, or where there are shortages of staff in terms of quantity or quality to allow you to do exactly what you need.

Managing people and project relationships

Weiss and Wysocki (1992) offer a 12-point guide for effective project leadership:

1. Do not over-direct, over-observe or over-report.

2. Recognise differences in individuals and have a keen appreciation of each person's unique contribution.

3. Help those you manage see 'problems' as 'changes'.

4. Encourage employees and stakeholders to think about how they might be more creative or if they would like to be more creative, and ask them what sort of creative contribution they would most like to make.

5. Allow more freedom for individuals to guide their work.

6. Train yourself and others to respond to the positive aspects of proposed ideas rather than react to the often easier to spot negative ones (this follows on from the principles of appreciative inquiry that we mentioned in Chapter 2).

7. Develop greater frustration tolerances for mistakes and errors.

8. Provide a safe atmosphere for failures as these are valuable learning experiences.

9. Be a resource person rather than a controller, a facilitator rather than 'the boss'.

10. Act as a buffer between employees and outside problems or 'higher up' demands.

11. Enhance your own creative ability through any opportunities to attend workshops or seminars, undertake specialised reading and learn how to practise creative exercises and games. This sets examples for employees and makes it easier for you to recognise and relate to the creative ability of others.

12. Make sure that innovative ideas are transmitted upwards and that feedback is given to ensure they are given a fair hearing and taken seriously.

Case study – innovation and progress: transforming services

Kent County Council streamlined the system for handling out-of-hours calls to social services, allowing social workers to concentrate on urgent cases. Contact centre advisers and managers have been trained to triage calls, so that only a minority need to be referred, reducing the number of social workers on duty out-of-hours to one or two. The social services team were close to breaking point, but listening to their ideas freed them up to concentrate on urgent work. (*The Guardian*, 25 November 2009)

Managing across functional boundaries

Projects within large care organisations involve working across a number of boundaries both internally and externally. In previous chapters some of the issues in working effectively across a number of disciplines were discussed. Project managers must communicate and sell ideas, negotiate and problem solve, and work to resolve a number of conflicts across functional and sometimes geographic boundaries. Project management often occurs between authority and control structures in a larger organisation, so managers will have to be adept at people skills as well as political skills. Some of the areas of skill development within your project management will involve:

- using different communication techniques
- team-building and group work
- conflict resolution strategies
- managing effective meetings.

Managing risk in your project

It is impossible to predict with certainty the outcome of your project but it is possible to take certain steps in advance to assess the possible range of outcomes. These principles were addressed when looking at business planning earlier on. Much of this is dependent upon the volume and quality of information available and gathered. This can then be used to answer questions about whether what is required is actually possible, likely or probable in the circumstances and in the desired timescales. It will also help to determine what is likely to go wrong, although we will see later on in Chapter 9 that risk assessment is very much an inexact science. Most decisions are given deadlines, and there is a balance to be struck between the volume and quality of information required and the deadline by which it is necessary. Decision trees are a tool that can help you to think through risk issues in your project and we will be looking at these and other decision-making tools in more detail in Chapter 8.

Many organisations tend not to review their successes, as they either take these for granted or else these are claimed by individual managers. In the history of social care it is also more likely that only failures are closely reviewed (Stanley and Manthorpe 2004). This is something for project managers to think about when closing projects. Taking time to evaluate the successes and problem areas that have occurred will facilitate the capture of any learning that can be derived from them.

Closing the project

Closing a project is frequently a neglected phase of project management. The major phases of project completion include obtaining approval of the work from your manager or the management team; documenting the project; evaluating and auditing; and issuing a final report. The rationale for closing a project is to terminate project team members' roles formally and obtain approval for the work done and the outcomes achieved. It is also a means of auditing the outcomes and objectives against the original project specification and associated resources. A final report can then be composed.

Questions to ask when closing your project

- Was the project goal achieved? Was it consistent with the overall goals of the organisation/service/team?

- Was the project work done on time, was it done within budget and was it done according to the original specifications?

- Were those involved satisfied with the project results and how can this be known or demonstrated?

- Did the organisation/team or service have the required skills to complete this project? If not, what gaps were there and how might these be addressed next time?

- How well was the project supported throughout its life? Are there any areas relating to specific departments/partnerships that could be reviewed in terms of working together better next time?

- Are the outcomes of the project actually useful and meaningful?

- What skills, knowledge and expertise did I acquire through my role in the project and what evidence have I provided to demonstrate these?

Your final project report

Your report serves as the memory or history of the project and it should be disseminated so that others involved or not involved can share in the learning from it, as well as to find out about its outcomes. This usually includes elements such as: overall success and performance of the project using some sort of audit information; the organisation and administration of the project; techniques used to accomplish the project results (that is, the number of training courses provided, the role played by technology); an assessment of the project's strengths and weaknesses and, finally, recommendations from the project manager and team for any next steps or future developments. Celebration at this stage is also very important!

People management and user involvement for successful delivery of projects

Some commentators (see Open University undated) have observed that the importance of budgets, time and quality to the success of projects means that they are often more likely to be managed as technical systems, rather than the utilisation of a more humanist approach. Yet giving inadequate attention to the softer people aspects of project management is as likely to contribute to their failure as neglect of the hard dimensions. As we saw in the stakeholder analysis earlier, the contributions and responses made by individuals such as sponsors, the project team, staff, users and providers are crucial. The interpersonal skills of the project manager are vital to communicate and manage effectively the different parties with a stake in the project. The chances of success will be increased by paying more attention to issues such as relationships between people through leadership and motivation, communication and facilitation of team-working, influencing and utilising political skills (as highlighted in Chapter 2). Boddy and Buchanan (1992) have identified six key activities from research they undertook into the effectiveness of project management and the roles of the project managers involved. These are outlined below:

1. **the importance of shaping goals** requiring project managers responsible for setting or implementing overall objectives to be very active in reacting to changes and clarifying any problems arising

2. **the obtaining of resources** by negotiating their release and managing their effective use within the context of the project

3. **building roles and structures** by clarifying project managers' own roles and those roles within the project team and with other functions and individuals

4. **establishing good communication** by linking together the diverse groups and individuals contributing to the project in order to obtain their support and commitment

5. **seeing the whole picture** by taking a 'helicopter' view, managing time and other resources, anticipating reactions from stakeholders, linking with other relevant activities and spotting unexpected events

6. **moving things forward** by taking action and risks to keep the project going especially through difficult phases.

Ensuring that all interested parties understand a project's goals and objectives may avoid potential misunderstandings which could impede communication. It is important to select the right medium, such as face-to-face presentations, meetings or written documents, and to ensure that this is sufficient and relevant without overloading with it detail which prevents busy staff from absorbing particularly important pieces of information. The avoidance of a proliferation of meetings will ensure that meetings remain focused and effective in facilitating proper discussion, and which do not deter people from attending. There should also be active resolution of conflict between project participants with attention to group work to reconcile priorities, goals and interests between parties coming from diverse backgrounds, professionally, personally and in their relationship to the project outcomes. Boddy and Buchanan (1992) particularly identify three aspects of a project for which a well-balanced project team will require appropriate skills. The *first* is content, where teams require expertise in the skills which the project concerns, for example ICT skills or experience of using services, awareness of the organisation's policies and strategies and operating knowledge. The *second* is about understanding process, which requires skills in team-building to help members of the group work together, paying attention to process as well as outcomes, and a willingness and ability to give time and commitment to the team. The *third* concerns control where the team appreciate a 'helicopter' view, which sets the project within its broader context and gives attention to deadlines and administration skills to ensure appropriate and timely project documentation.

The role of senior management

Senior management have a crucial sponsoring role to play both during the planning and the implementation of projects, in terms of establishing their legitimacy, making project resources available and endorsing project progress. For this reason, those involved in a project must be proactive about securing and maintaining senior management support throughout its lifetime and this is where the project overview statement discussed earlier is useful. There are a number of issues that can arise that need to be anticipated to ensure that there is no sabotage of the project. Project managers can take a number of actions to improve the project team's relationship with senior management and to deflect unnecessary and unhelpful involvement in the project such as micro-managing or underestimating or overestimating the significance of the project and making unrealistic demands. The execution of a project may depend on the involvement and cooperation of several departments or functions within an organisation. Senior managers have an important role to play in sponsoring and encouraging good relations with all interested parties across the organisation in order to get their support for the project. This may not be a straightforward issue, since each function will have its own priorities and interests; they may be indifferent or even downright hostile to the project. Not surprisingly, the larger the project task, the more difficult the job of maintaining good relationships with all interested parties, especially if the project involves more than one site.

Of course, there may be times when your project is not successful. Social care has witnessed its fair share of failed projects including risk-taking when pilot projects are not completed, but which then go on to inform much larger organisational change due to urgent economic or political pressures. It is important to learn from these challenges and an effective post-project review is one way of doing this.

Disseminating knowledge from your post-project review

Earlier we referred to the importance of closing your project, and this final section will take this one step further and consider post-project review as an integral component of project management and its contribution towards organisational learning cycles. It is not only the project review, but the dissemination of the learning from project team members' knowledge and experience that helps to build future organisational capabilities. Rezania and Lingham (2009) stress the importance of storytelling, dialogue and conversation, in building a bridge between individual and organisational learning. Their own research demonstrates that prior to becoming a 'performing entity', project teams develop the norms, values and beliefs (implicitly or explicitly) which guide their group behaviour. They assert that several aspects of this experience can be captured and used as a foundation for further reflection and conversation. They recommend a social constructionist approach to project evaluation and suggest a role for an impartial evaluator within organisations which frequently use project management as a tool for organisational design. Social constructionists believe that personal experience and meaning is not created by the individual alone but is embedded and shaped by their culture (Burr 1995). During the life of the project, the project manager constantly needs to negotiate between the project and its stakeholders taking up a lot of their time and energy. As a project operates within an engrained organisational culture, ethos or a set of moral codes, values and rules, this narrative becomes an important source of organisational learning.

Chapter summary

This chapter has introduced you to the key concepts underpinning project management and attempted to provide a practical outline of some of the techniques and tools that can be used to manage specific projects within your strategy or business plan. There are many specialist areas within project management, which is a discipline in itself, but it is hoped that you may have also realised that *everything* is potentially a project and the mix of skills required embody principles of good management planning and people management. You may have the opportunity to undertake further training in more formal project management techniques or to access project management software packages to discover how they might help in more detail. Where some projects are repeatable, this gives more scope for evaluating and improving a project each time it runs but other projects may be extremely complex and may not always run successfully. Social care is by nature characterised by ambiguity and unpredictability.

Prescriptive top-down approaches may be less helpful than approaches to defining and managing your project which foster critical reasoning in a climate of uncertainty. Utilise everyone's contribution within the project in a considered way, which is where developing structures that encompass both hard and soft elements can assist you.

Manager's comment

One of the numerous projects I have been involved in was the development of a reflective learning programme in the workplace to improve reflective learning and practice. The overall aim was to improve outcomes for children. It was a collaborative project in partnership between a social care and a voluntary organisation with mutual benefits.

By the time I became involved in the project, funding had been agreed and senior managers in both agencies had identified SMART goals and agreed the basic purpose, definition of the partnership and what it sought to achieve. To achieve practice improvements a maximum number of 12 practitioners (divided into two groups) were asked to attend monthly consultation groups with prepared case studies for discussion. The group was supported by the attendance of two experts and external coaching support within the workplace. Regular managers' meetings took place to assess progress and take corrective action when required.

Having not been involved in the initial discussions and preparation of the project's overview statement, I recognised that whilst support and commitment at a senior level was essential for effective collaboration, account needed to be taken of a non-hierarchical structure where power to make decisions regarding purpose and vision should be shared. I therefore recognised the need to engage stakeholders at a local level and consider how service users might become involved.

It was helpful to undertake a SWOT analysis to determine the key strengths, weaknesses, opportunities and threats. One of the key strengths and opportunities was the chance to develop the practitioner's use of self, their understanding of relation-based practice and encouragement of reflective practice. The weaknesses and threats to the project were reflected within the organisational culture – whether the social care practitioners were able to commit themselves to exposure and scrutiny of practice in order to grow in self-awareness. Other potential barriers to success were identified as the procedural issues of accountability and confidentiality. A number of social care workers were asked to take part in the project, but were initially reluctant to do so, due to fears that they were being singled out as poor performers. As their practice had recently been subject to an inspection which was not positive, they were already feeling under threat, devalued and demotivated as a consequence. The culture of the organisation was one where many practitioners worked independently and were perceived by family members and professionals involved as powerful individuals. Being able to share their status and power and to make key decisions *with* children and parents, rather than *for* them, were areas where we were hoping to transform practice and improve partnership.

Open communication with all practitioners was essential in their engagement with the project. This optimistic and inclusive approach worked well. There had been gains during the initial period evidenced during consultation meetings and coaching, but it was difficult to evidence that practice quality had improved.

I think having a clear model to work with, particularly a WBS to detail activities and tasks and Weiss and Wysocki's 12 points in this chapter, can definitely help in managing a project. In my own situation, it can be difficult to manage a project where much of the purpose and structure had previously been agreed by senior management. This was compounded by a lack of written information about the project. I therefore agree that it is important not to mirror this process with the participants, stakeholders and beneficiaries.

Having sufficient management time and access to resources to make sure the project progressed well would have enabled me to take a more active leadership role. As it was, this was difficult due to competing demands on my time and geographical distance. Although service managers in other areas were delegated responsibility for the staff involved in the project, it faltered at times due to poor engagement by some participants. For example, some consultations had to be cancelled due to a failure to prepare case studies on time, and attendance at consultation groups and coaching sessions was not always 100 per cent. This caused some conflict and irritation between the partners at subsequent review meetings. Having enough time to follow through these concerns with individuals and spend time on inputs would have made a difference to the outcomes for all.

Time was taken to evaluate the successes and difficulties of the project via a research paper. Whilst the project ran to time, was completed within budget and stayed within the original project plan it was difficult to evidence the outcomes and learning. We used a comparison of assessment reports, case plans and completed questionnaires by participants and stakeholders to provide evidence of success.

Lucy Titmuss is a manager for CAFCASS a social care organisation working with children and their families.

CHAPTER 6

The Commissioning and Contracting Process

When you have worked through this chapter you will be able to:

- describe the basic principles of the commissioning and contracting process
- draw up a service specification and contract for services to meet the objectives of your business plan
- identify the dilemmas and tensions involved in developing an outcome-based approach
- consider your overall approach in working towards outcomes which meets standards for equality and diversity in a strategic context.

Introduction

The central role that commissioning plays in strategy and business planning has only relatively recently been properly recognised within mainstream management. Whilst not many managers would view themselves as commissioners, this chapter aims to illuminate the different roles that operational managers have to play in the commissioning cycle. The chapter begins by defining and explaining the concept of commissioning within its strategic context. Commissioning in very broad terms is often used interchangeably with contracting, purchasing or procurement (Richardson 2006). We will also be exploring the concept of outcomes or what is often referred to within commissioning as the 'outcomes-based approach'. These terms are frequently cited in policy and regulatory developments in social care and considered as vital in helping to achieve clarity of purpose for all stakeholders involved in delivering services.

Within a strategic context, commissioning and contracting enable an organisation to engage providers fairly and transparently in their business plan. This process is one which takes into account the current 'fit' between needs, aspirations and services at a locality or team level and to make best use of the information available. There have been a number of critiques over the last decade or so on the ineffectiveness of commissioning for change. This has been criticised for being no more than contracting for more or less of the same service within a narrow, mechanistic, almost static modelling (Fletcher 2008). Some of these debates will be examined towards the end of the chapter with a closer look at how commissioning is central to addressing the government's transformation and personalisation agenda and to support the role of social enterprise and co-production in some commissioning models.

What is commissioning?

The Audit Commission (1997) describes commissioning as:

the process of specifying, securing and monitoring services to meet people's needs at a strategic level. This applies to all services, whether they are provided by the local authority, NHS, other public agencies, or by the private and voluntary sectors. (Audit Commision 1997, p.5)

According to Richardson (2006), this definition has three particular strengths which emphasise:

- the cyclical nature of the activities involved, from understanding needs and analysing capacity, to monitoring services which makes commissioning an ongoing process, not just a one-off event

- the importance of meeting needs at a strategic level for whole groups of service users/patients and/or whole populations, and this is what distinguishes commissioning from simply contracting for individual services

- the importance of commissioning services to meet the needs of service users/patients, no matter who provides them in the public, private or voluntary sector.

There are a number of models of commissioning, most of which have similar characteristics in that they describe a cyclical process of activities encompassing needs analysis, aligning resources to meet needs, developing services and monitoring performance. However, the Institute of Public Care's (IPC) framework, illustrated in Figure 6.1, is based upon four key performance management elements – analyse, plan, do and review.

Figure 6.1 *Institute of Public Care joint commisioning model for public care*
From *Care Services Improvement and Institute of Public Care 2006.*

The IPC approach sees a key component of effective commissioning as the development of comprehensive commissioning strategies. These strategies in turn drive contracting arrangements, with systems to ensure strategies are implemented and effective use of monitoring to assess and evaluate progress. The key activities involved in the IPC cycle and the principles that underpin it consist of:

- All of the four elements of the cycle (analyse, plan, do and review). These are sequential and of equal importance, for example commissioners and contractors should spend equal time, energy and attention on the four elements.

- A written joint commissioning strategy per user population or group should be developed, which focuses on that user group's needs across a range of different agencies such as housing, education, health or social care.

- The commissioning cycle (the outer circle in the diagram) should drive the purchasing and contracting activities (the inner circle). However, the contracting experience must inform the ongoing development of commissioning.

- The commissioning process should be equitable and transparent, and open to influence from all stakeholders via an ongoing dialogue with patients/service users and providers. (Richardson 2006)

Commissioning is therefore a very complex activity and should be located within a strategic framework to maximise the scope for collaborative commissioning with a range of partners as well as within the current political parameters for the development of commissioning activity in your area. This, for example, might take account of the degree of investment in the independent sector and of the legal or policy framework in children's or adult services and the standards and outcomes by which commissioning strategies will be measured (Improvement and Development Agency 2008). Commissioning requires expertise in needs analysis, service review, planning and contracting. Commissioning can also be joint, using the flexibilities enshrined in the Health Act 1999 where two or more organisations pool their resources into one budget and/or develop a system of 'lead' commissioning to implement a common strategy for providing services. Collaborative commissioning has led to more integrated provision where two or more agencies co-collaborate and develop strategies for using their resources.

Translating this vision into a reality can prove difficult due to significant restraints. Not least there may be problems with conflicting internal priorities between agencies due to differing governance agendas, alignment, organisational and jurisdictional boundaries and budgets. There are also tensions in relation to the continuing policy of charging for social care where other agencies, such as health do not, and the persistence of differing professional and organisational cultures (Godwin 2007). One cannot talk about commissioning without referring to the concept of decommissioning. This is the process of planning and managing service activity or terminating a contract in line with commissioning objectives and cost effectiveness. It is relevant to the government's transformation agenda (Department of Health 2008a), as achieving the right balance may require disinvestment and decommissioning, for example away from institutional care and towards community-based services and support. It is worth pointing out, however, that it is anticipated that the largest efficiencies will come from what is commissioned if sufficient preventative services are available (Social Care Institute for Excellence 2009).

There are several stages involved in the commissioning process (adapted from Crampton and Ricketts 2007; Fletcher 2008; Needham and Carr 2009; Richardson 2006) as follows:

- **Resource mapping** – for example understanding, mapping and forecasting the nature of supply and demand within the current market and how this meets both current and evolving and future needs of the users/recipients of care services, as well as meeting statutory requirements and local objectives. This will also involve reviewing services across agencies to understand provider strengths and weaknesses, and by identifying opportunities for improvement or change in providers and supporting the development of new ones.

- **Consideration of 'best value' principles** – by ensuring that the resources across the system are applied for the best effect and within the resources available. This includes benchmarking and application of fair and transparent principles in selecting the most appropriate providers as well as enabling viable market conditions. Pooling of resources and shared responsibility may be needed to achieve the best possible returns on any investment. This might involve some challenging decisions about key investments including where your organisation will not invest or no longer invests.

- **Gap analysis** – ensuring that the market is developed in terms of both choice and the range of services on offer and the development of new or different services in response to users' needs. This should proactively address any intelligence on current inequities and access for marginalised groups. People who use services are experts in determining their own requirements. A co-productive approach will recognise that rather than positioning them as passive dependents, people who use services can be enabled to play a more active role in meeting their own needs in line with the move towards personalisation of care services.

- **Priority setting** – involving all the system partners (including end users and service providers) in the development of vision and goals to ensure that priorities are clarified, whether local or national, and that these are based on any research or best practice.

- **Service redesign** – the creation of new structures, regulatory and commissioning practices and financial streams to embed new approaches, particularly those which recognise co-production as a long-term rather than ad hoc solution. This will involve developing a dynamic model that is able to take on board a range of sources as well as the level and balance of services to be commissioned using scenario planning. In Chapter 2, we already considered the impact for example of developing more integrated care and the importance of supporting continuing financial viability of providers, whilst developing their capacity to respond to self-directed care. Capitalising on new technologies and evaluating the impact of any changes within the system on designated user groups or priorities is essential to service redesign.

There are four further steps in the strategic commissioning cycle, those of drawing up a service specification, service procurement, contracting, and monitoring, reviewing and evaluation which we will return to shortly and which are illustrated in Figure 6.2 below. Before this, we will consider the imperative to develop an outcomes-based approach to commissioning.

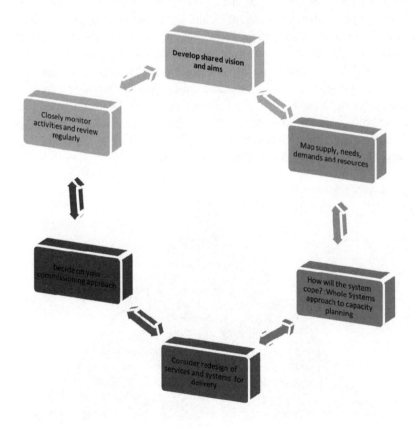

Figure 6.2 The strategic commisioning cycle

Developing outcomes-focused social care

Glasby and Littlechild (2009) remind us that whilst achieving choice and control are important ends in themselves, the practical focus should be on the increased ability for people using services to make changes in their lives and to achieve outcomes that are meaningful to them. These should be set 'against which the experience of individuals can be measured and tested' (Department of Health 2005a, pp.25–6), as opposed to practitioner and provider concerns. This is coupled with the duty to purchase services which offer overall best value to tax payers and service users alike as opposed to the cheapest option. Outcomes are the changes, benefits or other effects that happen as a result of an organisation's activities. Service outcomes have been linked to broad quality of life domains in recent key documents, specifically *Every Child Matters* (HM Government 2003) and *Our Health, Our Care, Our Say* (Department of Health 2006a) and, following the passage of the Health and Social Care Act 2008, are now firmly linked to performance assessment. Adopting an outcomes approach allows a provider and its funders to find out what effects the services provided are having and whether it is successful in achieving its aims, as illustrated in Figure 6.3 below. Outcomes can therefore provide a common language, bridging the separate worlds of public policy, administration and accountability on the one hand, and of urgent needs, social commitment and community action on the other (Charities Evaluation Services 2006). The Charities Evaluation Services planning triangle below illustrates how outcomes relate to the aims of an organisation.

Figure 6.3 Charities Evaluation Services planning triangle
From Charities Evaluation Services 2006.

The focus on outcomes raises both practical and conceptual challenges. Since the implementation of the legislative and policy reforms in relation to community care in 1993 professionals have traditionally conducted individual assessments of need and procured services available from the local authority's contracts with provider organisations in the mixed economy of care. These services have to be consistent with users' aspirations, and services that deliver desired outcomes require multiple, highly effective, channels of communication between users, service commissioners, contracts managers, front-line professionals and both managers and provider services. This is not an easy task and is resource intensive. The identification, measurement and auditing of outcomes is also challenging, especially if outcomes are to be personalised to reflect individual priorities. New information systems to record desired outcomes and progress towards their achievement are equally challenging (Glendinning et al. 2008). Glendinning et al. define three clusters of desired outcomes:

1. **change outcomes** – those relating to improvements in physical, mental or emotional functioning. Based on extensive research done by Qureshi et al. (1998), they can include improvements in symptoms such as depression or anxiety linked to social exclusion, physical functioning, confidence and morale

2. **maintenance outcomes** – those which prevent or delay deterioration in health, wellbeing or quality of life and may include meeting environmental needs, physical needs and social inclusion

3. **process outcomes** – those which refer to the actual experience of seeking, obtaining and using services. These might include feeling valued and respected, or by having a say and control over services, as well as value for money and compatibility with cultural preferences and informal sources of support.

The government has long argued that health, social care, education, housing and other organisations need to be brought together in a coordinated way to serve the best interests of service users and the community. They implied that this would naturally emerge as the logic in the system encouraged innovative and more flexible commissioning (Godwin 2007). Commissioners at the different individual, locality and strategic levels require differing but complementary skills as Table 6.1 below indicates. Managers will need training, support and time if the approach is to be uniformly and successfully adopted. Such developments will also involve considerable changes to tendering and contracting processes across a local authority or health commissioning body (Kerslake 2006).

Table 6.1 Commissioning at different levels
From the Improvement and Development Agency

Levels at which commissioning takes place	Activity – skills and knowledge required
Individual	Enabling individuals and their families to focus on identifying and addressing the barriers to achieving their potential.
	Tailoring interventions and combination of responses which build on, rather than undermine, the strengths of individuals and families.
	Striking a balance between risks and opportunities, independence and interdependence, choice and control.
	Formulating desired outcomes and the required service responses that are feasible, deliverable and accountable.
	Handling different degrees of user control and utilising direct payments, individual budgets and brokerage arrangements.
	Facilitating users to collaborate and to create scope for user-led provision.
	Identifying and feedback of shortfalls in individual-led commissioning to inform locality and strategic commissioning.
Locality	Ability to collate and analyse information from a wide variety of sources about all of the interacting forces in a given locality.
	Managing processes to aggregate and evaluate intelligence from individual commissioning.
	Understanding of how organisational, social and political processes may be influenced or changed.
	Creativity in developing new locality-specific solutions.
	Networking skills with key players at the local level to promote change.
	Working with user groups and existing and potential service providers to identify changing requirements, preferences and improved ways of working.
	Refocusing on community dimensions and specialist versus generic commissioning within a locality.

Levels at which commissioning takes place	Activity – skills and knowledge required
Strategic	Capacity to provide transformational leadership to achieve radical change necessary for person-centred and outcomes-led commissioning.
	People skills to engage users, carers and staff in change strategy.
	Organisational skills in workforce training and development.
	Analytical skills to discern patterns, trends and shortfalls.
	Research skills to learn from best noticeable practice externally.
	Strategic networking skills and ability to forge inter-agency alliances.
	Commitment to evidence-based performance management.

Outcomes are derived from a variety of sources such as national and local government requirements in relation to performance, research, past practice and evidence of need. Whatever outcomes are defined, however, the commissioning body needs to be clear about their rationale and, importantly, give sufficient time for providers to think through the outcomes to be achieved and allow opportunities for them to be rigorously tested in debate (Kerslake 2006). This will include the question of whether outcomes justify the cost, as illustrated in the case study below.

Case study – the relationship between costs and outcomes

Beecham and Sinclair (2007) reviewed 14 studies to explore the relationship between costs and outcomes in children's social care and examined the 'business' case for some services in terms of the relationship between costs and effectiveness. Whilst Beecham and Sinclair focused on the financial dimensions of services and practice, they argued that financial costs could not be seen as the sole determinant when planning services but that the wider social and emotional costs of difficulties faced by individual children and their families must be considered by policy makers and commissioners.

Their study drew out some of the complexities in trying to link early intervention and cost effectiveness. For example, in some therapeutic services for families, whilst there was no significant change, there was a high level of user satisfaction. They also found that a substantial proportion of resources were spent on a defined group of children with complex needs, highlighting the tensions between prevention and access thresholds. Fragmented and uncoordinated delivery of services to children also makes the task of assessing and measuring effectiveness difficult, as many prevention services are hidden within the overall sector and information about the service use and history of the families is not always accurately or consistently recorded. Beecham and Sinclair conclude that as the integration agenda moves forward, more robust research is required into the outcomes of children's services. This should particularly examine the causes of wide cost variations and investment into the systems needed to improving coordination and information for effective commissioning (Beecham and Sinclair 2007).

Kerslake (2006) reminds us that applying outcomes-based principles is at its simplest when contracting for a new service from a new service provider. Changing the nature of the contracting relationship with existing providers can cause tensions where there is insufficient choice. At the initial stage, meeting with existing providers to think through current achievements and to look at how they can be expressed as outcomes are useful. Providing seminars and training for providers on developing and adopting outcomes-based approaches may also be helpful.

Commissioning from the third sector – issues for consideration

As partnerships with many voluntary sector and community-based organisations have become a common feature and a policy imperative (HM Government 2007a), the lack of a shared framework (of authority, accountability and procedures) has been raised. Voluntary organisations have long faced dilemmas about accountability to funders and cross-sectoral partnerships, which can at times place voluntary organisations at reputational and financial risk. Where this happens it can undermine their own accountabilities to stakeholders, and the voluntary sector's ability to contribute effectively to the partnership depends very much on the dynamics between the various partners involved (National Council for Voluntary Organisations undated). Within the strategic commissioning context, partnerships bring people together with diverse skills and resources, different work cultures and substantial disparity in their income and power. Where commissioning takes place within tight timescales, poor internal governance within partnerships and a lack of accountability between partners may result. The National Council for Voluntary Organisations (undated) has set out the following guidelines for the third sector in order to enhance its own accountability:

- Be clear about the various ways in which it is accountable to the full range of stakeholders including funders, partners, regulators or service users.

- Be clear about the nature of its relationship with those it defines as its primary stakeholder group.

- Have open and transparent mechanisms for user involvement via governance mechanisms and other activities.

- Be aware of its own strengths and weaknesses in relation to issues of accountability and be committed to continuous improvement.

- Be clear about its reasons for entering into any partnership and about what it is it has to offer.

- Ensure that trustees are well informed and central to any decision to enter into partnership. (National Council for Voluntary Organisations undated, pp.ii–iii)

Partnerships involving the third sector need sufficient time to develop trust and sound internal governance, with performance mechanisms which are clear from the outset, proportionate to the level of funding given and which take account of local circumstance. Peck and Dickinson (2008) refer to the 'steering' of collaborative partnerships by government and, using the example of NHS and local authorities, look at how they are having to divest themselves of provision which has encouraged contestability as much as collaboration. They conclude that these commissioning organisations are 'puzzling over the appropriate local balance in a context where the political messages over support for competition can be mixed' (Peck and Dickinson 2008, p.16). Further, the increasing uptake of direct payments and individual budgets has put significant amounts of commissioning responsibility and resources in the hands of private agencies and individual citizens, which both necessitate new models of commissioning partnerships and a reorientation of primary care trusts, and local authorities to become more embedded in and fundamental to their local communities (Glasby, Smith and Dickinson 2006). Also, given the different democratic structures of some commissioning organisations, they will have to confront a number of cross-cutting challenges working with other key local stakeholders to engage the population and produce a vision of their local community.

Commissioning for personalisation

Whilst direct payments have transformed the way in which people receive support, they have not yet changed the way in which people access services, the way they are assessed, the prevailing culture or the way in which the bulk of the social care budget is spent (Glasby and Littlechild 2009). The notion of personal budgets, however, offer greater potential for transforming the system as a whole, to develop a new 'operating system', which is 'open source in nature' and which develops new bottom-up approaches that build on the realities of service users and front-line staff (Glasby and Littlechild 2009; Waters 2007). Whilst commissioners continue to play a direct role in specifying and procuring services, there will be a strategic shift away from task- and time-based contracting towards outcomes-focused and person-centred approaches (Social Care Institute for Excellence 2009). Glasby and Littlechild (2009) helpfully summarise the seven steps to self-directed support based on the In Control model and principles behind the development of personalisation (Waters 2007).

> **Step 1** – set personal budget; using In Control's resource allocation system (RAS), everyone is told their financial allocation or personal budget, and they decide what level of control they wish to take over their budget.
>
> **Step 2** – plan support; people plan how they will use their personal budget to get the help that is best for them; if they need help to plan, then advocates, brokers or others can support them.
>
> **Step 3** – agree plan; the local authority helps people to create good support plans, checks they are safe and makes sure that people have any necessary representation.
>
> **Step 4** – manage personal budget; people control their personal budget to the extent they want (there are currently six distinct degrees of control, ranging from direct payments at one extreme to local authority control at the other).
>
> **Step 5** – organise support; people can use their personal budget flexibly (including for statutory services). Indeed, the only real restriction is that the budget must be used for needs the state recognises as legitimate and must be spent on something legal.
>
> **Step 6** – live life; people use their personal budget to achieve the outcomes that are important to them in the context of their whole life and their role and contribution within the wider community.
>
> **Step 7** – review and learn; the authority continues to check that people are okay, shares what is being learned and can change things if people are not achieving the outcomes they need to achieve. (Glasby and Littlechild 2009, p.79)

The upshot of these types of developments are a likely reduction in block contracting for many services, as this can reduce the choice available to people, and new contractual models that support the move to personalisation. The Social Care Institute for Excellence's guidance (2009) written specifically for commissioners recommends three different types of developments:

- **Framework contracts and approved provider lists** – where people opting for the council to manage their personal budget can draw upon a range of 'approved' services. It is important that people have the information, support and guidance to purchase services outside these contracts if they wish, with a clear understanding of any implications, risks and benefits. Contracting practice should not unnecessarily restrict the choices available to those who cannot manage or do not opt for a direct payment.

- **Person-centred contracting** – where anonymised information from individual support plans is used in 'mini-tenders' (either from within the framework or outside) and individuals and families are supported to be involved in evaluating successful bids to deliver the support they need.

- **Individual service funds (ISFs)** – where the personal budget is held by the provider and the person using the services establishes the timing and the actual tasks to be carried out. (Social Care Institute for Excellence 2009)

Personal budgets also have significant implications for children with disabilities, for young people with support needs and children's services more generally and should start as soon as people need additional support at a point of transition or change (Glasby and Littlechild 2009).

Case study – developing a flexible commissioning strategy

Council X decided it was time to revise its commissioning strategy for older people. Over a long period, the council had built up a pattern of commissioning typified by cost and volume and block contracts. The JSNA and a local consultation on personalisation raised a number of significant issues including low numbers of older people using personal budgets and direct payments; a lack of support planning and brokerage services available for older people; an increase in the uptake of residential care placements despite older people saying that living in the community is their top priority; poor usage of leisure facilities by older people; a steep decrease in the numbers of older people using day centre facilities and an under-representation of older people from black and minority ethnic groups in all services.

In response, the council developed a strategy to commission local user-led organisations to provide information, advice, support planning and brokerage services for older people using personal budgets and direct payments. It replaced block contracts for domiciliary care and other services with outcomes-focused framework contracts, underpinned by individual service funds (ISFs). It then systematically disinvested in residential care, and reinvested in re-ablement, assistive technologies, low-level preventative services and supported housing.

Alongside this Council X reviewed all its leisure facilities to ensure they cater for and are accessible to older people and explored ways of matching people with similar interests so they can pool budgets and do more of the things they want during the day. In addition, the budget was allocated in a way that attempted to redress the balance in relation to black and minority ethnic elders. Local councillors agreed that the scrutiny committee would monitor the implementation and impact of the new strategy with adjustments to budgets expected as more older people take up personal budgets (Social Care Institute for Excellence 2009).

Service specifications, contracting and procurement

The contract or service agreement is a one of the key mechanisms for generating quality improvements in service provision. This section deals with the process, content and value of contracts in the pursuit of quality services. A contract is a bargain between two parties, whereby one party agrees or promises to do something in return for the promise of the other party to pay the price of those services. There are typical kinds of contract used commonly in social care. First there are contracts between the commissioning agency, such as the children's trust, local authority or primary care trust who are often acting both as purchasers and providers. Some contracts might actually be negotiated at national level, for example through the criminal justice board for youth justice services or through the National Drug Treatment Agency. As stated earlier, many of these arrangements are changing with the personalisation agenda. The contract will include the price of the services to be provided along with a description of those services. Virtually anything can be included in the contract as long as it is not unlawful or 'contrary to public policy'. A description of the services (which may form a schedule to the main agreement) should therefore include the number of service users or services provided for, but also the agreed outline of what the services will look like. For example, a contract could include the 'key indicators' used within the performance assessment framework, such as timescales for seeing service users, waiting times and number of people seen within a specified period of time. There are a number of different types of contract used in social care, the most common ones being block and cost and volume, which we are going to look at in more detail. Before doing so, it is useful to mention spot contracts commonly used to agree an individual unit of services, such as a residential placement designed to meet a specific circumstance or need and to be purchased quickly

Block contracts

Under this form of contract the commissioners pay the service provider an annual fee, in instalments, in return for a defined range of (usually core) services. Such contracts may include some form of indicative workload agreement or fixed volume. For example, for a fixed price, a residential home may agree to take all service users in a given locality during the year. There are two variants of the block contract, simple and sophisticated. The sophisticated block includes indicative service activity targets or thresholds with 'floors' and 'ceilings' as well as agreed mechanisms if targets are exceeded. Such contracts should include quality performance aims and agreements on how the quality, efficiency and outcomes of the service are monitored. Block contracts bring benefits to both purchasers and providers. Purchasers benefit from the increased influence that the size of their contracts will bring, as well as competitive pricing which should result in cost efficiency. As we saw in the last chapter, providers benefit from the business planning advantages of block contracts, which ensure a steady income and allow for longer term planning of resources. However, providers may carry out more activity than budgeted for, with no expectation of additional income. The issue of full cost recovery for the voluntary sector is one such issue for the voluntary sector and was the subject of an agreement with the government in 2002 and subject to a full review in 2007 (National Audit Office 2007). This aimed to encourage the recovery of the full costs of a project or service within a contract, in addition to the direct costs, such as staff and equipment and the overhead costs associated with finance, human resource management and ICT systems integral to provision.

Cost and volume

Under this type of contract, the outputs are specified in terms of services provided, rather than in terms of the access to services and facilities available. The provider undertakes to provide a clearly defined number of services for a fixed 'baseline' price. Beyond that number, funding would be on a cost per service basis, at a level agreed in advance, up to a volume ceiling. From the provider's point of view, the 'baseline' activity would assist in planning. It also ensures the payment of a reasonable amount for work actually done. For the purchaser, such contracts also allow for budget planning while leaving a degree of flexibility. If moving away from simple block contracts there is a need for greater data quality and more accurate costing information.

Developing a contract framework – some guidance

Description of parties

This sets out who the contract is between, for example the local authority and a voluntary organisation. This section may also include who the parties to the contract are, for example the director of children's services and chief executive of a housing trust.

Objectives

The objectives of the contract should state the services which are to be provided, for example the provision of a defined range of services. In addition, it may be appropriate to specify that the services will be provided to a defined agreed level of quality. It may be appropriate to insert any nationally or locally agreed targets, for example from a policy document or national service framework. Chapter 7 on performance management will be considering what quality measures might trigger payment of fair market fees and the arguments for using star ratings and other national performance measures to achieve fairness, consistency and scope.

Range of services provided

This section should include a general description of the service or services to be provided. This may vary considerably according to speciality and, if necessary, could form a comprehensive list to be added as a schedule to the main contract. At the end of this section, the parties should have a clear idea of the range and scope of services to be provided.

Quality specification

This section may be considered the most important part of the contract. In discussing quality issues, the contracting parties have the opportunity and the flexibility to negotiate to achieve the maximum benefit for the service users they represent, improve wellbeing and possibly reduce the purchaser's overall costs in the longer term. This could incorporate preventative services for example. Of course, there will always be resource constraints and where this is the case, priority should be given to services which have measurable outcomes and demonstrable benefits. The practical use of evaluation techniques will be examined in Chapter 10.

Volume and mix

This section should state the amount of work to be covered by the contract. The development of the contracting process should enable the parties to predict the volume of activity accurately. The mix could be based on different levels of need and to ensure that the services to be commissioned are those which are targeted to particular user need.

Prices

The increasing sophistication of contracts from block to cost and volume allows parties to build in greater flexibility and user choice. For example in relation to personalisation, fluctuations might be allowed in the actual number required to facilitate choice and to agree any additional services on a cost per person or service basis. It is important to ensure that all quality and outcome measures are included, regardless of which pricing basis is the most suitable. Pricing also has an indirect impact on the service user, for example if price, price review and payment terms too closely favour the purchaser, there is a possibility of a business becoming unsustainable, with potentially devastating effects on service users and carers (Clogg 2006).

Case study – calculating a fair market price for care

Laing's 2008 survey found that weighted average pay for unqualified care assistants outside London was £6.07 per hour with a premium of about 20p per hour for those with a National Vocational Award at level two and a further 70p for senior carers. In addition to these low pay rates, hourly staff employed by private home operators typically received statutory sick pay only and no employer's pension contributions. Voluntary sector providers offered somewhat more generous terms and conditions. The report recommended that residential homes rated following an inspection as 'good' or 'excellent' and who meet the 2002 physical environment new management standards for new homes should qualify for the ceiling rate. Homes classified as 'adequate' or 'poor' should be paid a discretionary rate with an incentivised payment to improve their star ratings.

They also found that the root cause of market instability was the unwillingness or inability of local authorities to pay fee levels adequate to cover provider costs and offer a reasonable return on investment. Threats to the stability of the local care markets can result in a decline in capacity and reduced local choice for state-funded care users since some may be unable to top up with their own income. For example, the position in 2008 was that fees paid by most social services departments throughout England remained below the fair market price rates and were inadequate to incentivise independent sector providers to develop the capacity of new care homes for 'frail older' and 'older mentally infirm' people dependent on state funding.

According to (2008) population ageing has now reasserted itself as a driver of growth in demand for care homes, following a decade in which local authorities effectively cut care home demand by tightening eligibility criteria and diverting demand to community-based services. Statistics strongly suggest that a point of inflection has been reached and that demand for care home places for frail older people is returning to an upward trend, one which will accelerate from the 2020s as population ageing intensifies.

Payment terms

This section of the contract sets out the payment arrangements, for example in 12 monthly instalments. Slow bureaucratic systems of payments that do not recognise business requirements for some providers, such as maintenance of cash flow and reduction of administrative overheads, can also militate against good contracting processes and partnership approaches. Commissioners should want to invest in building up long-term partnerships in order to ensure that the right services are in place for the right people at the right time. When coming to the end of a life of a contract, negotiations on contract renewal should be planned well ahead to ensure all aspects can be reviewed and discussed fully between the parties (Clogg 2006).

Variations to contract terms

This sets out what should happen if the contract is not being fulfilled due to circumstances beyond the control of both parties, for example significant changes in the anticipated workload. Thought needs to be given to some specific areas such as temporary absence of service users through hospitalisation, death or how complaints are dealt with. A balancing act may be required to address the needs of the service user against inappropriate use of limited public funds or lack of capacity for others awaiting care and support. Emphasis should be placed on the 'reasonableness of all parties' and it is important for contract clauses to build on underpinning partnership relationships (Clogg 2006).

Monitoring arrangements

Agreement should be reached between the parties as to how the contract performance will be monitored and what information should be exchanged to facilitate future contract development and needs assessment, such as that arising from a significant audit. A key part of the monitoring process involves a regular meeting between commissioners and providers. Moreover, regular communications may help to prevent any misunderstanding or dispute arising.

Disputes and arbitration

Any contracts where there is not a direct management relationship between the parties are not legally enforceable and, where possible, should be settled by 'in-house' arbitration. This section should specify the procedures to be followed if either party breaches any of the contract terms; for example, if the provider fails to provide agreed audit data. It may be agreed that if one party considers that the other has underperformed its agreed obligations, that party will instigate a meeting with the other within two weeks following the meeting, and the non-performing party may be given an agreed time to resolve the issue to the satisfaction of the other party. If the dispute has not been specified within the agreed period, the other party will have the right of recourse to arbitration. In the event that a dispute cannot be settled, it is open to parties to agree on an external person or body to act as an arbitrator.

Content of a well-written cost and volume contract

1. It is well defined in terms of service user group.

2. It is comprehensive in terms of providers and services for its care group/issue.

3. It is strategic but stable, anticipating planned service changes.

4. It is shared with providers, particularly care professionals.

5. It is affordable within cash limits.

6. It is integrated and user-centred, enabling continuity of care and support and demonstrating different providers' responsibilities.

7. It offers a means of monitoring and raising service quality, given existing information.

8. The content is relevant to local circumstances, including professional and user/carer views.

9. The contract is informed by needs assessment and challenging to providers to improve service quality and value for money. (Semple Piggot 2002, p.132)

The contracting process

Properly managed tendering processes have high transaction costs. Tendering also relates to the current structure of the market for care services in that it is imperfect, in the sense that most local authority purchasers occupy a dominant positive vis-à-vis providers.

Several clear steps can be identified in any contracting process. A suitable approach may be to consider the following steps.

Step 1 – invitation to tender

The contracts team will invite organisations to tender (bid) for a range of services on a block, cost and volume or cost per case basis. The tender document (purchasing intentions and /or purchasing plans) should specify the number of services and quality parameters (such as times and types of processes) required. Perhaps you can consider how useful the invitation to tender below is in attracting its potential tenders:

> Sunnyside is seeking expression of interests from experienced, suitably qualified provider organisations to provide office-based, outreach and/or interactive virtual hub services for carers in Sunnyside. We will consider expressions of interest from all organisations who can bid as one or together to provide services. This is a three-year contract.

> Sunnyside Council and the PCT are committed to supporting carers in their caring role. Carers must have information that is relevant, up to date, and accessible and delivered on time. The aim of the service is to ensure carers have access to independent advice, advocacy, information, assessment and resources to, support their general wellbeing and promote their independence.

> For more information please contact Ms X at Sunnyside below.

When preparing the tender document, which should include as much detail as possible, the contracts manager will need to involve managers in specifying the service required as they are in the best position to know how to meet needs. But this first stage of the contract process is not driven solely by the commissioner. Providers must ensure that they are invited to bid for the services in the first place. Providers will need to develop marketing approaches that highlight the range and quality of services they are able to provide.

Step 2 – the offer

Having received and considered the invitation to tender, the provider will then submit a statement of the services it is willing and able to provide, and the price of those services (the service specification). This 'offer' document will have been drawn up following detailed discussions between the contracts staff and the providers of the service. Services will not be sold on cost alone as standards will need to be met and costs of facilitating this should be built into the contract.

Step 3 – negotiation and decision

It is likely that there will be a number of terms in the contract needing clarification or discussion. Further negotiations between the two parties will be required to iron these out. Following these discussions the commissioner will be in a position to consider the final competing bids. The decision on which provider to choose will take into account the providers' ability to meet the quality criteria laid down at an acceptable price.

Step 4 – signing

Once the decision has been made to accept an offer, and each party agrees to all terms of the contract, then the duly authorised representative of each party will sign the contract document.

Step 5 – monitoring quality and outcomes

In order to ensure that users' and carers' needs are being met, commissioners will wish to monitor the performance of the provider. There are a number of ways that this can be done including the use of audit and questionnaires, reports, looking at the number and types of complaints received, comparison of outcomes with other providers, national averages, best practice and so on. Some of these approaches will be covered in more detail in Chapter 7 on performance management and in Chapter 10 on evaluation.

Involvement and participation

In summary, the development of a written strategy when commissioning and contracting can act as a catalyst to galvanise effort, resources and thinking about how to meet needs, and acts as a valuable statement of intent to service users, carers and providers (Walker 2007). It should be a fluid and dynamic document that can be reviewed and revised as additional evidence or policy comes to light. The assumptions underpinning any commissioning strategy and activity and the rationale behind them must be open to scrutiny and challenge, with a logical flow from the evidence about what needs to be commissioned and why. The key to a successful contracting process is the involvement at every stage of those purchasing or providing the service. Attention to detail within the process should be focused and strong on analysis with less emphasis on describing the service (Walker 2007). Only by involving those directly responsible for referring service users and providing the services will contracts fully address the needs of the user.

Semple Piggot (2002) offers some further useful tips:

- Get out and about to meet the people with whom you are contracting.
- Involve both managers and staff in the negotiating meetings.
- Use negotiation – not confrontation (look for win-win solutions).
- Build in quality standards in contracts, measures and outcomes.

Social enterprise

The government made a commitment in *Our Health, Our Care, Our Say* to support social enterprise as a source of more innovative provision in health and social care and to minimise the barriers social enterprises might face in setting up and competing fairly. In Chapter 3, we introduced the concept of social enterprises as business-like entrepreneurial organisations with primarily social objectives. Their surpluses are mostly reinvested back into their business or the community to help achieve these objectives and change people's lives for the better. Social enterprises are not driven by the need to maximise profit for shareholders and owners. In essence, social enterprises use business solutions to achieve public good. They tackle a wide range of social and environmental issues and operate in all parts of the economy, helping to make it stronger, more sustainable and socially inclusive (Department of Health 2007c). Any social enterprise will want to adopt the best possible model for serving its customers and values and within the context of this chapter we examine some of the legal options in which social enterprises can enter the commissioning and contracting environment.

What legal form is right for your enterprise?

'Legal form' is the term used to describe the way in which any business is set up and the rules and regulations that govern it. Whether a social enterprise is new or wants to make changes to its existing structure, there are several legal forms open. The choice made will depend on a range of different factors including: the social purpose of the enterprise; the people and stakeholders involved; the scale on which it intends to operate and the way it is financed. Choosing the most appropriate legal structure is vital. Getting it right first time will ensure the organisation has the scope to function legally and effectively, both now and well into the future. In brief, the legal forms for social enterprises are:

- **limited liability company** – either as a company limited by shares, where shares are sold to private investors or to the general public in public limited companies (PLCs)

- **company limited by guarantee** – where there are no shareholders and the members give a 'guarantee' to cover the company's liability. In these companies, profits are generally reinvested back into the company

- **community interest company (CIC)** – a new type of company, designed for social enterprises that want to use their profits and assets for the public good. CICs have all the flexibility and certainty of the company form, but with some special features to ensure they are working for the benefit of the community. Becoming a cooperative community interest company enables CICs to operate under cooperative principles also

- **industrial and provident society** – for businesses without share capital, such as various forms of cooperatives and some social enterprises. Societies can take two forms. They can either be run as a cooperative society for the mutual benefit of their members. Here, any surplus is usually ploughed back into the organisation to provide better services and facilities. Alternatively, they can be run as a community benefit society to provide services for the community rather than its individual members

- **limited liability partnership (LLP)** – these share many of the features of a normal partnership, but unlike ordinary partnerships, the LLP itself rather than the individual partners is responsible for any debts that it runs up

- **charitable incorporated organisation (CIO)** – a new form which will only be available to charities. Members and managers of a CIO will be protected from the financial liabilities of their organisation. It will be easier for people dealing with a CIO to assess any potential credit risk, benefiting both the body and those dealing with it.

Having considered many of the strategic and practical issues involved in contracting and commissioning within care services, this chapter concludes with a brief look at some of the 'hot topics'. Given that commissioning is seen as a vital key to transforming services, practice is still a very mixed in terms of analysing need, demand and supply; in relationships with stakeholders; and in commissioning for quality with involvement of local people (Walker 2007).

Transformation and the concept of brokerage

The government's unambiguous commitment to individualised budgets has brought with it both a foregrounding and official endorsement of 'brokerage', placing it firmly with the mainstream social care discourse and this is an issue for commissioners (Scourfield 2010). According to the Commission for Social Care Inspection (2006):

> It is not yet clear where brokers will come from, who will recruit train and pay them (and on what basis), whether they will be self-employed or employed by a service provider or by the council or whether the brokerage function will be operated by a social care professional. (Commission for Social Care Inspection 2006, p.iv)

In his extensive review of models of support brokerage, Scourfield (2010) identifies that there is no single model of support brokerage but there are six different models which have been used in the UK, all of which involve different degrees of professional input. These include:

1. independent brokers who are either self-employed or who are working for a local or national voluntary agency which does not provide direct support services itself

2. independent advocacy agencies which either employ brokers or where advocates act as brokers for some of their time

3. service-providing agencies which provide support brokerage for people using the services of other agencies

4. local authorities where care managers carry out the support brokerage function or where the function is separated out from the resource allocation responsibilities within the authority

5. families who carry out the support brokerage responsibilities for their family members, or where families or disabled individuals form small local organisations to deliver support brokerage and other functions to a wider group of family members in a single community

6. a local authority or a prescribed area within a local authority where the full mix of all of the types of support brokerage is encouraged. (Research in Practice for Adults 2008, p.3)

Workforce development and employment

Any commissioning and contracting process must consider the terms and conditions of employment, staff remuneration, opportunities for training and qualifications and the general adequacy of local pay conditions to bring about the creation of a more qualified and professionalised social care workforce, as widely advocated within social care workforce policy. Staffing is one of the largest cost items in business planning and is the product of pay rates, on-costs per hour and staff hours. Staff turnover costs may be incurred in a new service or from induction to new roles and responsibilities. Unskilled staff turnover results from competition for unqualified staff from all sectors of the economy including retail. The gap in pay and conditions between care providers and other sectors for similar skilled jobs is likely to remain a potent factor leading to staff turnover, until it is more affordable to equalise pay and conditions. Organisations recognise that staffing is a major concern and that there are difficulties in recruiting a qualified workforce at an affordable price. This is likely to become more pressing as demography changes and the workforce ages.

In relation to leadership and management skills, the role of managers in commissioning calls for new and different skills from those managers in traditional operational services. These changes require a wider understanding of supply and demand to commission provision effectively ensuring appropriate levels of trained staff and the need to develop new ways of working. It calls for the ability to lead and to be innovative, so as to be able to work with a wide range of providers, service users and carers. Most importantly, leaders and managers need good analytical skills and to be willing to challenge organisations when their activities need to shift to meet agreed strategic and policy outcomes (Walker 2007).

Chapter summary

This chapter has introduced the basic principles of the commissioning and contracting process and taken you through some of the more practical issues involved in managing the process. This involves acknowledgement of asymmetrical power relations and different professional discourses in relation to taking steps to make sure all stakeholders understand and engage with the government's shift towards an outcomes-based approach.

Until recently service users have had a relatively powerless voice in service provision. Commissioning in this sense is a means to secure the best possible outcomes for people and a means of promoting equality. There is considerable interdependency in achieving outcomes for service users through integrated, joint or parallel arrangements between the partnerships involved. When working in partnerships within the strategic commissioning context, it is useful to reflect with the key stakeholders that you are directly involved with the ways in which they and their partners organise themselves and the different values, rituals and priorities that are at play. Leadership is also crucial to effective stakeholder participation that explores what can be learnt from the expertise, interest and developing a leadership approach that is flexible enough to ensure that stakeholder participation is useful in meeting the diversity of local need (Social Care Institute for Excellence 2009).

Manager's comment

The commissioning and contracting process is fundamental to the successful running of services for adults with learning disabilities. Whether at the micro level of a service user or carer commissioning or contracting a personal assistant to provide one-to-one support, or at the macro level of a local authority's commissioning process, the effectiveness dictates the quality of service. This has been my experience, whether managing service provision for adults with learning disabilities or working within a local authority community learning disability team or, as I am now, helping to manage a social enterprise providing services for adults with learning disabilities.

As a social worker, or social work manager, commissioning has always been crucial to the variety and quality of services you are able to access on behalf of the service user. If services did not meet the requirements of local authority commissioning, then you were often unable to access them, despite any negative impact upon the rights, independence, choice and inclusion of service users.Within my current role the limitations to choice are still all too clearly present, despite the government's encouragement to set up social enterprises and desire that:

> Everyone who receives social care support, regardless of their level of need, in any setting, whether from statutory services, the third and community or private sector or by funding it themselves, will have choice and control over how that support is delivered. It will mean that people are able to live their own lives as they wish, confident that services are of high quality, are safe and promote their own individual requirements for independence, well-being and dignity. (Department of Health 2008, p.4)

My own experience of the personalisation agenda, referred to above, has highlighted the fact that inherent problems within old style 'block contracts', anathema to person-centred social work and service provision, can still effectively be present as a result of tendering requirements of local authorities. As social enterprises, we understand the need for achieving 'best value', but we would be more welcoming if it were best value for the service user. Limiting the options of service users to organisations that have met the often exhausting demands of tendering can go against the principles of personalisation. What constitutes best value for service users in the short, medium and long term does not always marry up with the financial restrictions a local authority insists upon. It would be desirable to see service users and carers actually involved in the tendering process to determine who should provide services, as they are the ultimate consumers/clients/service users.

The demystification of the commissioning and contracting process, as contained in this chapter, is essential for the involvement of social enterprises in the personalisation process. People starting up social enterprises are not always entrepreneurs imbued with an innate sense of business; and it can be a huge challenge negotiating the complexities of 'business speak' local authorities regularly employ. I spent ten years in business prior to working in the social care sector; and I have found it to be a massive challenge. However, when this challenge is met, the end result can be 'change that could not even have been conceived in the recent past' (Beresford and Croft 2004, p.63). Something we should all be aiming for, and something that effective commissioning of services can facilitate.

John MacDonough is a founder member of Richmond Care, a social enterprise run by and for people with learning disabilities.

CHAPTER 7

Managing Performance

When you have worked through this chapter you will be able to:

- describe how quality assurance and performance management has developed within social care and some of the key issues and debates

- identify mechanisms for setting, measuring and managing the performance of services you are responsible for

- develop a range of indicators including formal performance indicators that enable you to evaluate how far your business plans are achieving their objectives

- consider some of the tensions and difficulties in measuring and evaluating quality and performance in services and the integral importance of user involvement.

Introduction

The terms 'quality' and 'performance' are used with high frequency within social work and social care and apply to all areas of the organisation: its people, processes, resources and environment (Schmidt *et al.* 2006). Wider public debate about quality issues and performance also tend to be highly charged and based on critical scrutiny. Such scrutiny is founded on the notion that infinite demand and finite resources require careful consideration of priorities, as well as a need for absolute transparency and equity in their allocation. This has become even more focused in the definition and measuring of 'outcomes' of care as we saw in the previous chapter.

There is no shortage of statements outlining the intentions behind monitoring performance in care settings, although some have highlighted the lack of actual evidence as to its benefits (Clarkson 2010). The search for ways to improve the performance of care services is reflected in many different initiatives to measure performance or to set standards. These include measurement of systems based on statute, such as the national performance assessment framework (PAF) (Department of Health 1999) as well as various quality assurance systems, which will be outlined in more detail later on in this chapter. This has led to a particular form of performance measurement in which public reporting has become 'de rigeur' (Clarkson 2010, p.171). According to Dummer (2007) there is a danger that different views of what constitutes good performance or quality will lead to conflicting objectives and diverging policy aims. This highlights the importance of ensuring continuity and consistency between both performance and planning for managers. In contrast, many approaches to performance management attempt to reduce the complexity, multiplicity and unpredictability of activities performed by public sector organisations to a single dimension (Hafford-Letchfield 2007).

On a more positive note, striving for quality can also be a key motivational factor for those participating. A well-designed quality service can empower and support members of the organisation in making service improvements. Having an active role in delivering quality services has direct benefits for staff, such as increased job satisfaction, reduced frustration, and being in receipt of good feedback from the people they work alongside as the reputation of their service or organisation improves (Hafford-Letchfield 2007).

The White Paper, *Modernising Social Services* (Department of Health 1998) made the measuring of performance a mandatory requirement and led to frameworks and measures by which the performance of social services authorities are judged nationally. This is generally accompanied by tough-sounding announcements from government concerning the consequences if departments do not improve performance (Challis, Clarkson and Warburton 2006). Star ratings and league tables and the publication of performance data are linked to reward and incentives, often in the form of financial reimbursement. In addition, the big stick of central takeover has been matched with a larger carrot in the form of 'earned autonomy' for organisations which perform well (Newman 2001). Whilst most quality and performance initiatives attempt to monitor and regulate public services at a national level, the real challenge is how to devise evaluation systems for use in a local context. Subsequent reforms in social care and political changes brought about since the 1980s (see Chapter 1) have continually emphasised the importance of monitoring social services performance from the viewpoint of the consumer within a national framework of standards. Quality assurance (QA) and performance measurement are both bound up with the emergence of a more market-orientated philosophy in social care. This is based on a competitive environment which requires stakeholders to have some grasp and accountabilities for how their activities fit into the overall provision. Knowing how services perform and whether they are achieving their objectives is one way of responding to budgetary restraints and competing pressures on expenditure (Challis *et al.*

2006). Greener (2009) helpfully summarises some of the reasons for the relatively recent growth of performance management in public services:

1. fiscal crisis and concerns about lack of scrutiny of services against resources used

2. a gap between policy formation and implementation and a need to ensure that these were carried out

3. a perceived failure of democracy and the need to create central accountability through performance management

4. concerns that decentralisation will mean loss of control for the government and to guarantee quality standards and accountability at a local level

5. wider availability of information technology and the ability to construct more complex information systems.

In summary, many definitions associated with central performance measurements sit uneasily with the aspirations of managers and practitioners who wish to have a more direct influence on how practice is appraised.

> Time pressures on managers, and high numbers of staff reporting to them without any method for mitigating this, result in a need to focus narrowly on tasks and processes, and on meeting indicators, at the expense of concentrating on outcomes for service users and the quality of service. (Department for Children, Schools and Families and Department of Health 2009b, p.32)

There continue to be a number of ideological arguments that performance indicators (PIs) serve only to contain costs and other aspects of care. This centres on whether achieving a PI means that one has met defined needs or whether services have been provided in an appropriate or timely way. This fuels the argument that further individualisation and customisation of service provision using business ethics or principles within the transformation agenda have, according to some, downgraded professional and practitioner expertise leading them away from the direct concerns of service users (Ferguson 2007; Scourfield 2010).

The pivotal role of external inspection of public services has also proved controversial. Whilst advocates of inspection see it as a powerful means for improving accountability and driving improvement, its detractors argue that it places a huge bureaucratic burden on those inspected, which diverts precious resources away from front-line service delivery (Davis and Martin 2009). Inspection, however, is only one of the mechanisms by which the public and government hold care services to account, as there are an array of regulatory methods used both to enable and control the quality and performance of care. Consideration needs to be given to how quality is to be built into the service before any form of measurement or assessment takes place. Before going on to look at these quality assessment mechanisms in more detail, it is important to acknowledge that performance in social care is multidimensional. Managing the quality aspects of a business plan requires an acute awareness of how different stakeholders will value different kinds of improvement. As we have seen in earlier chapters, there is potential for conflict between national and local priorities. In developing quality services, managers will be looking to shape their own local services with citizens and service users' priorities at the forefront.

What do we mean by quality services?

Accountability for practice involves moving with the times and delivering the services that people need in the right place, at the right time and which provide value for money. These may seem like common-sense notions when we think of our own expectations of services and we probably all know from first-hand experience what we consider to be either a poor-quality or a high-quality service. Yet achieving a common definition is important, as it drives the whole implementation process and forms the basis for setting standards and measuring services against them when developing a local strategy or business plan. Various dictionary definitions and those offered by quality 'gurus' include definitions of quality such as:

delighting the customer by fully meeting their needs and expectations. (Department of Trade and Industry undated)

the totality of features or characteristics of a service that bears on its ability to satisfy a given need. It must be explicitly designed and built into a service; it cannot be inspected at the time, or after, delivery. (Davis and Hinton 1993, p.51)

These are generic definitions which are not easily put into operation given the tensions between 'care' and 'control' inherent in the statutory duties that drive some aspects of social work and social care. For example, which aspects of the assessment and delivery of safeguarding practices would one consider building quality into where there are contested interventions and unwilling participants? Resource constraints and the need to prioritise particular service users' needs over others have the potential to compromise the quality of service users' and carers' experiences or the extent of services provided. Having a set of minimum standards or benchmarks, if met, does not actually guarantee quality but it may be a matter of staff or the organisation 'going the extra mile' to deliver a quality service.

We can build on Moullin's (2003) definitions of quality derived from the management literature in order to define what specific features are unique to developing a quality service in social care:

- the importance of providing services capable of meeting the exact needs of service users and carers

- services easy to access or obtain, in the right place, at the right time, and at the right level

- equality in access and provision regardless of social, ethnic or cultural background

- reliability, consistency and continuity

- services that have a clear purpose and rationale contained within a statement of their aims and objectives and a description of the minimum standards or level that people could expect

- services that are in keeping with the legislative and policy framework and the outcomes expected to be achieved

- services provided within the costs and resources available but which are efficient, effective and give value for money

- being delivered by people who are committed and competent and who receive good-quality training, supervision and support to do the best job possible

- services that are socially acceptable, inclusive and involve service users and carers in their design, delivery and evaluation. (Hafford-Letchfield 2007, pp.28–29).

The disaggregated approach described above recognises that quality is complex and multidimensional (Donabedian 1980). Each individual component of quality provides a partial picture when viewed on its own, but offers more specificity in defining quality when viewed in combination. Further, any definition of quality must incorporate the views of service users, commissioners and service providers. To be effective, the organisation must have a reliable and robust system in which it can assess and understand the needs and expectations of its service users. This involves developing internal processes (between departments, teams or colleagues) and external processes (involving other agencies, providers or suppliers) to make this happen effectively. Martin and Henderson (2001) refer to this as the 'quality chain' (p.180) which in turn is just one element within a more systematic approach to developing quality. A strategic framework for performance measurement is illustrated in Figure 7.1.

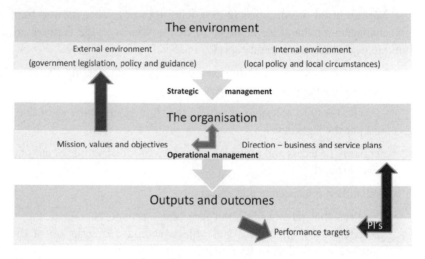

Figure 7.1 Strategic context for performance measurement

Quality assurance and performance management systems – key issues and debates

The term 'quality assurance' is often used interchangeably with 'quality control'. The latter describes activities and techniques employed to achieve and maintain the quality of a service but in itself contributes only one step towards quality assurance. Quality control involves monitoring activities that can detect and eliminate any causes of poor quality and is the process through which organisations measure actual performance by comparing it with the standards set and then acting on the difference. Management audit is one example of the rectification of errors and shortcomings, maintenance through standard-setting (Adams 2002, p.288). Managerial audit is one example of quality control.

Saario and Stepney's (2009) comparative study into the use of managerial audit of mental health services highlights a central paradox: where on the one hand a systematic audit can provide illuminating data necessary for the efficient deployment of resources and quality improvement but on the other, it might be said that at a time of limited resources and high-profile incidents, managers and policy makers may have a vested interest in light-touch monitoring of practitioners' performance so that they can distance themselves from its consequences, 'especially when something goes wrong' (p.42). They conclude that whilst management audit systems are developed or 'good causes' are associated with quality improvement, they may simultaneously produce diverse and unintentional consequences at the micro level of practice (Saario and Stepney 2009). This is illustrated in their quotation from a social work practitioner wanting to be sensitive to demand and yet see as many users as possible by keeping the reception time short:

> In those kinds of situations when I feel that I have many...yes, too many clients, I feel very anxious and stressed. I don't know exactly how many clients I'm having right now, but I guess maybe 40 to 60 at any particular time. I can't respond to everybody with the same amount of enthusiasm and concentration. Somebody is always suffering because not everyone gets equal treatment. (Quoted in Saario and Stepney 2009, p.48)

Performance measurement and the use of its associated indicators draws largely on the theory of management accounting, which uses information to summarise the organisation's actions and activities in quantitative terms. Performance management systems allow managers to track whether activities and processes are working as planned and are designed to drive out inefficiency and minimise deviation. This is often facilitated by technology as we shall see later on. Many serious case reviews and reviews of serious incidents have suggested that we need to look more closely at the tensions between control and autonomy in order to be able to manage the multiple pressures that are embodied within audit and performance review systems (Stanley and Manthorpe 2004). These often result in public disparagement and political criticism only when failures are retrospectively discovered. Professionals spend considerable time meeting administrative targets, whilst at the same time managing risk in the community and fulfilling statutory roles in which they are expected to use their professional knowledge (Foster 2005). This sets up contradictory roles for practitioners as both budgetary calculators and care facilitators (Saario and Stepney 2009).

> Having the right legislation, policies, systems and structures does matter. But they are not enough. What matters most to children, young people and families is the day-to-day support they receive from services. Above all, we need consistently high quality practice, working to high quality standards, firmly focused on what will make a real difference to children's lives. (HM Government 2009b, p.5)

As the above quotation from the government's response to Lord Laming's investigation into child protection in England implies, managing quality to achieve excellence requires a more holistic approach to achieve excellence in management within an organisation. In a quality assurance system, the search for excellence is ideally driven from within the organisation rather than being imposed from the outside. This is supposed to incorporate a never-ending improvement cycle to ensure that an organisation learns from its results, systematically standardises and documents what it does well and improves the way it operates and what it delivers – all from what it learns (Department of Trade and Industry undated). Therefore a quality assurance system entails taking a planned, systematic and conscientious approach to creating a climate and culture of quality and excellence that permeates the whole organisation. We are now going to look at some specific aspects of this 'system' before examining the various quality frameworks in current use in social care.

Innovation in social care

Innovation is often referred to in government policy and guidance, based on the premise that this is the key to empowering and modernising services for the community. Innovation involves doing things differently by changing paradigms, services and processes through exploration with stakeholders, particularly service users such as in the co-production model formerly explored in Chapter 1. According to Dowler (2008), the challenge to innovate is writ large if one takes into account the complexity of integrated partnerships. Whilst all partners might have a common aim, the different cultures, priorities, working methods and vocabulary between all the agencies involved need to be reconciled (Dowler 2008). One might argue that this is the opposite of innovation and a balance is required. Conceiving performance measurement as a learning rather than control system, as referred to earlier, is one approach. Experimentation and exploration are anathema to a control system that focuses on efficiency and optimisation (Delbridge et al. 2006). Measurement systems can lock organisations into particular structures and processes, repetition and instruction. These are generally short term, whereas innovation requires rapid responses to emerging opportunities, with more long-term goals. The collection and analysis of management information, for example, can provide insight into what is and isn't working and help to develop insight or lateral thinking about better ways of working.

Case study – managing the recession creatively

We are entering a period where there will be great pressure on public spending. It is reasonable to expect that all budgets will face cuts over the next couple of years. But I believe there is a strong case to exempt some youth justice spending from this – particularly prevention and early intervention – where a pound spent now could save much more in years to come. Equally there is a very strong economic case for investing in services for young people leaving custody, good resettlement plans and services will reduce the likelihood of reoffending. We have seen significant falls in numbers of first-time offenders, frequency of reoffending, and numbers of children and young people in custody. This is good news for children and young people who offend and good news for local communities. (John Drew, Youth Justice Board, quoted in *Community Care*, 1 December 2009)

Setting standards

The use of standards was illustrated briefly in Chapter 6 when we looked at commissioning and contracting, as they provide some way of judging and comparing standards for people bidding to deliver services. Standards describe the level of service to be achieved and once the standard of service is set, indicators can then be developed and established to measure the extent to which these standards have been achieved. The formulation and application of standards of quality are not only internal to particular organisations and individuals but are universal to the whole system of care. The introduction of national minimum standards and national service frameworks (NSFs) involve extensive analysis of the quality of care that must be provided by specific services. NSFs are defined in a way that enables them to be measured by using indicators of quality and performance or by identifying shortfalls in provision.

The key characteristics of a service standard are:

- It can be measured, monitored and evaluated.

- It is realistic and attainable within available resources.

- It is expressed clearly and unambiguously and tells people what they can expect.

- It is consistent with service aims and values.

- It is set in conjunction with the people asked to achieve it.

- It reflects what people say they value most. (Martin and Henderson 2001, pp.194–195)

Within a business plan, setting clear standards can help to assess the level of service you are providing and communicates expectations by making explicit what professionals do. When devising or writing your own standards, it is helpful to start by working backwards using outcome criteria. Outcome criteria are descriptive statements of the performance, behaviours or circumstances that represent a satisfactory, positive or excellent state of affirms. A criterion is a variable selected as a relevant indicator of the quality of care and must be measurable, specific, relevant, clearly understandable, clearly and simply stated, achievable, professionally sound and reflective of all aspects of those it is applied to, taking into account their physiological, psychological and social circumstances (Hafford-Letchfield 2007).

Outcomes can be measured using both quantitative and qualitative measurements and the measurements are required at both the individual and the service level. Performance indicators are therefore just one aspect of measuring outcomes and when combined with more qualitative measures or research, such data can powerfully illuminate aspects of professional practice or measurement (Tilbury 2004). We shall be looking at some of these qualitative and broader evaluative aspects in Chapter 10.

Developing performance indicators

Much of the previous discussion has focused on the national requirements to measure performance and provide information to central government in respect of national league tables and adherence to national policy and performance frameworks. Here, we will address the question of how initiatives around quality can be translated into a mechanism which seeks to address quality at a local level. This involves a staged approach as demonstrated in Figure 7.2. The first stage involves accurately describing those services and standards that are the subject of the quality improvement. Donabedian's model can be helpful here. Donabedian (1980) considered that there were three important components when describing quality of care: structure, process and outcomes. These he identified as the structure in which care is delivered, for example the staffing arrangements, financial resources, management roles and hierarchical positions. The stability of a structure can increase or affect the probability of achieving quality. Donabedian also considered the process where the interactions and relationships between practitioners, service users and managers all contribute towards how the design, delivery and evaluation of care and support services are embedded in the organisational values, policies and procedures. Outcomes are Donabedian's third component as discussed earlier. His findings are still highly valued, forming the basis of much current work on quality assurance in both health and social care.

Indicators are used by managers to assess the work of a service or organisation against policy priorities, local circumstances and national guidance. Theoretically, they can be used to motivate staff and explore the extent to which services conform to their expected use and to bring to light concerns about quality in service provision. Measures have to be designed with reference to the environment in which they are to operate, as the measuring phase in Figure 7.2 illustrates. During the design stage and in subsequent analysis, measures must, on the one hand, be simple and understandable for their users and, on the other, be able to be generalised to a wider context.

Performance measures must support enquiries into the way services operate and help raise questions concerning different aspects of the care service system. Indicators often do this indirectly by drawing attention to aspects that deviate from what is expected or by reference to important policy concerns. Once analysed and interpreted, these measures have a range of uses, from commenting on efficiency and effectiveness to judging services according to user-defined criteria of choice and acceptability (Challis *et al.* 2006).

As illustrated earlier, using techniques that enable output to be measured against the objectives of the organisation on the basis that corrective action can be taken if there is deviation from these objectives are insufficient measures of quality. Unlike private enterprise, performance in health and social care is difficult to measure, as what is being measured is often contested. There are no broad overall measures, leaving us with a challenge, as well as significant questions, concerning the purposes and success of evaluating care and support provided. There have been a number of inquiries, for example, where regulatory inspection did not pick up serious issues, leading to later organisational failure (Department of Health 2002; Laming 2009). An effective framework will enable managers to move beyond operational management functions, such as monitoring costs and activity, towards a strategic focus. These latter activities enable managers to comment on the organisation's long-term objectives as well as the unique circumstance and characteristics of social care. Such objectives can be set in terms of PIs which can then be used to compare performance, both internally and against other authorities or organisations in terms of national data. The advantage of a framework is to ensure that changes in policy and practice are assimilated. Figure 7.2 illustrates one staged approach to developing such a framework.

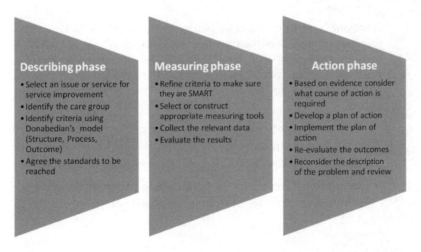

Describing phase
- Select an issue or service for service improvement
- Identify the care group
- Identify criteria using Donabedian's model (Structure, Process, Outcome)
- Agree the standards to be reached

Measuring phase
- Refine criteria to make sure they are SMART
- Select or construct appropriate measuring tools
- Collect the relevant data
- Evaluate the results

Action phase
- Based on evidence consider what course of action is required
- Develop a plan of action
- Implement the plan of action
- Re-evaluate the outcomes
- Reconsider the description of the problem and review

Figure 7.2 Developing a staged approach to quality (building on a description by Kitson 1988)

At a national level, the performance assessment framework attempts to shape the delivery of care at a local level. In Chapter 2 when we looked at the joint strategic needs assessment (JSNA) and the setting of local objectives in your business plan, it became clear that some local decisions will need to be made about competing priorities and to enable services to be flexible and responsive to a variety of changing and local needs. Planning inevitably involves measurement, and targets need to be set in advance and modified in the light of new information (Challis *et al.* 2006). The case study below illustrates some of the ways of monitoring policy implementation at a national level and some of the continuing challenges in interpreting such information.

Case study – measuring preparedness for an ageing population?

In 2005, the Audit Commission introduced its comprehensive performance assessment (CPA), which was replaced by comprehensive area asessment in 2009 as a result of the local government White Paper, *Strong and Prosperous Communities* (HM Government 2006). One of the shared priorities in the corporate assessment element of CPA is 'older people'. The lines of enquiry for older people assess how well a council works with its partners to:

- develop a strategic approach to older people that goes beyond health and social care and covers the areas that older people say are most important

- undertake meaningful engagement with older people and their representative groups on all aspects of the strategic approach and service provision

- deliver a comprehensive, coordinated range of services to older people.

A national analysis of the older people shared priorities in 111 corporate assessments published between September 2005 and May 2008 revealed that more than two-thirds of councils needed to improve their services for older people and that there is no straight forward correlation between preparedness and/or the proportion of older people.

- Twenty-eight per cent of councils were performing well and had meaningful engagement with the older community, well developed cross-cutting strategies with a coordinated range of services.

- Forty-five per cent of councils had started to make progress but were at an early stage of strategic development.

- Twenty-seven per cent of councils focused solely on social care and made no other provision for older people. (Audit Commision 2008)

The table below shows some of the potential contradictions in performance measurement.

Table 7.1 Contradictions in performance measurement

Highest performing councils on older people shared priorities	Councils with the most improvements to make
Have a CPA score of 3 or 4 stars Perform well in Adult Social Care, scoring 3 or 4 stars in the CSCI assessments Spend more than average on social care for older people (19 out of 31) But: 2 high performers have below average social care spend per head	Have a range of performance on CPA (21 scored 3 or 4 stars; 9 scored 2 stars) Have a range of performance on Adult Social Care (22 of 30 were 2 or 3 star and 8 were 2 star) Spend less per head than average on social care for older people (18 out of 30) But: 8 low performers are 4 star councils overall 11 low performers have an above average social care spend per head

(From: Audit Commission 2008)

The case study above illustrates the complexity of performance measurement. Most councils measure the cost of an ageing population in terms of social care spending, but measuring the costs and savings associated with an ageing population is more complex and may require spending on preventative services as well as generic services other than social care that promote well being in later life (Audit Commission 2008). It is this breadth and depth of thinking within a strategic framework that will enable quality services to be developed.

Different types of performance indicators

In a detailed study of how to develop performance indicators at a local level, Challis et al. (2006) have provided a useful review of the different aspects involved in their design. They categorise these as follows:

Resource inputs

This entails looking at what resources you have, for example inputs such as labour and capital, which can more easily be measured. Less easy to measure are quality dimensions of labour such as how you would assess and account for training, support and adequacy of staff coverage or supervision. The range of inputs must reflect the operational realities of the organisation and have costs attached to them, which should be included when working out any unit costs for services. Unit costs are usually taken to be an indicator of efficiency. Achieving a lower unit cost might represent the more efficient use of resources, but one needs to be aware of the underlying assumptions and how these are affected by external factors. Using a Best Value approach allows further questioning of cost data when comparing services. This is then supplemented with information about the influence on costs of other variables in order to analyse true efficiency (you are referred back to Chapter 4 here on resource management).

Non-resource inputs

These refer to less tangible determinants of outputs, such as aspects of the care environment, including the attitudes of staff. This may have implications for costs, for example if you were dealing with a constant number of complaints about staff. Non-resource inputs are in a dynamic relationship with resource inputs into care. Exploring their associations with resource use and costs can then provide insights into how care services operate. Devising indicators of non-resource inputs remain, however, difficult to operationalise.

Need indicators

There has been a lot of academic and practice debate about the difficulties in defining need (Bradshaw 1994). Need is an expression of an individual's state of wellbeing, often focused on anticipating how they might be in the future, and involves relative priorities (Asadi-Lari, Packham and Gray 2003). We should however be able to define need in order to match service provision to local needs and to distribute resources explicitly. There is a tendency to use broad definitions of need, for example those categorised within *Fair Access to Care Services* (Department of Health 2003) which assume relative importance of some needs over others using categories such as 'critical', 'substantial', 'moderate' and 'low'. Similarly, using these tools to target and allocate resources does not operate in a vacuum, as meeting different types of prioritised need is directly related to achieving the objectives of specific social policies.

Intermediate inputs

These relate to indicators of service activity, are more easily specified and measured and therefore relatively easy to use in the planning process. Knapp (1983) distinguished types of intermediate output as levels of provision and throughput measures. An example is the number of admissions or discharges which express the rate of production of a service and which have theoretical or empirical links with other indicators of input, expenditure or costs. Intermediate outcomes represent the achievement of service-level objectives such as providing all the services specified in a care plan rather than the impact that these services actually have on the service users' wellbeing.

Care outcomes

We defined 'outcomes' in Chapter 6 and established that this represents the ultimate effectiveness of a programme of care and is very difficult to measure. Measuring outcomes must include perspectives from service users themselves and requires a multivariate analysis of all the factors that contribute to the final outcome, which may be beyond the scope of care itself. The concept of 'outcome' does not easily transfer to routing collection of information on a day-to-day operational basis and numerous difficulties arise in translation. This explains why there has been a marked tendency for indicators in social care to concentrate merely on inputs and outputs. Outcome criteria are descriptive statements of the performance, behaviours or circumstances that represent a satisfactory, positive or excellent state of affairs. A criterion is a variable selected as a relevant indicator of the quality of care. It must be measurable, specific, relevant, clearly understandable, clearly and simply stated, achievable, professionally sound and reflective of all aspects of those it is applied to, taking into account their physiological, psychological and social circumstances (Hafford-Letchfield 2007). Outcomes can be measured using both quantitative and qualitative measurements and the measurements are required at both the individual and the service level.

Problems in measurement

Despite tough warnings and consequences for authorities that do not achieve national performance standards, there are some real problems in collecting the relevant information and in analysing performance information:

> Some of these problems are at the conceptual level, concerning which aspects of performance need to be monitored; some are concerned with measurement issues, such as how to devise relevant data and

> analyse it effectively; and others are at a technical level, such as how to disseminate information effectively within authorities. (Challis *et al.* 2006, p.2)

Conceptual difficulties in measuring effectiveness of social care reflect practical problems of stakeholders in defining what they are working towards. The problems can be summarised as follows:

- There are multiple, often conflicting objectives in social care as exemplified in both the enabling and safeguarding tensions involved in self-directed care.

- Measuring 'quality' involves coming to an agreement about definition and expressing this clearly in more tangible terms.

- There is organisational complexity involved in developing systems for measuring quality and performance that are realistic and owned by those involved. This becomes even more complex where there are a number of stakeholders involved where each is dependent on the other for doing their bit.

- The criteria by which social care is evaluated are wide-ranging. Efficiency is important but so too are equality of access, standards of care and so on.

- There is a difficulty in finding indicators that are both relevant and operational.

- There will always be dispute and political compromise. Indicators are far from neutral and accusations have been made that these represent tools of central government control (as we saw in Chapter 1).

- There is a problem in measuring the final outcome of social care services and proxy measures may be needed in the absence of individualised measures of user satisfaction. (Adapted from Challis *et al.* 2006)

Quality frameworks

Within the quality assurance literature, there are three key performance frameworks or 'off the shelf' quality approaches likely to be familiar to managers working with quality and performance issues. These are illustrated in Figure 7.3. Any quality system selected depends on the nature of the organisation and what it seeks to achieve. Some of the systems summarised in Figure 7.3 can complement each other. There will also be likely costs associated with achieving standards against a particularly quality system, such as purchase of the standards, cost of guidance materials, training and external consultancy, self-assessment and external recognition fees, cover for routing tasks and of course the costs involved in introducing any changes. It is definitely not a paper exercise and will involve a lot of staff time and resources as well as commitment to reviewing and maintaining performance. There are a number of charter marks available for organisations dealing with the public, including voluntary organisations dealing with the public sector. These involve an assessment which looks at the quality of service delivery, checking that customers are placed at the centre of everything it does. The standard is externally assessed, with reassessment every three years. Applicants are encouraged to network with others working to achieve the award through quality networks and events around the UK.

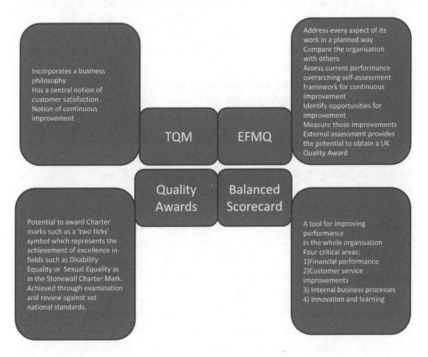

Figure 7.3 Different types of quality systems

Case study – the Stonewall Diversity Charter Mark

Stonewall is an organisation that campaigns and works with a range of agencies to address equality within the lesbian, gay men and bisexual (LGB) community and the needs of transgendered population. They have created the 'Workplace Equality Index', which is a benchmarking tool for employers to use when developing a more robust model of good practice in LGB equality and diversity. The tool provides a baseline assessment against which employers can compare their human resource and workplace practices and make positive improvements. Members subscribing to the workplace equality index have someone allocated a 'client account manager' who can help them explore the outcomes of the agency's result against the index and to give advice and help from Stonewall using Stonewall's own expertise and knowledge. There is also the potential to chart their progress over time. Stonewall publishes the results of member organisations in their 'Top 100 employers' every year to celebrate those that are successful.

As the results of the Stonewall Top 100 Employers 2010 demonstrate, even at a time of economic turmoil the best employers are choosing to recruit and retain the very best talent regardless of their sexual orientation. Every employer in this booklet has an employee network group to provide support, advice, networking and development for LGB staff. Every employer in this booklet understands that lesbian, gay and bisexual equality benefits both individuals and organisations. (Stonewall 2010, p.1)

The relationship of technology with performance management

Measurement systems backed by sophisticated information technologies, such as computer technologies, generally support managerial goals, as they allow the collection and collation of information in standardised formats, as well as being able to monitor and evaluate staff and organisational performance (Kirkpatrick, Ackroyd and Walker 2005). However, there has been much discussion and debate about the potential misuse of IT systems in social care. 'The process of making human services including social work "auditable" is in danger of being destructive, creating a simplistic description of practice and focusing on achieving service outputs with little attention to user outcomes' (Munro 2004, p.1075).

Performance measurement has been characterised as one part of the managerial assault on social work, a monitoring technology that ignores the role of traditional values in practice (Clarkson 2010; Watson 2004). Innovative decision support systems such as those involving ICT should allow practitioners to work more efficiently and to record data in a more systematic fashion, leading to better assessments and interventions as well as releasing time for more direct contact work with their service users and communities (Schoech and Toole 1988). However, having a system in place will never replace professional and user expertise, as a number of research studies are beginning to identify that increasing emphasis now being placed on entering data on an IT system has the effect of reinforcing certain ways of working or excludes others (Burton and Van den Broek 2009; Holmes et al. 2009; Scott, Moore and Ward 2005). Such studies have questioned the purpose of gathering some sources of information.

They assert that these are designed primarily to meet the administrative needs of the organisation and question the extent to which these then serve to influence the content of the work done with service users. Scott *et al.* (2005) have observed that many information systems have been designed to store and record data, with little attention being given to how they might be used to support practice or decision-making. Performance management systems that rely on ICT are said to have refocused on auditing and cross-checking professional behaviour, rather than facilitating more robust involvement of the practitioners in the services that they themselves provide (Munro 2004).

This begs the question of who is involved in designing quality assurance and performance management systems applied within care contexts using new information technologies. Outcomes from research to date suggest that social workers' experience and knowledge of service delivery should be more proactively integrated into the design and application of technology. Adequate training and commensurate ongoing training on such systems is another issue (Burton and Van den Broek 2009). This is a political challenge. As we saw earlier there are some perverse incentives that have developed which link performance measures to recognition and reward systems, particularly financial ones. Combined with the increasing use of technology, this has led to documented examples of responding to measures in social care where information is manipulated at the expense of the wider interests of the organisation or service.

> There are assessments that need to be done on the computer but when you look in reality as a social worker, at what you are doing you say to yourself, 'what is this really doing for the client who needs some help right now?' It's more of a management tracking system for government legislation than any help. It doesn't speak to people's needs and how we are going to get to meet them. (Senior welfare worker and union activist, Nova Scotia, cited in Baines 2004, p.277)

In a study conducted by Holmes *et al.* (2009) on how social workers spend their time, practitioners and managers all consistently reported that it was not possible to complete their work within their contracted hours. A lower proportion of practitioners' time was also spent in direct contact with the children and families they were working with. Practitioners were shown to experience an increase in hours spent on administrative activities and indirect processes, however, to which the implementation of the Integrated Children's System (ICS) has contributed. Practitioners perceived that

ICS exemplars were further compounded by the way the supporting IT systems had been set up as the implementation of a substantial system takes a great deal of planning and time. The slowness of this process was also cited as a point of frustration by a number of the participants in the study. However, many of the difficulties raised were implementation issues associated with a new system in general, rather than specific to ICS or electronic recording. One key factor in the time spent inputting data into electronic recording systems was familiarity with the whole system or individual report sections. It is accepted that issues regarding navigating electronic records and IT proficiency would improve, reducing time on administrative tasks, as workers become more familiar with the systems in place and electronic recording becomes more embedded in social work culture.

Looking at the extent to which e-government and changes in technology have already impacted on organisational structures and processes in public services and, in particular social care, should lead us to examine the extent to which the e-revolution agenda has been directed, for example, towards service improvement and improving coordination and relationships between those involved in assessing and delivering care. The data handling focus has highlighted the negative consequences of managing information badly, but there are just as many risks in not sharing information and huge opportunities that we are only starting to understand in terms of exploiting information as an asset (Ceeney 2009). The introduction of new technologies (Burton and Van den Broek 2009) and reappraisal of technologies and functions of the public sector, and implementation of new techniques for judging the operation of services are still unclear. Performance review and measurement have reflected these changes, as accountability now requires a quantitative element as a basis for planning and monitoring. Technological measures risk creating a false sense of security. Most breaches of information are the result of quite mundane physical factors, and are essentially caused by process failures and/or people simply not knowing what to do. (Ceeney 2009; Poynter 2008) Organisations can have all of the policies and processes they like, but according to Poynter (2008) if culture and values, management systems and scrutiny are not joined up in a clear governance framework, this lack of integration lends itself to data security issues. Failures in information management are not therefore always attributable to technology itself, but may be primarily a cultural and governance issue.

Chapter summary

Developing quality services is not a technical, value-free activity which simply requires good management combined with encouragement and a commitment to implement and be effective in its application (Watson 2004). Professional codes of practice and ethics in social care (General Social Care Council 2002) place accountability to service users clearly above the concerns of employing organisations (Burton and Van den Broek 2009). Measurement of social work and social care therefore cannot take the place of relational and caring aspects of the work but we need to find a balance between accountability towards service users, employing organisations, the community and professions (Sheafor and Horejsi 2005) at both a local and national level. Local approaches require their own incentives, not only to collect the right data, but also to engage practitioners and managers in their use (Clarkson 2010). We need to make knowledge work for us in a number of different ways (and we will expand on this in Chapter 10 when looking at evaluation techniques). This should utilise more intangible assets such as building professional networks and communities of practice in order to experiment and take advantage of emergent opportunities.

As illustrated in the last section of this chapter, the introduction of new information technologies has led to substantial changes in expectations and accountabilities – 'what gets measured, gets done'. Not conforming to performance measurement requirements is clearly not an option, particularly in light of the range of regulation and inspection emanating from legislative and policy requirements. But forward-looking management practice will involve thinking about how one plans for quality and performance and what needs to be put in place to support improving performance rather than about how to review it. This requires a number of strategies: first, systems thinking to analyse and understand complexity; second, to build capacity and capability within the organisation, service or team so that a culture develops which responds positively to change and stimulates innovation and commitment to develop quality services. Third, reviewing performance management data should focus a manager's and their team's mind more on looking for answers, rather than being concerned with how to perfect the data using performance indicators alone.

The valuing of tacit and experiential knowledge alongside technical knowledge is important to finding ways of sharing this within the organisation, service or team in a collaborative way. When identifying poor performance, prompt and positive responses by managers, particularly those which involve redesigning *processes* that are unnecessarily burdensome and bureaucratic will help to shape people's engagement with performance management at the front line. Team and service business plans can be used as a means to connect overall strategic intents to activity in service delivery in a way that aligns the motivations of practitioners with the wider concerns of organisations (Clarkson 2010).

In reviews of social services in Wales over a decade (Care and Social Services Inspectorate Wales 2009), monthly or quarterly reporting of team performance was seen to have variable impact, particularly where those managers who had a say in the content and design of performance reporting were more likely to take the feedback seriously. It was also found that comprehensive and reliable information was more likely to be used to good effect where there was a clear connection to the organisation's strategies and priorities and there had been full involvement of front-line managers in determining information priorities and requirements. In other words, information was designed to be of use operationally and not just to feed external reporting demands. Further, systems are required to bring together a number of information sources, for example about budgets, costs, quality and service activity in conjunction with information about trends and using benchmarking in order to make fair comparisons (Care and Social Services Inspectorate Wales 2009).

Finally, whilst it has come a long way, feedback from people using services and from carers remains unsystematic and could certainly be more creative. Without active listening to people and connecting this feedback to management thinking, services can become out of touch. Feedback from front-line staff in constant touch with people receiving services is a valued source of information. People's experience of services should be an important element of determining standards and performance measurement alongside using imaginative approaches to get feedback from different user groups.

Manager's comment

Quality assurance and managing performance has for the last few years been high on everyone's agenda. Quality Protects and Best Value for example allowed for the allocation of more resources to achieve increasingly stretched targets. As managers, targets and inspections have led to increasing pressures on the staff and services we provide.

One of the benefits of this has been the increased anxiety of staff to ensure that case records and information on service users are up to date. It may seem odd to argue this as a benefit but workers feel less stressed when they have their work up to date and complete. It is therefore the manager's role to ensure that strategies are in place for the workers to manage time effectively to achieve positive outcomes. One of the most effective ways I have found is to allow staff to work from home and not be contactable. This can cause extra work for those left in the office but as they all now do it, they are effectively supporting each other. This has caused less stress and anxiety for the staff concerned.

Having stretched targets and unannounced inspections causes obvious anxieties. But the overall benefit is that rather than having announced inspections and there being panic to get work up to date before the inspectors come, the workers and managers work together, constantly monitoring the output and outcomes for service users and staff alike. This provides consistency and transparency for all stakeholders.

Service users are now more readily asked for their views and opinions about the service provided, which can only improve the outcomes for services as a whole. We cannot truly assess the effectiveness of services without the views of the key stakeholders for the services we provide.

Angie Lymer-Cox is a manager with Leicestershire County Council and manages a team of staff who work with young people who are in care or care leavers.

CHAPTER 8

The Process of Decision-Making

When you have worked through this chapter you will be able to:

- understand the theory behind management decision-making and critically examine rational decision-making models

- appreciate the complexity of decision-making process in the social care environment and the practical limitations of managerial decision-making in the context of ethical and practice dilemmas

- consider different management tools and approaches used to develop participatory and inclusive decision-making.

Introduction

Decision-making is not the sole prerogative of managers and it is important to be aware of how those who make decisions well arrive at such decisions. In this chapter we will define what we mean by decision-making and critically examine a model that characterises the process as a rational one. It is often assumed that managers are supposed to act rationally, which fails to take into account the practical limitations of managerial decision-making, the impact of power and situational constraints as well as opportunities and best practice.

Decision-making is the conscious process of making choices among several alternatives with the intention of moving towards some desired course of action (Bratton *et al.* 2007). We may also refer to decision-making as problem-solving. Problem-solving assumes a fuller analysis of issues than pure decision-making because it relies on trying to discover the root cause. Conversely, as Armstrong (1990) notes, there are no real problems, only opportunities! This implies that focusing on problems alone tends to promote the more negative aspects of management work.

Decision-making is probably one of the most important functions of management and has been identified by management theorists as a rational aspect of management behaviour. At whatever level the decision is required, there are certain fundamental considerations that have to be made if the process is to be effective and successful. Current decisions and patterns of decisions typically arise from that which has previously occurred, combined with the pressures of the present situation. Decisions taken in the present will also have a direct impact and implications on the future (Pettinger 2001).

According to Bratton et al. (2007), organisational decision-making can be studied at different levels: at the individual, group and organisational. Thinking of decisions in this way can encourage managers to draw on relevant theories that might underpin decisions such as organisational structure, culture and leadership at the strategic level; team dynamics and team roles at the operational level and professional knowledge and interventions at the individual level. Decision-making is a complex phenomenon because it involves dealing with technical issues as well as ethical ones. We will always be subject to human biases and errors but the manager's role in decision-making and your practice around this is at the heart of managing people through the promotion of participation, diversity and the appropriate use of authority. One cannot deny, however, that decision-making may also be associated with a bureaucratic command-and-control vision of management as well as with oppression and omnipotence.

Managers and professionals working in social care not only have to consider the needs, wants and rights of service users when making decisions. They also have to consider a range of issues such as resource allocation, efficiency, values and equalities, legislation, policy and practice guidance and professional codes of practice (General Social Care Council 2002), to mention just a few. Assumptions inevitably enter analysis of decision-making, which is why the rational model is not always appropriate. At worst, rhetoric to justify decisions by managers at the very top of an organisational bureaucracy is used to reinforce their claims to knowledge and competence. Delbridge et al. (2006) highlight the notion of 'cognitive competence' (p.9) for effective decision-making by considering the way in which individuals and groups make sense of their world and the mental processes used to process information and acquire knowledge. This normative model of decision-making is rarely realised fully or extensively in practice. In social work and social care we are more likely to use a wide range of evidence to inform our decision-making by utilising different forms of knowledge including tacit, experiential and practice knowledge, and that recognised as formal (Eraut 1994).

Pettinger (2001) divides decision-making into 'programmed' and 'non-programmed'. He considers that good management practice is to have as many decisions as possible in the first category provided that this does not diminish effectiveness of managerial activity, nor ignore changing circumstances and factors beyond the manager's control. Programmed decisions are simply those taken automatically in any given set of circumstances and are normally taken to address simple and relatively certain operational issues. In the increasingly complex, ambiguous and shifting environment of social care, however, the art and science of decision-making is crucial in a bewildering flow of information (Delbridge *et al.* 2006). Fundamentally, there are limits to the amount of information individual managers and others can process and because of these limitations, they rarely reach optimal solutions. This chapter will look at just some of the numerous remedies that managers can deploy to counteract these shortcomings and different tools that can help overcome personal biases and other constraints (Delbridge *et al.* 2006).

Rational-technical decision-making model

To outline briefly the rational-technical decision-making model, consider the approach below as a means of examining a recent problem requiring a decision. This approach seeks resolution through the following steps:

1. Identify problem or problem definition as a starting point.

2. What information will you gather, from which sources?

3. What criteria and weighting will be given or assumptions made?

4. Storm or generate the potential different solutions.

5. What evidence or research will you consider? Who did you consult or involve?

6. Evaluate these and the alternatives.

7. Consider what resources will be required, for example are there time and cost constraints?

8. Choose a solution.

9. Decide how to implement it.

10. Decide how to evaluate or test the decision made.

Whilst the above rational-technical approach was relatively straightforward, it is suggested that this would be an inadequate method to capture fully the nature of social care practice. A purely rational approach might result in the colonisation of decision-making in which making judgements inevitably involves selectivity and power imbalances because of the nature of the decisions required. The lived experience of working in a care organisation means that many decision-making processes are actually messy, unpredictable and chaotic. They are commonly influenced by the need to make quick and on-the-spot decisions in unusual places during times when stress is running high and those involved feel quite overwhelmed.

The very nature of managerialism within social care organisations can lead to avoidance of making important decisions as these might just be too difficult for the organisation to face up to. This is particularly difficult when they concern demands for change in the face of few resources (Hughes and Wearing 2007). Diffuse and empowered styles of managerial leadership, as we shall see later on, require meaningful decision-making, enabling staff to have more influence over their work and the conditions in which decisions are taken. A manager's role should support emergent process in organisations which encourage autonomy and create opportunities for staff to interconnect in ways that traditional structures fail to enable (Hafford-Letchfield *et al.* 2008).

According to Taylor and White (2006), most social workers have been trained to use 'knowledge' to create certainty out of uncertainty. Equipping them with the skills to exercise 'wise judgement under conditions of uncertainty' (p.937), however, also means helping them to interrogate their own knowledge and case reasoning in a more reflexive way. They argue that the current preoccupation with searching for certainty is actually misplaced. Scientific evidence, for example, is rarely available in interactive situations with service users and their helpers, despite the ongoing development of schedules, proformas and procedures put in place to guide practice. This links to some of the debates around evidence-based practice which will be discussed more fully in our last chapter on evaluation. As we saw in earlier chapters when looking at tools for analysis, these will always have a limited role. As a manager, therefore, you will need to foster a democratic culture which facilitates the interpretive abilities of all staff through learning and support and encourages insight and critical reflection within your own management practice.

Critical incident analysis techniques

Tools for critical reflective techniques, such as critical incident analysis, can be used to consider positive incidents rather than just negative ones. Enhancing critical reflection helps to consider ethical issues and values in decision-making. They are, for example, encouraged as an aid within professional supervision where the use of reflective frameworks help balance educative and pastoral support for staff in the front line as well as managerial and administrative accountabilities (Crisp and Green Lister 2007). There has been a lot written about critical reflection in the caring professions. Reflection is a special form of thought leading to some type of action. It is a wholehearted approach during which one considers management practice carefully in order to develop a conscious response. This is not only a process of critical self-determination (Habermas 1973) but a process of becoming aware of the wider influences of societal and ideological assumptions, and the ethical and moral beliefs which lie behind professional practice. Ruch (2000) has identified four types of reflection from the literature:

1. **Technical reflection** which refers to technical rationality in decision-making and to an empirical analytic level of knowing. It involves decision-making or problem-solving by immediate behaviours or skills and draws on analytic thinking techniques.

2. **Practical reflection** which refers to a means of identifying and modifying one's own professionals' personal assumptions underpinning practice. This type of reflection looks for alternative responses, enhances professional understanding and facilitates personal insight (Schön 1983; Ruch 2000). Schön (1983) refers to a reflective practitioner being in possession of three important levels of reflectivity within practical reflection:

   (a) *knowing in action*: being aware of what you have done and what might need to be done

   (b) *reflection in action*: making choices and using research-based theories and techniques to effect change

   (c) *reflection on reflection in action*: being able to reflect on the effect of your reflections leading to considerable enhancement of practice.

   Yip (2006) likens this to peeling off the layers of an onion, where reflection can go deeper and deeper, starting from being aware of one's performance, to critically assessing the ideology and belief behind one's thinking and feeling in the action.

3. **Process reflection** with its roots in psychodynamic theory. This type of reflection focuses on both the unconscious and conscious aspects involved in reflection. It takes account of transference and countertransference between the professional and other people (Ruch 2000). This approach inevitably involves the development of a 'reflexive' self in interaction with others.

4. **Critical reflection** goes further than examining the 'personal' and is aimed at transforming one's professional practice by taking a wider view and challenging existing social, political and cultural

conditions (Habermas 1973; Mezirow 1981). It also involves ethical and moral criticism and judgements because it relies on one's own thinking, perceiving and acting. Within this model, managers should be able to analyse their own potential for reflexivity and develop a deep form of critical reflectivity about their ethical and moral assumptions behind practice (Mezirow 1981; Yip, 2006). The deeper the reflection, the stronger is the individual's awareness of his or her affectation, experiences and cognition. It is also a 'process of self-evaluation, self-analysis, self-recall, self-observation and self-dialogue. In reflective practice, the individual evaluates his or her own performance, thinking, feeling and response in practice' (Yip 2006, p.780).

Achieving critical reflection, however, within certain organisational cultures can be a double-edged sword: 'a potent way of confronting sticking points or previous irresolvable dilemmas but its effectiveness may be limited because of the misunderstanding, resistance and anxiety which can result when deep seated assumptions are questioned' (Fook and Askeland 2007, p.521).

As stated earlier, reflection becomes 'critical' when it focuses on power, a common feature within management and managerialism. This focus enables managers to link personal experiences with cultural and structural ones. This is difficult to achieve in task-centred cultures where staff may not have time to reflect or may feel uncomfortable in having their practice scrutinised. Fook and Askeland (2007) remind us that the more proceduralised or regulation-based workplace cultures become, the more likely they are to cause tensions between bureaucratic and professional demands. This highlights the importance of giving as much value to those skills gained through socialisation as through action. The vital importance of service user involvement in decisions about their own lives and the involvement of practitioners throughout the whole process will improve the quality of any decision-making. Furthermore, some of the features of management or leadership style can enhance decision-making such as:

1. **charisma** – developing a vision, engendering pride, respect and trust and using influence

2. **inspiration** – motivating by creating high expectations, modelling appropriate behaviour, and using symbols to focus efforts and looking beyond self-interests

3. **individualised consideration** – giving personal attention to followers, giving them respect and responsibility, including the

use of emotional intelligence to foster cooperation within highly emotional interpersonal relationships to achieve better conditions for change

4. **intellection stimulation** – engaging with expertise wherever it exists within the organisation rather than seeking this only through formal position or role and continually challenging staff with new ideas and approaches. (Bass 1990; Hafford-Letchfield *et al.* 2008)

So far we have identified that one of the weaknesses of the rational model of decision-making is its neglect of social and cultural factors. Tactics that can improve decision-making include the setting of objectives, encouraging individuals to become engaged in critical and creative thinking and the use of group techniques such as those identified in Chapter 2. All of the topics in this book so far should have stimulated your thinking about how management processes can improve decision-making for those involved, if conducted in an ethical and reflective way. Managers should also actively engage with professional knowledge, research, evidence and skills alongside service delivery information. This inevitably involves the appropriate acknowledgement and use of power, a topic to which we will now turn.

The use of power in decision-making

There has been much debate about the impact of decentralisation and delegation of decision-making within health and social care in relation to decision-making. This has focused on the issue of the distribution of power between national, regional and national levels (Clarke 2004). Despite a number of reforms giving rise to the delegation of power for decision-making from central government to a local level (as illustrated in Chapter 1), at a strategic level, it is still perceived that a number of decisions affecting social care remain at ministry level. The extent to which power is devolved is therefore variable. In relation to our discussion here, we will focus on the ways in which power operates and is distributed within the organisation itself and particularly in relation to equity issues and the implications for managers.

One useful differentiation of types of power is provided by Hales (1997) who describes power as lying within:

1. physical power

2. economic power

3. knowledge power including administrative knowledge about how an institution works, or technical knowledge concerned with how tasks are performed

4. normative power, for example personal qualities, or the 'aura of office'. (Hales 1997, p.25)

Hoyle (1986) gives us a similar list relevant to management power.

- structural: power as a property of a person's office or structural position

- personality: power as a function of personal characteristics, such as charisma or leadership qualities

- expertise: power as a function of specialised knowledge or skill or access to information

- opportunity: power as a function of the occupancy of roles which even though they may rank low in the hierarchy, provide the opportunity to exert power through the control of information, or key organisational tasks. (Hoyle 1986, p.74)

It is useful to differentiate power as a concept from the two related concepts of authority and influence. Power is overarching, but authority relates to the legal or statutory right to exert power, whilst influence relates to the more informal power that individuals may have (Coleman and Earley 2005). For example, a senior manager in your organisation may exercise power with authority because of her status, whilst individual members of staff may exercise more unofficial aspects of power, such as influence, and which is often linked to personal charisma.

Our understanding of power and authority in bureaucracies is based on the work of Max Weber (1972) who was particularly concerned that decisions taken by officials in bureaucracies tend to support the survival of the organisation rather than respond to the desires of the other stakeholders. Therefore, managers are given legitimate power through their position in the bureaucracy and this 'legal authority' will always support the existence and influence of the bureaucratic structure. This is not to say that all managers have agency and contingency which they can use as they see fit (Gunn 2008), as power is not a linear, rational phenomenon that somebody has or can exercise through choice (Lawler and Bilson 2010).

Foucault (1982) made a significant contribution to the way in which we conceptualise power and its discourses within government agencies and its organisations. Foucault's key concepts of 'archaeology' and 'governmentality' are used to investigate the way in which power is operationalised through different levels of everyday life. Foucault referred particularly to the unquestioning of everyday discourses which relate to the arrangements we make to deliver care. These are present within policy decisions made higher up and can permeate right down to the front line of care practice. For example, in the assessment process and allocation of resources, there lies a set of assumptions about what can be said and thought on a certain issue or set of issues which are embedded within organisational structures and cultures. Foucault therefore puts specific emphasis on the relational aspects of power, and on those silent aspects of power acquiesced in everyday policy-making and practice.

Democracy and participation in decision-making

In respect of service users, Gunn (2008) notes the increasing move by local authorities towards viewing their service users as consumers, and on how democratic processes are retained for decision-making based on citizenship principles. He reminds us that neither citizenship, a term often used to describe democracy through the ballot box, nor consumerism, which is built upon individual choice, clearly dominates decision-making. Local authority departments may use both concepts in their participatory decision-making when they involve users in policy-making. A number of academics have also examined the development of different terminology used in British social work to describe the relationship between those who assess and commission services and their recipients (McLaughlin 2009; Scourfield 2007). As we saw in Chapter 1, such critiques find the different terminologies increasingly problematic for explaining and ensuring how the perspectives of people using services are effectively taken into account.

Case study – the power to shape decisions through participation

Gunn (2008) gathered data from a sample of four groups of stakeholders which included young people, front-line workers, managers and local politicians across three different social services departments in diverse locations. These research participants were asked to reflect on their experiences of their involvement in participation, and particularly on their perceptions of their past, present and predicted involvement in local government policy development. Following this, they were then asked to rank their own group and other groups' ability to influence policy. Using a particular theory of power derived from Levin (1997), a brief summary of Gunn's conclusions from the interviews and ranking exercise are found below:

Young people were perceived as having the least influence on policy-making, whilst managers and local politicians vie for the most powerful position. Managers perceive themselves as having the most power and this is borne out by young people. Front-line workers, who do not have a day-to-day relationship with local politicians, think that they have the most influence over policy-making as do local politicians themselves. From the interviews with young people, generally whilst they mostly spoke positively about participation, they were given little feedback about the results of their input and were consequently hazy about the effects they were having. Young people interviewed did not demonstrate an understanding of the mechanics of the process they were involved in. This meant that their influence was dependent upon the support of adults who could withdraw at any time. Gunn concluded that young people ultimately did not have an independent power base to work from and had little contact with each other. Neither were they able to describe how the managers and local politicians saw their participation developing.

Managers, on the other hand, were recognised by all groups as having the power to make changes and control how the department worked and when participation happened. Setting up participation to address service-related issues, rather than as empowerment strategies was seen as a way of making change without presenting a serious challenge to the status quo. Selecting young people on the basis of their abilities to fit in with departmental structures, and the role of support workers in helping them frame their requests for change, were often to ensure that any participation developed fitted with departmental norms. In these situations, Gunn found that young people would dissent with their feet rather than by confronting the organisation about the way they were involved.

Local politicians were seen as most powerful by front-line workers, particularly over resources. Every group involved in the study, however, perceived politicians as not having sufficient information about the day-to-day working of the department or of young people's experiences. Local politicians, although supportive of young people's participation, were also not really sure how this worked in practice.

Front-line workers were perceived to be the lowliest in the decision-making hierarchy both by service users and themselves. Tensions were expressed between workers' own lack of involvement in decision-making whilst they saw that users' involvement was increasing in their organisations. Workers were, however, felt to be committed to participation in terms of their professional ethos. Overall, this shared reality of having little real influence tended to bind users and workers together.

Gunn's study is an interesting one in that it concluded that mechanisms used to facilitate participation and the culture of the organisation where participation takes place are important factors in the decision-making process. A clearer understanding of power and how it operates could therefore be used to help sustain participation with the different stakeholders and to avoid tokenism or the most powerful stakeholders from framing the agenda.

There are three main arguments used to increase user involvement in decision-making: political, legal and social (Wistow and Barnes 1993). The political case for participation acknowledges the benefits of involvement where services can be improved, democracy strengthened and the insights, skills and opportunities developed during the process. The legal case is evident from the creation of new structures, regulatory and commissioning practices and financial streams necessary (as described in Chapters 1, 2 and 6) to embed co-production as a long-term requirement of all current legislation and policy in social care. The social case is focused on the 'rights' to participation and relates to the generation of social capital, the reciprocal relationships that build trust, peer support and social activism within communities (Needham and Carr 2009). Co-production models are used to argue that partnerships between front-line staff naturally evolve from their repeated interaction and expertise with service users (Needham 2007a). However, as we saw earlier in Gunn's study, these need to be balanced with the constraints and pressures that can lead to street-level bureaucratic responses when making decisions at the front-line. Aspirations towards co-production should be viewed in the context of the continuing power inequalities between the state, its employees and the users of social care (Simmons *et al.* 2009).

Managers and power in decision-making

Coleman and Earley (2005) identify three further models in the exercise of power which, they state, do not exist independently. Each model contains elements of all three, but one style may predominate. These are: collegiality, bureaucracy and micropolitics.

Collegiality tends to be normative and thought to be one of the best ways of managing, and is particularly appropriate to organisations where there are professionals. It assumes a common set of values such as the General Social Care Council's codes of practice for employers and employees in social care (General Social Care Council 2002). Underpinning the code of practice, which has both a code for employers and employees, lies the assumption that there are systems of democratic representations which facilitated consensus decision-making. This was one of the issues highlighted by Laming in his inquiry into the death of baby Peter Connolly in Haringey (Laming 2009). Most, if not all organisations in social care aspire to collegiality but in reality are torn by the demands on them to be strong and efficient and to keep power centralised within the organisation or service in order not to waste professionals' time. For example, this can be seen in front-line workers who occupy an ambivalent position between management and service users and operate a delegated form of bureaucracy with reference to an organisation's legislation, policies and procedures. On the other hand, the core values, professional knowledge and practice theories arising from professionalism can facilitate empowerment by utilising the workers' own sense of agency and ability to make meaningful relationships with users that impact on their relationships and subsequent interventions. Therefore, an aspiration towards collegiality requires time to develop the appropriate structures that will support empowerment.

Bureaucratic models, on the other hand, have a more hierarchical authority structure with formal chains of command and are focused on the goals of the organisation using a rational-technical process. Such organisations are often divided into specialist roles where decisions are governed by rules and regulations which feature neutral and impersonal relations between staff. Bureaucracy is not necessarily seen as a negative aspect but as a way of striving continuously for maximum efficiency through rationally defined structures and processes. For example, formality protects individuals in the organisation from being arbitrarily treated, for example in procedures used in recruitment and selection. For users this might involve the application of eligibility criteria and financial assessments, so that the organisation is seen to be transparent and fair in the decisions around access and provision of services.

Micropolitical styles of management involve the use of influence to further the interests of individuals. This was discussed in Chapter 2 in relation to the types of political skills needed by managers during strategic development. Here, there is a focus on the immediate work group rather than on the organisation as a whole. This may reflect differences in values and aims between the interest groups within the organisation and also conflict management. Decisions are made through negotiation and bargaining and those holding power are the key to decision-making.

Coleman and Earley (2005) highlight the influence of external power exerting itself outside the institution and rebounding on the relationships within it. This may be particularly evident where power is developed but where there is a disparity between the view of the government and the view of professionals. Micropolitical theory focuses on the interaction of groups both formal and informal such as those which reflect the subcultures within the dominant culture of the organisation. One example might be the conflict arising between groups when bidding for limited resources. Limiting the harmful effects of micropolitical behaviour can be done through examining the overall effectiveness within the organisation, that is, keeping focused on the bigger picture and engineering frequent interaction and communication between groups to encourage collaboration and reinforcement of these principles. Rotation of staff and strategies to increase mutual understanding between competing groups can also emphasise the sharing and pooling of resources.

Tools to aid decision-making

This chapter started by looking at rational-technical models of decision-making and has considered some of the complexities of the decision-making process in the social care environment. We have highlighted the practical limitations of managerial decision-making in the context of ethical and practice dilemmas in relation to user involvement and resources. We will return here to some of the common practical tools that might be used to aid decision-making. Within the context of business development, some managers make use of sophisticated, mathematical and computer-based techniques to try to take some of the risk out of their decision-making. However, you will have realised by now that these are only tools to aid management and can never replace actual judgement and evaluation of information and the situations presented.

The tools outlined below might be ones that managers can use to involve different stakeholders in the process of decision-making. The most basic methods use facilitated activities such as thought showering followed by questioning techniques, which examine people's ideas or responses more closely in order to get to the root of the problem. Working with groups, however, is not without its problems. Research by Janis (1982) has identified the phenomena of 'groupthink'. Janis found that individuals in groups tend to conform to the majority decision because they do not feel comfortable being an outsider; meaning that less creative solutions may be offered or false optimism is created. These issues have arisen in the examination of case conferences or multi-stakeholder meetings where the result of group pressure prevents members testing the reality or using individual judgement to decide whether something is good or not for fear of standing out (Barr and Dowding 2008). Janis identifies the following characteristics of groupthink:

- illusion of invulnerability
- belief in integrity of the group
- negative views of competitors
- sanctity of agreement
- erecting a protective shield. (cited in Barr and Dowding 2008, p.127)

> The consequences that flow from groupthink are synonymous with those of poor decision processes. As leaders need to bring out diversity of ideas to address problem solving they should perhaps

work towards counterbalancing the possibility of groupthink within their team. (Barr and Dowding 2008, p.128)

Some decision-making tools

Decision tree

One such tool involves the use of decision trees which provide a visual means of making informed choices. These tools are available on several software packages which may be obtainable within your organisation, but here we are going to look at a more simple 'pen and paper' approach.

The decision tree is a visual tool for helping you choose between several courses of action and to explore options and investigate the possible outcomes of choosing those options. A decision tree helps to lay out the problem clearly so that all options can be challenged, and provides a framework to quantify the values of each outcome and the probabilities of achieving them. Decision trees are started by outlining the decision that you need to make and placing this in a box on the left-hand side of your diagram. Figure 8.1 below represents an example of this process.

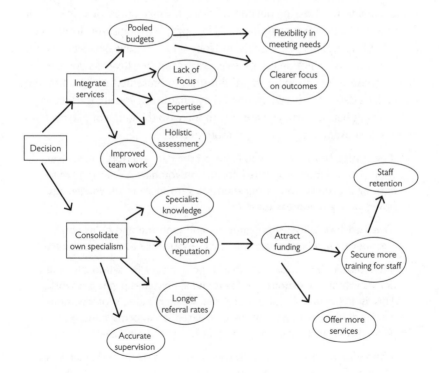

Figure 8.1 Decision-making tree

From this box draw arrows out towards the right for each possible outcome and insert your outcome in the circle. From each circle, draw further lines and circles to generate lots of outcomes. Keep doing this until you have exhausted the process and have generated as many outcomes as possible. You may use different colours or shapes to represent preferred or less preferred outcomes as a further visual cue. The whole point of the exercise is to storm and record your own and your team's thoughts in a more accessible way, allowing you to trace ideas.

Some people assign values to the different options identified and by weighting or giving them a 'worth' so to speak. Assigning values helps make decision-making more transparent and evaluative. Some organisations also have computer-based packages to try to gauge the effects of the range of possible outcomes in advance of decisions being taken. Whatever approach you use, decision trees are just one simple aspect of helping to make decisions. They can ideally be used with a team or management team to maximise storming of both ideas and in weighing up solutions.

Edward De Bono's 'six thinking hats'

This is a technique developed by De Bono (1990) aimed to help people think outside the box, or outside of one's normal range of thinking or predisposition to ways of thinking. The approach helps you to appreciate the full complexity of a decision from very different perspectives, for example rational, emotional, intuitive, creative or negative. As you can see below, these different styles of thinking are represented by the different colour hats described by De Bono and by imagining you are the wearer of the different hats in turn, you are able to increase the range of perspectives taken when examining an issue in more detail:

> **The white hat** is where you focus on the data available and look at what you can learn from the information you have. Wearing a white hat might prompt you to question the gaps in your knowledge and how you might address these.
>
> **The red hat** utilises your intuition and emotion and helps you to consider how other people will react emotionally to your decisions.
>
> **The black hat** looks at things pessimistically, cautiously and defensively and questions why ideas and approaches might not work. This is important in eliminating the weaker aspects of decision-making and how these can be eliminated or informs contingency plans. Black hat thinking prepares you for difficulties, flaws and risk.
>
> **The yellow hat** is the optimistic viewpoint that spots opportunities and benefits and is motivational in its approach.
>
> **The green hat** stands for creative solutions and generating new

ideas.

The blue hat is worn by those who are in control of the process by inviting the other colour hats to come in with their unique perspective, thus keeping up the momentum and encouraging creativity. It is the hat worn by people chairing meetings or as project manager.

The six thinking hats approach can be used on your own or within a team or group and is a particularly useful technique for defusing disagreements. It offers a method for looking at the effects of a decision from a number of different viewpoints as well as adding different qualitative dimensions to rational decision-making techniques.

Force field analysis

Force field analysis (Lewin 1947) is a diagnostic technique applied to facilitate weighting of the variables involved in making a decision. It is generally used during change management to determine the potential for organisational change. It is based on the concept of 'forces', and how people in the organisation might perceive particular forces and their influence. It involves looking at opposing forces, such as those forces driving a situation and attempting to push it in a particular direction alongside resisting forces used to restrain or decrease the driving forces. A state of equilibrium is reached when there is equal balance between these two forces. This is illustrated in Figure 8.2 when looking at the decision to relocate services for example.

Lewin formulated three fundamental assertions about force field and change. First, increasing the driving forces results in an increase in the resisting forces and so the current equilibrium does not change but is maintained under increased tension. Second, reducing resisting forces is preferable because it allows movement towards the desired state, without increasing tension. Third, group norms are an important force in resisting and shaping organisational change. For the model to be of use, the forces need to be identified perceptively, rigorously and objectively, and the means identified of addressing the resisting forces need to be creative (Iles and Sutherland 2000). This is an important point as many practising managers will be able to reflect on occasions in their own experience when they have aimed to increase the driving forces, rather than reduce the resisting ones; and have increased the resistance and the tension as a result.

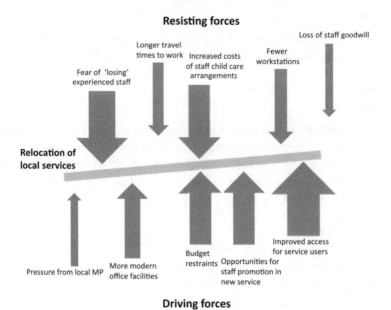

Figure 8.2 *Force field analysis for a possible relocation of local services*

Scenario planning

A key danger for individuals and groups when making decisions is their dependence on fixed mental models which only represent their own under-standing of their organisation and its environment. These mental models may remain relatively static even in turbulent environments (Delbridge *et al.* 2006). Changes to business conditions may not be obvious until it is too late and this is where scenario planning can be useful. Considered use of scenario-based techniques to ponder medium- to long-term develop-ments in economic, social, technological and political fields perhaps using the PESTL analysis tool (described in Chapter 2) can be helpful. This can enable the team or organisation to detect the start of a crisis and to roll out contingency plans quickly. Material from your PESTL analysis can be used to develop a series of scenarios or stylised portraits to depict a range of plausible futures.

Reviewing decisions

It is important to review decisions, particularly successful ones, as well as to learn from mistakes and challenges. Some of the reasons for unsuccess-ful outcomes are because of insufficient attention to problem definition or the consequences of following particular courses of action. Supporting the implementation of a decision will require creating suitable conditions and support systems and the establishment of proper aims and objectives along the way. Very often, short-term results are prioritised at the expense of long-term activities. A common example in social care is the frequent overconsumption of resources in the short term or making reductions in expenditure that have long-term implications but short-term impact. Artificial constraints and deadlines driven by resource issues and reporting relationships that can be unrealistically demanding and heavy handed with little actual gain for service users and staff, as we saw in the previous chapter on performance management, may take over an organisation's original aims and objectives as well as setting unreasonable deadlines (Pettinger 2001). Likewise, procrastination or complacency can sometimes lead to feeling unable to choose a particular direction. Abdicated leadership arises from this scenario in which an absence of leadership leaves people with a lack of direction and decision-making. This results in a poorly motivated work culture where conflict or indifference thrives (Martin 2008).

In short, there will always be strengths and weaknesses when deploying any management techniques for planning and decision-making. Not all decisions are of equal importance and thus need different skills and levels of risk or resources. The quality of decision-making is always dependent on a variety of factors such as ethics, values and personal beliefs, the organisational culture, levels of accountability and personal vulnerability, alongside professional knowledge, skills and experience. In the next chapter we will be looking at decision-making in relation to risk assessment and risk management affecting strategy and business planning. This involves other pressures on decision-making such as limitations of law and policy, public interests and public values, lobbying from political, social or environmental groups, health and safety and workplace bargaining. Needless to say, seeking specialist advice and addressing the specific needs of particular groups are an essential element of decision-making.

Chapter summary

Decision-making is said to be perhaps one of the most important management functions and central to this ability is management influence at different levels. Decision-making in social work and social care is primarily concerned with the allocation of resources and the exercise of power, as well as technical ability. Reflexivity is important to avoid unethical and poorly informed decision-making. Managers can minimise some of these dynamics by involving others appropriately in their decision-making process in an empowering way. As we saw earlier, groups can often make higher quality decisions than individuals because of their potential capacity to generate and evaluate more ideas and evidence. There are a number of strategies, tools and techniques that can greatly improve the quality of individual and group decision-making processes. However, as Delbridge *et al.* (2006) highlight, these are highly dependent on context, especially the degree to which the culture of the organisation, together with its wider external political, legal, economic and social environment, are conducive to their use. Humanist approaches that promote creativity within all levels of the organisation can go some way to create more pluralistic and interdependent approaches to management decision-making.

Manager's comment

As a Service Manager in a social care organisation I am often confronted with making decisions daily at an organisational, team as well as individual level. As a manager I am expected to provide, for the most part, immediate answers, as that is perceived as the manager's main function. This chapter emphasises some key points that I find very relevant in my role; for example, it speaks to me about decisions which need to be taken on a daily basis and makes me aware of how these mainly occur at a 'programmed level', with limited conscious thought as to how I make those decisions. One example would be within my informal supervision where an instant response is required from me by the practitioner. This then raises the question about what the key driving forces are which enable me to make those decisions when I don't always have the opportunity for reflection and about whether the decisions I make are the best possible decisions for the children we are working with. Further questions arise for me about decisions in terms of whether they are sufficiently evidence informed, insightful and ethical.

Decision-making is expected in all managerial roles at different levels and on reflection I am able to draw from a wide range of experience, knowledge and skill to make safe decisions. The skill of decision-making therefore must create a 'certainty out of uncertainty'. As managers we are encouraged to develop critical reflection; we are not only expected to consider practice issues but also organisational demands and policy and procedures. For example, a recent increase in case referrals has meant that it is not possible to allocate all the unallocated casework. The practitioners already have significant caseloads. The partners of the organisation expect the cases to be allocated, whilst also supporting the practitioners' views that the organisation's expectations of them are too great to adhere to practice standards and social work values. If the partners are very influential then it is agreed that allocation should increase. However, as a management group we have to make a decision about how we can successfully implement this. To achieve this, the use of the 'rational decision-making model' and 'the six thinking hats' can be useful. In these situations, issues of power are apparent – that is, the power to shape future allocation through staff participation is not indicators. In the short term, results are immediate, unallocated cases are reduced. In the longer term, however, it is possible that higher sickness levels and these types of management approaches lead to a more disenchanted workforce. The use of Lewin's model by increasing the driving forces, rather than reducing the resisting ones' might increase tensions as a result. Therefore it is important for me and my management team to ensure involvement at all levels of the organisation and sharing of the power at different levels. This should lead to a more collegial decision-making process to encourage a more creative and qualitative decision-making process. I am not saying that this is easy, of course, but it is ultimately desirable.

Lucy Titmuss is a manager for CAFCASS, a social care organisation working with children and their familes.

CHAPTER 9

Risk Assessment and Risk Management

By the end of this chapter, you should be able to:

- identify the key risks that impact on organisations and the contingency arrangements or corrective actions that might help to mitigate risk

- consider the notion of adverse events and institutional risk management issues in relation to service users and staff.

Introduction

This chapter draws on a number of key concepts and issues from previous chapters to help develop your thinking further about the overall impact of organisational strategies in care services. As discussed earlier, there has been an increasing focus over the last few years on the safety, accountability and improvement of services delivered by social care and health organisations. This has led to a clearer expectation from those who receive services which together with the responsibilities and statutory duties placed on organisations and its individual members means that decisions made to ensure the delivery of safe and effective support and care are crucial. Whilst sometimes controversial, inspection, regulation and performance management are necessarily important aspects of social care governance.

Governance is the term used to describe the overall system of accountabilities and assurances that are put in place to ensure the organisation discharges its functions legally, ethically and effectively. Through mechanisms that legitimise authority, it informs both corporate and local strategies, policies and procedures. Care governance is a continuous process rather than a single event. It could be defined as a framework through which organisations are accountable for continuously improving the quality of their services and safeguarding high standards of care by creating an environment in which excellence is encouraged. It also includes taking corporate responsibility for performance (Simmons 2007). Governance covers the organisation's systems and processes for monitoring services. It provides a route for accounting for the quality of services to its governing body and applies to all commissioned services, statutory services, the independent sector and the third sector within the social and political environment in which they operate. Peck and Dickinson (2008) highlight how within networks of organisations, governance now serves to distribute involvement in legitimisation around a selected range of interests. Traditional accountability to elected national politicians and local councillors is supplemented more and more by appointed boards, neighbourhood councils, and the co-option of service users. In summary, care governance involves virtually everybody involved in the delivery of care and support.

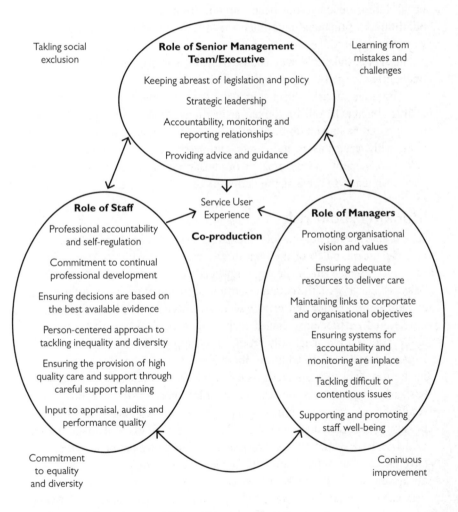

Figure 9.1 *Roles and responsibilities within a governance framework*

The core values that underpin care governance include respecting the independence, choice and dignity of service users and employees; ensuring that the working environment is safe and secure and that employees are valued even when difficult or controversial issues are raised. Aspirations towards these values point to the need for a sound knowledge of risk management and health and safety, as well as the ability to learn from mistakes and challenges when there are adverse incidents or near misses. We are all familiar with the different corporate scandals in both public and private sectors that come to public attention now and again and have served to underline the importance of good corporate governance and the regular ongoing public inquiries into failed care (Cooper 2005; Webb 2006). Local authorities have not been immune from scandals, for example the questioning of financial investments made abroad by local authorities that were affected in the economic downturn of 2009, and the jeopardising of public sector stakeholder pensions. In short, everyday public debates are frequently charged with dialogues on risk.

The issue of risk within a governance framework is the main topic of this chapter. It will be looked at in the context of strategic decision-making and its impact on business planning as well as in relation to direct work with service users and carers. Ultimately, the consequences of poor risk management in any area of organisational practice will ultimately have an impact on them as the end users of public services.

Thinking about risk

Risk is an essential but unavoidable part of everyday life but in social work and social care, much of the literature is associated with the risk of harm to service users. Within the organisational context there are a number of risks associated with the commitment and securing of resources influencing statutory, third sector and private sector relationships within strategic and operational partnerships. Issues such as demand and capacity; efficiency and productivity, particularly around the supply side, are a distinct challenge in social care. In addition, there is the notion of adverse events and institutional risk management issues in relation to service users and staff. Risk arises out of uncertainty, from either internal or external sources. As a result of pursuing or not pursuing a particular course of action, there is the possibility of economic or financial loss or gain, physical damage, injury or delay. 'Risk' is defined as the chance of something happening that will have an adverse impact upon the achievement of objectives. There will always be some risk involved in anything we choose to do. The choice is between the actions we dare to take, given the level of risk we will accept, and the different factors in the environment that enable us to tolerate risk or not at any particular point in time.

Risk has two key elements:

- the *likelihood* of something happening
- the *consequences* if it happens.

The level of risk is the relationship between the likelihood of something happening and the consequences if it does. Action taken to address the level of risk must address the likelihood of the event occurring, or the consequences if it does occur, or both.

There is a developing and growing literature emanating from inquiries and events from the social work research community which are proving to be a powerful means of evaluating and learning about safety issues at an institutional level. For example, in the government's response to Lord Laming's independent report of progress on national safeguarding arrangements for children, it was stated:

> Lord Laming's report confirmed that robust legislative, structural and policy foundations are in place and that our Every Child Matters reforms set the right direction and are widely supported... He challenged us all – central government, local government, national and local partners, and the public – to do more. Lord Laming's report set out a compelling analysis and a comprehensive set of recommendations to ensure best practice is universally applied in every area of the country, to strengthen national and local leadership and accountability, and to provide more support to local leaders and for the frontline workforce. (HM Government 2009b, p.3)

Likewise, the investigation and report into standards of care in Cornwall Partnership NHS Trust of widespread institutional abuse blamed a number of factors for the abuse, including ineffective management within the health trust; poor employment practices, such as a lack of training for staff; a breakdown of communication between health and social services; the failure of social services to provide needs assessments; and the non-implementation of adult protection policies by all agencies. Services described as assessment and treatment centres had slipped into being long-stay hospitals, and supported living services were described as 'being run as unregistered care homes, which did not meet accepted standards' (Commission for Social Care Inspection and Healthcare Commission 2006, p.6).

These reports and Lord Laming's previous report into the circumstances of the death of Victoria Climbié (Laming 2003) inevitably raised questions about the roles and responsibilities of politicians, policy makers, senior managers and service designers as well as front-line staff for the effectiveness of front-line practice. A common theme of the critical risk literature is that risk operates as a predominantly morally conservative and repressive social, political and cultural force in contemporary care work (Stanford 2008). Here, the concept of risk operates as 'semiology of catastrophe to impress the seriousness and severity of the existing and looming financial crises of state funded welfare' (Culpit 1999, p.37).

Cooper's (2005) examination of the recommendations of Lord Laming's (2003) report, into the death of Victoria Climbié notes the imbalance in the concerns of policy makers. These tend to focus on structures, procedures and protocols with much less attention to the actual conditions of practice and the complex realities of staff working on the front line. Cooper (2005) refers to the 'untold stories' (p.4) in the public reporting of the Climbié case. He notes the recommendations of 'surface instruments to guide practice' (p.7) and a predominant focus on bureaucratic rather than human factors. He calls for more 'detailed emotional observation' (p.7) through promoting organisational interest in constructing the narratives of service users; the role of quality supervision, with attention to the transactions that take place between managers and staff, and for more qualitative studies on how social workers actually do their work.

The role of professional registration and regulation provides another dynamic. For example, McLaughlin (2010) refers to the shift from the 1990s, when protection of the public and professional regulation tended to be seen as the employers' responsibility, a situation that was criticised for leading to diverse approaches to the management, supervision and censure of staff. This is now managed through the registration and regulation of social care workers with the General Social Care Council (General Social Care Council 2002). This responsibility becomes more complex when working with integrated teams with differing registration requirements.

Managing mistakes and challenges

Public enquiries are therefore a useful source of data for examining everyday professional practice. Risk management programmes that promote learning from adverse events and near misses have proved to be a powerful means of improving safety (Bostock *et al.* 2005). Root cause analysis (RCA) techniques are sometimes used in public services to try to understand the underlying causes of incidents rather than identifying individual failure. Within the health service, for example, professionals are positively encouraged to report adverse events and near misses to improve patients' safety. RCA is aimed at performance improvement measures at the level of root causes, on the basis that this is more effective than treating the symptoms of the problem. This lies at the heart of some of the government's preventative strategies in care.

To be effective, RCA must be performed systematically, by attempting to draw conclusions which can be backed up by documented evidence. As we often find from hindsight, there will be more than one potential root cause for any given problem and a number of identifiable causal relationships between the root cause(s) and the defined problems. The attraction of RCA is that it facilitates changes in culture by attempting to identify and resolve problems before they escalate. RCA assumes that systems and events are interrelated. An action in one area triggers an action in another, and another, and so on. By tracing back these actions, it is possible to discover where the problem started and how it grew into the phenomenon now being faced.

Three types of causes have been identified in the RCA literature:

1. **physical** – a tangible material item that has failed in some way, for example equipment failure

2. **human** – where the individual failed to do something or made an error. Human errors can typically lead to physical causes, for example by not reporting the failure of equipment

3. **organisational** – where a system, process or policy that people use to make decisions was not good enough or failed, for example not having someone responsible for checking equipment on a regular basis.

RCA infers that by repeatedly asking the question 'why', you can peel away the layers of an issue or problem like an onion, to get to the root cause. Questioning the reason for one problem can often lead to deeper questioning and you may need to ask the question repeatedly before getting to the origin of a problem. The real key is to avoid assumptions and a logic trap, and encourage teams to keep drilling down to the real issues that are perhaps constantly evaded, particularly in organisations where there is a more defensive or risk adverse culture.

Good communication is essential to RCA and developing systems to improve communication helps to move away from a quick 'fix it' mode of solution. Status, organisational or cultural issues, particularly those arising from issues around integration or multi-disciplinary working, all impact on communication within care services. Hall and Slembrouck (2009) in their study of everyday communication noted the way in which communication is embedded into institutional processes and routines. Likewise, it may be embedded within 'the administrative infrastructure, its documents, databases and other resources' (Mäkitalo and Säljö 2002, p.161). Managers and professionals thus tend to categorise information in accordance with their own institutional priorities and concerns. The point being made is that good communication extends beyond those tools used to facilitate it and has to include the softer aspects, such as the human factors involved. Whilst the centrality of 'good' communication is exhorted within a number of policies and is being increasingly regulated through the introduction of user databases and information management systems, according to Hall and Slembrouck (2009) these are often couched in quantitative terms (that is, 'being well-informed' and 'having all the information available' p.281). Such terms also have a tendency to express neutrality or impartiality which lies unchallenged.

Garrett (2009) has investigated some of the recommendations and competing visions that have come out of inquiries into serious case reviews. He concluded that key aspects of the New Labour 'transformation' strategy have been destabilised and rendered vulnerable by public and media focus on 'incompetent' child welfare professionals. He highlights how these have not been challenged or, in some situations, were even endorsed by the government. Garrett identified a number of thematic domains which may provide terrain for debate, some of which were covered in previous chapters but are worth reiterating here. These include: the fixation with quantitative assessments of 'performance'; the way in which ICTs (information and communication technologies) and modes of electronic working have begun to dominate social work and erode the ability of individual workers to engage meaningfully with children and their families; how the government has tended to inflate the ability of social care services to 'deliver' certain 'outcomes'; and how the pervasive neoliberal framing strategy for New Labour's 'transformation' of social care actually prevents staff within care and support services from providing effective interventions.

A report commissioned by the Social Care Institute for Excellence (Bostock *et al.* 2005), into organisational approaches to learning from mistakes, took a systems perspective on organisational failure (errors and accidents) based on the work of psychologist Reason (2000). They distinguished between 'active failures' and 'latent failures' to express the multilevel nature of accident causation. Reason had argued that the effects of active failures or errors are felt almost immediately and are associated with the actions of front-line workers whereas latent failures lie deeper in the system and only become visible when they combine with other factors to create error. These type of failures are more often due to the actions of people not in front-line work such as policy makers, senior managers and designers (Bostock *et al.* 2005). The report makes some useful recommendations for safety management in three areas.

Policy

This advocates using root cause analysis techniques in social care to promote an open and fair culture, which encourages all staff and other stakeholders, such as politicians and policy makers, to understand their role in decision-making and preventing error. Capacity would need to be increased within local authorities to adopt a systems approach, by introducing critical reporting systems or forums and root cause analysis techniques for understanding why things do, or almost, go wrong.

Research

The use of regular surveys and evaluations may help to move more towards a culture of learning within local authority and partner agencies charged with safeguarding service users. These could focus on efforts to tackle any blame culture that has developed; on forums for reflection and on how well front-line workers are supported in their efforts to create safe working practices. Latent failures embedded within organisations, as well as active failures made by front-line staff, could be explored by going beyond surface errors towards identifying underlying patterns in order to devise better solutions.

Practice development

The introduction of critical incident reporting within services can help to explore how best to promote an open and blame-free approach to learning from safeguarding incidents. As we saw in the manager's comment in Chapter 5, the development of a professional network for referral and assessment workers can promote good practice in complex decision-making if managed well.

Risk management within business planning

A particularly prominent feature of any strategy or business plan is the increasing concern with how to manage risk in an environment which is already politically, socially, psychologically and economically risk averse. There are also some advantages to embracing risk in order to exploit any potential to stimulate innovation and creativity. In Chapter 2 we looked at SWOT and PESTL analyses which facilitate the identification of the risks associated with developing key services, particularly new ones; the impact of legislation and policy and critical success factors. These tools can be useful in analysing risks inherent within business planning, for example by attributing weighting to the likelihoods and consequences of going down a particular pathway and whether these constitute major or minor risks. Risk assessment also involves looking at the existing controls in place and their adequacy, then the likelihood and consequences with these in place and whether the level of risk can be mitigated by internal controls and systems. Whatever analysis is done, as has already become apparent in the previous chapter on decision-making, there will always be a place for using professional experience, judgement and intuition.

The need to understand patterns of spend on care services that match local priorities and decisions and which might affect whether one out-sources a service or not all lead to risks. As we saw in Chapter 4, managing resources is undertaken within a complex scenario where spending in other service areas, such as leisure or transport, might all be making a contribution to the quality of life of those needing care and support (Department of Health 2009c).

Investment in and use of available technology to support business processes is another area where managers need to ensure that the business drives the technology and not vice versa, as we saw in Chapter 7 on performance management. All organisations need clear information risk policies and this may include the development of policies which also cover partners such as local independent contractors. An information risk policy would need to define how the organisation and its delivery partners will manage information risk and how risk management effectiveness will be assessed and measured. The policy should support the organisation's strategic business aims and objectives and should enable staff to identify an acceptable level of risk, beyond which escalation of risk management decisions is always necessary. Information risk policy should sit within the organisation's overall business risk management framework and not be managed separately from other business risks, but should be considered a fundamental component of effective care services, as well as being resourced adequately.

It is hoped that you will be able to identify that most of the areas covered so far all bear some relation to minimising and managing risk within the strategic and business planning process. It goes without saying that this is an enormously complex area for which there are no guarantees or formulas for avoiding risk altogether. There are a number of perspectives in the social science literature such as in the work of Giddens (1990, 1998) and Beck (1992). Enormous resources within contemporary society are devoted to risk prediction and planning as well as for scrutiny when things go wrong. Sennet (2006), for example, traces the decline of long-term, sustained and deep relationships within the actual organisation of work which affect people's identities under conditions of increased risk and flexibility. The increasing orientation within care organisations towards short-term projects and contracts leads to a series of losses, which affect how people feel towards the work itself; reducing loyalties to the organisation and diminishing trust between colleagues, particularly between management and staff as referred to earlier. The ability to focus quickly on new tasks can count more than the valuing of experience (or expertise) itself, and where resistance to change is then perceived as a sign of failure.

Tracking resources

A number of challenges are faced in social care in relation to achieving a balance between care and control, between prevention and meeting a high level of complex needs in the community whilst achieving equity and equality. Tracking the use of resources and the impact their deployment is making to the community has to be a consideration of both resource management and commissioning and contracting plans. These in turn involve a number of ethical problems and dilemmas. One example is taking decisions or following policy imperatives to outsource care services, which can make particular types of services more vulnerable, such as domiciliary care and residential care where there are recruitment difficulties and a high public profile (Improvement and Development Agency 2008). The outsourcing of services can lead to low morale for those staff involved, particularly where services may have to be outsourced due to budgetary constraints rather than for reasons of service innovation. Appropriate use of consultants and agency staff is another example in which additional resources may be used to address gaps in skills and knowledge or to achieve better value for money. However, consideration must also be given to how such consultants work alongside staff in an organisation to build capacity and learning.

The terms 'efficiencies' and 'savings' are often bandied about rather loosely in discussions about preventative care. Cashable savings refers to those that are tangible and can be physically reinvested elsewhere or used to achieve spending reductions. Non-cashable refers to situations where better use can be made of existing resources, for example to build capacity (known as capacity gain). Managers and staff need to appreciate not only how to manage their budgets on a day-to-day basis but also be able to develop the insight into those dynamics and external factors influencing the use of resources. They need to be clear about the type of efficiency savings being made and their ethical implications. 'Any risk management involves making a balance between competing economic and social objectives' (Taylor 2009, p.380).

In a Department of Health (2009b) guide to local authorities on the use of resources in social care, the following advice is given:

- Demonstrate how priority is given for social care within other competing priorities.

- Clarify how the distribution of resources is proportioned between different groups of people.

- Regularly analyse the patterns of spend and costs for services and how these deliver quality outcomes and meet predicted demands.

- Develop a commissioning strategy that ensures an affordable supply of services that support independence as well as alternatives.

- Develop partnerships that facilitate the sharing of investments that work towards outcomes for the community with an agreement of how the benefits and risks will be shared.

- Ensure the achievement of efficiencies through a system focused on early intervention, prevention and re-ablement. These should be supported by good information and advice; practical support, appropriate housing options, etc. which reduce the need for ongoing support for people from social care as well as enabling them to live more fulfilled and independent lives.

- Develop an efficiency plan which achieves saving whilst re-shaping services and makes a strategic shift towards prevention, rather than making cuts in services.

- Move towards personalisation of services in a measured way, with a transparent and sustainable mechanism for allocating resources to individuals.

- Procure services in a way that is mindful of both the needs of service users and the ability of providers to deliver good-quality care.

- Have robust systems in place to monitor and review the effectiveness of procurement and contracting arrangements so that underperformance of commissioned services can be identified early and remedied.

- Develop a strategy to work with other agencies and partners that harnesses their activities and resources in order to achieve the greatest efficiencies in addressing shared outcomes for people who have care and support needs.

As you may appreciate, these measures involve a high degree of management knowledge and skill as well as leadership. We will now address one final area of risk management in relation to resources, that associated with public private partnerships (Department of Health 2009b, pp.5–6).

Public private partnerships (PPPs)

In 1992, the Conservative government developed the concept of public private partnerships. The public finance initiative (PFI) is its most common form whereby the public sector can access capital assets such as buildings, schemes or services through capital investment. The private investor through capital investment in these assets by public companies, over a lengthy contracted period, can recoup their initial investment plus profits on related services and maintenance over a 25- to 30-year period, or sometimes a 60-year period. Contracts set up under PFI are usually for both assets and services. The attraction of PFI for the government is that it avoids making expensive one-off capital payments for unaffordable major projects which would present an initial cost to the taxpayer. The private sector operator also manages the risk involved in the initial raising of money, building and operating the project and bears the risk and liability for financial penalties. Within the most recent economic recession, however, there have been a number of criticisms of public private partnerships: 'PFI has also failed to shift fully the risk of project failure onto the private sector, even though risk transfer is one of the founding principles of PFI' (Bowcott 2009).

Whilst we have been focusing on partnerships in providing care, the type of 'partnerships' which describe the relationship between the private and public sector in this context very much emphasise the contractual obligation involved: 'a public private partnership is a risk sharing relationship between the public and private sectors based upon a shared aspiration to bring about a desired public policy outcome' (Institute of Public Policy Research 2001, p.40).

At the government level, there is a widespread assumption that the private sector can provide services more cheaply than the public sector. However, research done by Hartley and Skelcher (2008) demonstrated that some private sector services were experienced by public sector managers as a factor that could effectively decrease their ability to control the flow of financial resources to service providers and, thus, reduce their ability to implement strategic plans. They found limited evidence of the development of strategies for maximising the benefits and minimising the pitfalls of using the private sector. Public sector managers are also likely to receive very limited advice in managing these strategies. Public sector organisations are critical to national competitiveness in creating the necessary conditions and infrastructure for private sector effectiveness at national, regional and local levels (Hartley and Skelcher 2008). They also play a role in leading and governing local communities and managing complex interrelationships between the state, market and society. Pressures for innovation have also come from service users' experiences and increasing expectations. One of the key points is that whilst there has been a top-down government drive to modernise services through the adoption of private sector management techniques and performance review, it may be timely to think about the influence of practice on developing these initiatives in a more dynamic way.

Chapter summary

In social care, we are charged with dealing with some very difficult and demanding decisions. Not all of these are necessarily complex but might be related to our lack of belief in ourselves, our current level of skill, our emotions and fear of uncertainty. Some of these decisions are going to involve employees directly, for example the need to make redundancies, relocate services, implement changes in operational roles and changes in organisational expectations. When making difficult decisions, it is best to try to face up to the issues and deal with emotions through listening to the concerns, recognising where they are coming from, and agreeing or conceding, anything that is genuinely legitimate and with the remit of authority on the spot. Risk has always been a concern in the caring services, it is just that this has been 'refracted through a social democratic lens' (Taylor 2009, p.380). Similarly, we need to recognise that risk is not always an objective, quantifiable phenomena (Bostock *et al.* 2005). There are no cookbooks or recipes for managers that tell them what to do best, or as Lawler and Bilson (2010) put it:

> An illusion, reinforced by successive reports into tragedies, that if we have sufficient guidelines, protocols and procedures, we will avoid major incidents of harm or ill treatment. We know that guidelines and procedures will not prevent tragedies…but [should] promote flexibility and encourage responsible action by practitioners and their managers. (Lawler and Bilson (2010, p.179)

Webb (2006) also reminds us of the practice of value within social care and the principles of virtue ethics where the role of perception and judgement is exercised. The integrity of social care employees is not found in taking consistent action with service users and carers, nor in carrying out agency policy or the law accurately, but is found in the consistency of a fundamental orientation of goodwill towards those whom one works for, and with, and towards the activities in which one engages.

Manager's comment

There are a number of strategic examples of how the agency I work in manages risk. We work in a period of significant change with reduced budgets, increased demand and expectations and with detailed government guidance about how we manage our 'duty' or 'intake' system for children referred to the Children and Families Court Assessment Service (Cafcass). Many of the drivers are aimed at our organisation to manage strategic risk at an operational level alongside the need to create increased effectiveness in use of resources. Other external drivers included outcomes from Ofsted inspections, learning from serious case reviews in children's services, research findings, and learning from our own quality improvement team. All of these combine to create a powerful combining force to review and change practice in the organisation constantly.

My own team has worked hard operationally to develop its local response to risk. This was through making sure the duty team completes tasks on cases prior to allocation; one of the areas specified in government guidance which highlights the importance of having a more nationally coherent and systematic approach to working toward the first hearing in the family courts. This path to our current practice has developed from what we have learnt from reviewing our internal practice and particularly from feedback from our partner agencies, which has led to a change in how we ring-fence specific aspects of the work. Constant review and conscious reflection on subsequent changes made and the impact of unintended consequences have combined to improve our awareness and response to risk. Having read this chapter, the use of root cause analysis is very helpful in this regard.

This whole process has been enabled by good data systems and constantly improving admin systems. The data we collect has had a national focus through using comparative intelligence and can be applied locally. We keep data that includes personal details about the families we work with; when issue went to court; the type of application; when reports are required; details about the safeguarding screening and checks that have been completed; when a case is allocated or closed and what specific orders are in place. This information provides our management team with detailed statistics, which facilitates accountability. Statistics are also used to demonstrate how issues are dealt with in the family courts, partly due to our improved data, which is then used to inform government and public through the national press. The systematic collection and use of national data then is the golden thread between the strategic and operational aspects of the service.

We have reviewed our duty system through strategic consultation with partner agencies and constant internal and external audit. SWOT analysis has also helped us to understand the strengths and weaknesses of the systems we operate alongside the potential threats. One example is that through SWOT we were able to identify early on in the process that where one agency working with families at risk changes its operational risk management, then this is likely to have an impact on other services (for example within a local authority). Other threats (and opportunities) have been the need to develop more robust risk assessment frameworks and staff training concurrent with any changes. We are always concerned about any time lags which can create an area of vulnerability and this needs to be understood better. Service user feedback has also been significant in shaping our systems through intelligence from complaints.

Ann Flynn is a service manager in Cafcass working in the area of Early Intervention.

CHAPTER 10

Evaluation

When you have worked through this chapter you will be able to:

- identify the key research and inquiry skills that managers need in order to commission or undertake evaluation using both quantitative and qualitative approaches

- critically evaluate the complex issues involved in demonstrating outcomes-based practice in social care against complex strategic objectives.

Introduction

Evaluation is a process which involves looking back systematically at what has been accomplished and measuring the present position against its original aims (Coleman and Earley 2005). It usually involves making some sort of judgement of success about how the original aims have been met and then using the feedback for improvement. Review is the action following an evaluation and which involves making a decision about whether we wish to continue with an activity or to reject or modify it in the light of the outcomes. As a management activity, evaluation is an integral part of the cycle of strategising, business planning and decision-making. Managers are likely to be at the interface between the many procedures and operations involved in making judgements about the value of alternative courses of action within a wide organisational context. On a micro level, managers may be asked to evaluate following a critical incident or complaint. It builds on the processes of performance management as part of regulation and statutory requirements. Commissioners commonly use evaluation as a control measure by monitoring service activities against a specification to check that the required standards have been reached (Hafford-Letchfield 2007).

The purpose of evaluation is not to prove, but to *im*prove. Evaluation also provides a formal process of judging the 'value' of something. The purpose of an evaluation is to assess the effects and effectiveness of something, typically some innovation, intervention, policy, practice or service (Byford and Sefton 2003). The growing profile given to evaluation also leads to expectations that 'real world' enquirers, such as managers and practitioners in social care, will be able to carry them out (Robson 1993) in the spirit of being research minded and critically reflective.

Evaluation is indistinguishable from other research in terms of design, data collection techniques and methods of analysis. But it must be remembered that there is a need for systematic information collection so that evaluation can be applied to a wide range of topics and for a wide variety of purposes. This requires attention to issues such as gaining clearance and permissions, negotiating with 'gatekeepers', considering the political nature of the study, ethical issues and the type of report required and, as Robson (1993) advises:

> Evaluation is intrinsically a very sensitive activity where there may be a risk (duty?) of revealing inadequacy or worse, and where your intentions may be misconstrued and your findings misused or ignored. The design implication is that you think through very carefully what you are doing and why. (Robson 1993, p.171)

To be effective, Byford and Sefton (2003) recommend that evaluation should meet the following criteria:

- **utility** – there is no point in doing an evaluation if there is no prospect of its being useful to some audience
- **feasibility** – an evaluation should only be done if it is feasible to conduct it in political, practical and cost-effectiveness terms
- **propriety** – an evaluation should only be done if you can demonstrate that it will be carried out fairly and ethically
- **technical adequacy** – given reassurance about utility, feasibility and proper conduct, the evaluation must then be carried out with technical skill and sensitivity.

There are problems associated with gathering and reviewing evidence about the efficacy of strategies in social care. As we have seen so far, within any strategy or business planning process, the impact is multidimensional. The measures of the effectiveness of any strategy or change management programme is that it must be capable of capturing all of these dimensions or the resulting picture will be incomplete. Any evaluation must also involve analysing the original issues, problems, in effect the drivers leading to strategy formulation, as well as the design and implementation of the strategy itself. Often this is an iterative process, with information gained during the implementation phase informing the subsequent review. Distinguishing between the outcomes of different stages of change and also between the skilfulness of the application and the underlying value of any tools requires the development of a sensitive set of measures. We have already covered some of these issues in previous chapters. This chapter specifically describes and reviews a broader range of approaches, models and tools, which managers and practitioners may be interested to learn more about as part of understanding and managing evaluation of their services and looking more critically at the outcomes of any strategic change process and planning. Figure 10.1 provides an overview of the evaluation structure.

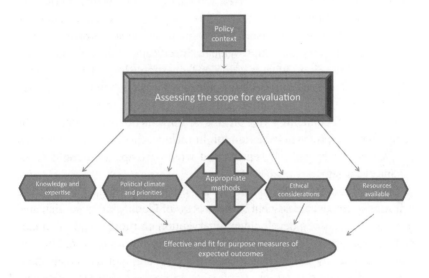

Figure 10.1 *Thinking about evaluation*

We will begin by identifying and defining some of the key terms and concepts from the evaluation literature.

Types of evaluation

There are generally four types of evaluation: formative, process, impact and outcome, and participatory. The first, formative evaluation, focuses on the process and is intended to help in the development of the programme, innovation or whatever is the focus of the evaluation. It needs to be carried out, and reported on, in time for modifications to be made as a result of the evaluation (Robson 1993). This would fall within your project management overview statement for example (see Figure 5.3 in Chapter 5). It usually involves stage-by-stage comparison between stated objectives or criteria and what is actually happening. It also helps to ensure interventions are developed in accordance with stakeholder and community needs and identifies how and why key decisions were made. According to Robson (1993) there is a tension between doing something 'cheap and nasty' (p.179), that is, more quickly with the likely outcome of low reliability and validity, with better quality work but where findings might come too late to meet important decision points in the development of the project. This makes feasibility an important consideration in evaluation and control of the process by those commissioning or managing it.

A process evaluation, on the other hand, focuses on what services were provided to whom and how. Its purpose is to describe how the programme was implemented, who was involved and what problems were experienced. A process evaluation is useful for monitoring programme implementation; for identifying changes to make the programme operate as planned; and, generally, for programme improvement. Specifically, it is concerned with answering a 'how?' or 'what is going on?' question (Robson 1993). It usually involves feedback during the course of a project, when things are still taking shape. Process evaluation can be carried out at, or near, the end of a project by documenting the process of implementing the project. The components of process evaluation might include: the number and type of people reached by an intervention and what participants thought about the intervention.

Impact and outcome evaluations are often called impact or outcome assessment. Impact assessment is the process of identifying the anticipated or actual impacts of a development intervention on those social, economic and environmental factors which the intervention is designed to affect or may inadvertently affect. It may take place before approval of an intervention, after completion, or at any stage in between. Impact assessment should start with the decision on aims and objectives. It is common to speak of short-term outcomes and long-term outcomes. Impact assessment identifies the main options for achieving the objective and analyses their likely impacts in the economic, environmental and social fields. For example, in public health, outcome evaluations are usually linked to the achievement of the objectives of the intervention. Components of outcome evaluation include changes in awareness, knowledge, attitudes, behaviours, policy and the social or physical environment. Most evaluations, however, incorporate both process and outcomes by having two aspects or phases, one focusing on the process (the way things are done) and the other on the outcomes (the consequences). Some evaluations are also entirely concerned with process (Greater Manchester Public Health Practice Unit 2007).

Finally, participatory evaluation involves the stakeholders and beneficiaries of a programme or project in the collective assessment of that programme or project. It is people-centred, as stakeholders and beneficiaries are the key factors of the evaluation process and not mere objects of it (Greater Manchester Public Health Practice Unit 2007). This fits more with the co-production model within social care in which the stakeholders, particularly service users and carers, participate substantively in the identification of the evaluation issues, the design of the evaluation, the collection and analysis of the data, and the action taken as a result of the evaluation findings. The strengths of a participatory evaluation are that it tends to draw on local resources and capacities and it recognises the wisdom and knowledge of end-users. Participatory evaluation also demonstrates the creativity and knowledge of end-users about their own environment, thus ensuring that stakeholders are part of the decision-making process and act as catalysts to ask key questions (Greater Manchester Public Health Practice Unit 2007). There are a number of roles that practitioners, service users and carers can take on during evaluation. This will be facilitated if managers routinely work with people who use services and who they can engage at short notice because they have established networks.

Undertaking evaluation: design, skills and implementation

Evaluation can utilise a quantitative or qualitative design or adopt a mixed method. Whatever design and methods are chosen, Robson (1993) identifies some of the key skills that managers might need to carry out an evaluation:

- writing a proposal
- clarifying the purpose of the evaluation
- identifying, organising and working with an evaluation team
- choice of design and data collection techniques
- interviewing
- questionnaire construction and use
- observation
- management of complex information systems
- data analysis
- report writing, including making of recommendations
- fostering utilisation of the findings
- sensitivity to political concerns. (Robson 1993, pp.182–183)

A good evaluation is one which has a clearly defined purpose, in which there is coherence between the evaluation topic and the methods or approaches used and which generates information and data which is valid and reliable. Evaluation of issues involving social care will always involve an element of the unknown and this is where qualitative approaches in particular can explore unanticipated issues as they emerge (Lewis 2007). It is also a continuing process which calls for constant review of decisions and approaches but which can never be a replacement for rigorous planning.

We will now look at two different approaches to evaluation, first, quantitative approaches using the specific example of economic evaluation and randomised controlled trials (RCTs), and then qualitative approaches including action research.

Economic evaluation

Economic evaluation has an important role in helping to make decisions about the use of scarce resources in an explicit and rational manner, yet economic evaluation is not well-developed in many areas of social care (Byford and Sefton 2003). In practice this involves a systematic attempt to identify, measure and compare all relevant costs and benefits in a fairly standard quantitative framework. Economic evaluation takes into account both the costs and benefits of policies with a view to identifying the most cost-effective way of achieving policy objectives. What distinguishes economic evaluation from other evaluation work is that it explicitly recognises the resource constraints faced by decision makers. The aim is to determine whether a particular intervention is cost effective, relative to other uses of the resources required, in other words identifying those services that produce the greatest or same level of benefit for less costs (Byford and Sefton 2003). Economic evaluation has played a significant role in the evaluation of health services, but less so in the field of social care mainly because of the inherent complexities. Standard approaches to economic evaluation may not always be appropriate, because of the nature of many social work or social care interventions and because evaluators need to be able to address a broader set of evaluation questions.

Economic evaluation is underpinned by a number of principles from welfare economics which seek to analyse the conditions under which policies might have improved societal wellbeing. It favours quantitative techniques and scientific robust study designs which are able to measure unbiased measures of costs and more 'scientific' or experimental approaches to evaluation. Barriers to applying these standard approaches in the social welfare field are partly to do with the nature of many social policies and partly to do with incompatibilities with other evaluation perspectives (Sefton 2000). Sefton, who has a research interest in the application of economic evaluation within health and social care, refers to the importance of identifying the components of the intervention in order to explore the mechanisms by which outcomes are influenced. There should also be a comparator within the methods of economic evaluation where one identifies the next best alternative(s) or normal way(s) in which any intervention is practised. This also might include 'doing nothing' as an option. This latter option, however, will have ethical considerations if a comparison group of services or service users are going to be utilised.

Some of the difficulties in this method of evaluation remain. For example, variability in effectiveness and the likelihood of success of interventions are crucially filtered through two sets of mediating factors which are, to some extent, independent of the mechanics of the intervention itself. These could, for example, be the enthusiasm, expertise and engagement of the staff carrying out the intervention, and the local delivery infrastructure. Unlike drug-based or technological interventions, social care initiatives often use multi-faceted approaches, making it more difficult to identify which elements of a programme may lead to change. Further, some social care interventions occur outside the care domain, particularly in the current integrated and partnership environment, which makes it more challenging to isolate specific contributing factors and their effectiveness. In complex situations where a number of people or agencies are involved, the cost of economic evaluation needs to be considered at the start, as this can be disproportionately high.

Common measures used to assess economic impact of using resources

Kelly *et al.* (2005) outline the different methods possible within economic evaluation. The first commonly used outcome measure is the QALY (Quality Adjusted Life Year) which incorporates the effects of quality and quantity of life, thus directing resources towards those interventions that incur the lowest cost per QALY ratio. The QALY measure may not be sufficient, however, to capture the complex impact and context of psychosocial outcomes. Other methods include:

- Cost–benefit analysis (CBA) which values all costs and benefits in the same (monetary) units. It looks at whether benefits exceed costs or vice versa in the same monetary units. CBAs are thus intrinsically attractive, and theoretically an ideal approach, but conducting them can be problematic because of the difficulties associated with valuing outcomes in monetary terms.

- Cost-effectiveness analysis (CEA) is also useful when comparing two interventions aimed at the same issue, for example if perhaps you are considering evaluating investment in counselling or talking therapies versus prescription drugs or other treatments for a mental health issue such as depression.

- Cost-consequence analysis is a final method which aims to present a range of outcome measures alongside the actual costs so that decision makers can make up their own minds based on this information.

It is unlikely that you will be undertaking economic evaluation without the necessary expertise of economists or statisticians who will need to be involved at a very early stage. Economic evaluation recognises that decisions are not made on the basis of cost-effectiveness alone but can be used alongside other types of evidence such as public perceptions or equity considerations. There are also questions as to whether success should be measured at an individual level or at a population level. Economists usually argue that the costs and benefits to individuals should be an integral part of economic evaluation. You will be asked, however, to help those evaluating to access useful sources of data. Both Kelly *et al.* (2005) and Sefton (2000) suggest sources such as user diaries; questionnaires that ascertain the use of resources in care settings; retrospective information obtained from electronic databases or case notes; and calculating or using existing unit costs of social care services. The case study below illustrates the potential usefulness of economic evaluation in care settings such as the workplace.

Case study – work place health promotion

There is good evidence, for instance, of the cost effectiveness of systematic, organisation-wide approaches to promote positive mental health at work and reduce work-related stress. These have recommended including staff support, two-way communication structures, enhanced job control, increased staff involvement and an improved working environment in programmes. An evaluation of employee assistance programmes in the USA which provide counselling services for employees and their families on a range of issues have been evaluated. These programmes have been found to be high cost savings with improvements in productivity and reduction in absenteeism which far outweighs the direct costs. The economic analysis is thought to be conservative as they do not take into account additional health and community benefits associated with maintaining employment. (Kelly et al. 2006, p.7)

Randomised controlled trials

Study designs to help solve the problem of cause and effect may bring problems of their own. Randomised controlled trials (RCTs), which are intended to eliminate bias, are often the preferred solution. However, it is important these trials are used pragmatically within social care, where they will be carried out in real-world settings, in order to test effectiveness and not just efficacy. RCTs may provide a way of eliminating bias and linking cause and effect, but are not without limitations.

Experimental approaches require at least two distinct treatment groups, where one group of users is exposed to the programme being evaluated and the other group is excluded or is exposed to a different programme, often seen as the current 'best' practice option. Outcomes for the 'experimental' and 'control' groups are then compared and any noted differences attributed to the effect of the 'experimental' programme. Extraneous factors that would have affected outcomes for both groups are then automatically stripped out (Sefton 2000). Researchers will often favour the use of RCTs, in which individuals or communities are randomly assigned to either the experimental or control groups to avoid bias or possibly unobserved differences between the underlying characteristics of the two groups. RCTs might be the most appropriate approach in evaluative research or in outcomes studies where the outcome or output of an intervention can be clearly specified in advance. For example, this might be where you are assessing the types and quantities of service provided, such as direct service versus direct payments, or as in the example given below.

Case study – Families and Schools Together: a social intervention programme evaluated using RCTs

The FAST Programme (Families and Schools Together) is a multi-family group prevention designed to build protective factors for children and empower parents to be the primary prevention agents for their own children. It was developed in the US in 1988. FAST is a two-year universal programme, designed for children aged 5–9. The programme serves 30–60 families at a time and addresses *Every Child Matters* priorities in extended schools.

Multi-family group activities for eight sessions use experiential learning, coaching and support, as parents try positive parenting approaches and repeat them weekly. Activities are designed to build deeper bonds between parents and their children and include embedded compliance requests, parent led family communication games and one-to-one responsive play. For parents, sharing meals, music and time to talk to other parents increases social capital and reduces stress. FAST helps parents feel respected; parents are assumed to love their children and want the best for them. They are not subjected to lectures, reading, entry requirements or exclusions. Across 1000 schools in eight countries, retention rates average 80 per cent for parents who come once. After eight weeks, graduated groups of parents lead monthly meetings; 86 per cent make a friend they see four years later. Four RCTs with low-income, minority families show improved family and child social, conduct and academic outcomes. The programme's design is based on social ecology of child development, family stress, family systems, attachment and learning. Practitioners participate in 12 training days over four months in teams alongside service user parents, with supervised practice. (Professor Lynn MacDonald, Families and Children Together, www.familiesandschools.org/international. php)

Qualitative approaches to evaluation

There is now a great deal of literature available from the social sciences on qualitative methodological issues in research that can be used in the evaluation of social care. Some of the more general issues are:

- Will the proposed methods address the aims of the evaluation?
- Will the sampling strategy enable the evaluator to obtain the right size and type of sample?
- Will the sample and measures produce reliable and valid evaluation outcomes?

The method of data collection needs to be appropriate to the sensitivity and scope of the subject. The approach also needs to ensure that the participants' wellbeing is safeguarded and that any ethical issues are addressed by gaining the correct approval if required.

The key defining quality of qualitative research is a naturalistic, interpretive approach concerned with understanding the meanings which people attach to phenomena (actions, decisions, beliefs, values and so on) within their social worlds (Snape and Spencer 2007). Certain data collection methods are identified with qualitative research such as: observational methods, in-depth interviewing, group discussions, narratives and the analysis of documentary evidence. These are aimed at providing an in-depth understanding of the social world by learning about participants' social and material circumstances, their experiences, perspectives and histories. Qualitative approaches are seen as suitable for research in care settings. There are few hard scientific 'objects' suitable for research from a positivist tradition meaning that the nature of situations being dealt with in social care, unlike some aspects of health care for example, are more abstract or less easy to measure. This is due to the nature of social care and potential intersubjectivity (Burgess, Sieminski and Arthur 2006). Qualitative approaches also have the potential to investigate service users' own narratives and increase their involvement. There is strong and increasing pressure for service user involvement in all aspects of research and evaluation from the government, from research funders, and health and social care service users themselves. 'Involve', for example, is an organisation specifically established to take forward such involvement in health, public health and social care (www.invo.org.uk).

A recent systematic review of the literature on public involvement in research revealed a number of impacts at all stages and levels on the members involved; on researchers and participants; on the community organisations and the wider community. The most striking finding was that involvement influenced whether the results of research brought about change (Staley 2009). Despite these developments, there remain some undercurrents affecting attitudes and responses to participatory research approaches, which Beresford (2007) states should not be underestimated and can cause tensions in spite of government imperatives. The aim is increasingly to shift and share professional knowledge, power and control to service users and to avoid the unequal relation of dominant researcher and subordinate research subject with an equalised relationship and much greater overlap between the two (Beresford 2007). Both qualitative research and user involvement go hand in hand as they capitalise on the value of experiential knowledge and 'lived' experience and its inherent political nature. Research by service users has already demonstrated a capacity to identify many inequalities relating to issues such as class, age, gender, disability, sexuality, ethnicity and culture which 'clearly come into collision with the positivist claims of "objectivity", "neutrality" and "distance", traditionally associated with scientific research' (Beresford 2007, p.308).

Snape and Spencer (2007) identify the methodological stances associated with qualitative research which include:

- the perspective of the researcher and researched which is more holistic and empathic

- the nature of the research design adopting a flexible strategy conducting naturalistic inquiry in the real world where naturally occurring or generated data can be captured

- the nature of data generation is sensitive to the social contexts in which data is produced and involves close contact between the research and the people being studied

- the nature of the research methods used as described earlier

- the nature of analysis and interpretation which reflect the complexity, detail and context of the data. Categories and theories can emerge with the potential to explain through paying attention to meaning making or what people attribute to different phenomena, rather than just trying to understand the cause. This can be helpful in both individual or cross-case analysis

- the nature of outputs where detailed description and mapped meanings are given from the perspectives of the participants. They answer 'what is?', 'how?' and 'why?' questions and allow consideration of the researchers' own perspectives.

Defining the evaluation question/s

Some questions are readily transformed into testable propositions and can be investigated using quantitative methods, perhaps by using existing user information systems and management information systems to answer questions about user characteristics, the nature of service provision and, to some extent, the outcomes of the service (Darlington and Scott 2002). Hypotheses about patterns of presentation to a service in relation to different sections of the community can be relatively easily investigated using local demographic profiles or the over- or under-representation of people from different backgrounds or characteristics. Similarly, using routine feedback from service users using pre-coded satisfaction surveys or looking at categories of complaints generally do not require more than a quantitative approach. Combining these with a qualitative approach can help to 'get behind the data' or to shape research or evaluation questions using a more inductive approach. Using qualitative approaches work by building on existing knowledge or ideas and developing tentative theories or conceptual frameworks (Miles and Huberman 1994), as opposed to the deductive model of a priori development of hypotheses to be tested through data collection (Lewis 2007).

Methodology, methods for data collection and data analysis will need to ensure rigour and utilise methods able to address the research question. Triangulation can be used to respond to the inevitable shortcomings and challenges in reconciling multiple positions in order to justify any claims in the most explicit way possible. Qualitative approaches can promote a multi-perspectival and multi-methodological view. They include methods strongly associated with the social rather than the physical sciences as underlying it are epistemological claims which do not intend to claim to capture truth or reality (Cohen, Manion and Morrison 2007). They include methods strongly associated with the social rather than the physi-cal sciences, as underlying qualitative research are epistemological claims (about how knowledge is developed in social care and its validity) that do not aim to claim to capture the truth or reality. It is worth bearing in mind that qualitative research offers an interpretation or version which is inevitably partial or situated (Taylor 2001). However, the presentation of claims and their justification must be made as systematically as possible within the conceptual structure of the theoretical problem or question with which the research or evaluation is concerned. Theoretical sensitivity involves questioning the investigative process itself and learning from it. 'Reflexivity does not only refer to the development of new theories but to the reflective process that the individual researcher attaches to its outcome' (Burgess *et al.* 2006, p.48).

The importance of being reflexive is acknowledged within all the literature on qualitative research and evaluation. Analysing data does not use neutral, mechanical nor decontextualised procedures (Mauthner and Doucet 2003). The process of sorting, organising and indexing qualitative data in a way that 'renders indivisible its interpersonal, social and institutional context' (p.415) provides an opportunity for reflexive inquiry and practice.

Selecting the settings for an inquiry and the population involves identifying those which by virtue of their relationship with the research questions are able to provide the most relevant, comprehensive and rich information (Lewis 2007). Comparison and control is another feature of design and is particularly relevant in evaluative studies where the design may involve comparison between an 'action' or 'treatment' group, which received or used the intervention being evaluated, and a control group that did not, so that the effect of the intervention can be investigated. This was demonstrated in the Families and Schools Together programme case study above. Lewis advises that the nature of comparison in qualitative research is very different from that of quantitative research, as the value is in understanding rather than measuring difference. She advises that qualitative research can contribute by:

- identifying the absence or presence of particular phenomena in the accounts of different groups
- exploring how the manifestations of phenomena vary between groups
- exploring how the reasons for, or explanations of, phenomena, or their different impacts and consequences vary between groups
- exploring the interaction between phenomena in different settings
- exploring more broadly differences in the contexts in which phenomena arise or the research issue is experienced. (Lewis 2007, pp.50–51)

Ethical considerations

The Department of Health issued its *Research Governance Framework for Health and Social Care* in 2005 (Department of Health 2005b). This acknowledged that research can involve an element of risk, both in terms of return on investment and sometimes for the safety and wellbeing of the research participants. Proper governance of research is essential to ensure that the public can have confidence in, and benefit from, quality research in health and social care (Department of Health 2005b). Research governance provides a set of general guidelines which highlights the requirement of all researchers and evaluators in ensuring the wellbeing of all participants, particularly those deemed vulnerable within legislation and policy. Good research governance should address questions of confidentiality, informed consent and anonymity, as well as investigating the methods used and how the resulting data will be analysed and disseminated.

Spicker (2007) identified four types of ethical considerations in published research governance guidelines:

- **Impact of research** – What can this research be used for? What effects could it have on participants? What effects could it have for non-participants? How will the data be analysed?

- **Treatment of participants** – How will you recruit participants? How will you ensure you obtain informed consent? How will you protect confidentiality and anonymity? How will you accommodate vulnerable participants?

- **Disciplinary considerations** – How will you ensure that the research is of high quality? In what way will this research inform policy or practice? What existing work has been done on this topic?

- **Research relationships** – What responsibilities do you have to the institution commissioning the research? What commitment do you have to other researchers? How will you maintain integrity in dealing with both participants and stakeholders?

Methods and the quality of research and evaluation echo some of the debates we covered in Chapter 7 around performance management in social care. These have been debated between those who place 'value for people' and 'value for use' above strictly epistemological and knowledge-building standards. Undertaking research or evaluation which makes a direct contribution to practice or pushes a social justice agenda is suggested to be of greater importance overall but requires 'rigour with relevance' (Shaw and Norton 2007, p.ix). Negotiating research relationships requires a great deal of investment of time and resources as well as patience and sensitivity. There are wider considerations in relation to being sensitive to the hierarchy or organisational structure, particularly getting clearance from 'gatekeepers'. As stressed earlier, cooperation is likely to be forthcoming if the objectives of the inquiry are seen as relevant by those invited to participate. This will include investment in considering diversity issues such as using appropriate language and the anticipation of any barriers to participation. As with any user-involvement strategies, giving thought to practical arrangements such as travel, provision of interpreters, sitters or child care will be part of both practical arrangements and sensitivity to the participants' cultureal and emotional needs (Lewis 2007). The issue of reciprocity and the need to maintain objectivity and neutrality is vitally important. Therefore the interpersonal and institutional contexts of research, as well as unpicking or trying to consider how to capture data that represents reality or contributes to social care knowledge within data collection, is important to think about when working through the research process. Taking responsibility for generating particular outcomes of research and their implications for process needs to be considered right through the process even as early as thinking how you collect and then analyse the data (Hammersley 2003).

We have only touched the surface regarding the details of implementing the process of evaluation, as this is a very complex process. It is probably unlikely that as a busy manager you will be undertaking the actual research yourself. However, it is useful to be informed about the relevant issues involved in an inquiry if you are commissioning or managing an evaluation. In summary, Robson (1993, p.191) provides us with a useful checklist for planning an evaluation:

1. **Reason, purposes and motivation** – Is the evaluation for yourself or someone else? Why is it being done? Who should have the information obtained?

2. **Value** – Can actions or decisions be taken as a result? Is somebody? or something going to stop it being carried out?

3. **Interpretation** – Is the nature of the evaluation agreed between those involved?

4. **Subject** – What kinds of information do you need?

Action research

Action research is a way of using research in an interventionist way so that the researcher is both a discoverer of problems and solutions, and is involved in decisions about what is to be done and why. It sees organisational changes as a cyclical process where theory guides practice and practice in turn informs theory. The concept of action research can be traced back to Lewin (1947). It elaborates on his transitional model of unfreezing, moving and refreezing by adding feedback loops (see Chapter 3) between the stages and promoting iteration between the thinking and acting processes of change management (Isles and Sutherland 2000).

Specifically action research is a process that involves:

- systematically collecting research data about an ongoing system relative to some objective, need or goal of that system

- feeding these data back into the system

- taking action by altering selected variables within the system based both on the data and on assumptions about how the system functions

- evaluating the results of actions by collecting more data.

It results from 'an involvement by the researcher with members of an organisation over a matter which is of genuine concern to them and in which there is an intent by the organisation members to take action based on the intervention' (Eden and Huxham 1996, p.75). In other words, it involves the researcher working as a consultant with a group of participants. The participants may be 'pure subjects' or 'full collaborating partners'. The principle is that if participants are engaged in understanding their situation more fully, they design actions that they themselves will take which will move them towards the aim of their change programme (Isles and Sutherland 2000). Action research enables managers and teams to learn on the basis of action and its observed effects, rather than on the basis of theory alone. Action research has been widely applied in management research first because during the change process it can demonstrate that what you are already doing is something worth doing and needs doing more of, or can be used to investigate why some aspects of practice are working well. Within change management theory, this approach is often referred to as 'first order' change and is mostly reversible. Second order change on the other hand is where one might do something significantly or fundamentally different and taking an investigative approach enables managers to demonstrate the impact of what aspects of the differences are having an impact and the type of impact felt by those involved. Success has been found to be largely dependent on organisational context with difficulties rooted in political and interpersonal conflict between researchers and managers.

Evaluation in the context of knowledge and information management

This chapter concludes with brief attention to the management and dissemination of the outcomes of an evaluation, as this will become an aspect of the organisational knowledge system. 'Knowledge' has become a central resource and a form of capital now commonly referred to in theories about organisations. Structures and institutions, which produce and require knowledge in the care sector, have vastly been extended and some critics see these moves as a form of regulation and uncritical solution to social problems. Knowledge production is embedded in the circulation and use of knowledge, through permanent reflection on the ways in which society and its associated institutions operate (Nassehi, von der Hagen-Demszky and Mayr 2007). Social care organisations, for example, have started to use information and communication technology for knowledge management purposes with the aim of improving service efficiency and effectiveness. Disseminating the outcomes of any formal research and evaluation is relevant here. Whilst knowledge management processes are widely discussed within industrial and business sectors, they are still relatively new to care organisations. Knowledge management can be generally defined as the collection of mechanisms and processes that govern the creation, collections, storage, retrieval, dissemination and utilisation of organisational knowledge that helps an organisation to compete or improve.

The literature on organisational and service development is large and growing, although it is unrealistic to expect all social care managers to be familiar with it in relation to their own professional knowledge base. Moreover, it is recognised that practising managers will be looking for approaches to research and evaluation that are useful and purposeful, rather than from a particular school of thought or theoretical perspective. Responsibility for generating evidence and developing theory may be seen by busy managers as an additional or even unsupportable burden, especially as the research skills they need do not come by easily. However, managers and leaders do have a responsibility to generate evidence about their strategic development and service developments, to present it in a form that can be useful to others, and to contribute to the development of theory. In order to do this, they must build this outcome into the design of strategic and operational interventions and where evaluation is an integral part of service development and service delivery (Isles and Sutherland 2000).

Nelson *et al.* (1998) argue that although measurement is essential if changes are to be made to improve the quality of planning and delivery of care, the measurements themselves must be defined pragmatically. They suggest that usefulness rather than perfection is the determining factor, and that the measurement chosen must fit the work environment, time limitations and cost constraints. As discussed earlier, they also advocate using a balanced set of process, outcome and cost measures, using qualitative and quantitative measures, small representative samples, and building measurement into the daily routine. This can be displayed in a manner so that it tells a story.

To work with knowledge and evidence requires managers to develop the skills and abilities to work in teams. Work should be understood as a process to collect, aggregate, analyse and present data on outcomes of care and processes of work, the design of care practices and protocols. It is an opportunity to develop a collaborative exchange with service users and carers and to work collaboratively with other managers up and down the hierarchy. One cannot underestimate the value of the social circumstances and relationships that can be nurtured in the workplace. One of the less understood or spoken about aspects of employee retention in social care is the vast loss to the organisation and its activities when people leave their jobs. Taking time to create a culture where knowledge and information exchange is encouraged from management (Nonaka 1994). One of the less understood aspects of employee retention is the vast loss of expertise when people leave an organisation. Much of our information and knowledge can never be independent of the social circumstances in which they have been generated, nor of the actors they have been created by (Nonaka 1994).

ICT systems with knowledge portals

Within the paradigm that knowledge is an object that can be physically managed, Willke (2002) differentiates between data, information and knowledge. Data can be created through any method of observation: investigation, analysis or inquiry, as we saw earlier. But Willke also stresses that data are not 'just out there' in the world to be observed, but are actively created by its observers through their theoretical approaches and their technical procedures.

Leung (2007) identifies two different types of knowledge management alongside what he terms 'an in-between one' (p.184). The first is technically orientated, involving the design and management of intelligence systems so that organisational knowledge can be better manipulated and deployed. This type of knowledge is represented in a number of physical artefacts, such as documents and databases, and therefore the use of ICT is critical. The second is more people-orientated and concerns capturing and promoting the tacit nature of knowledge held by individuals or groups arising from their subjective practice experiences, which can then be shared through networks or communities of practice. Socio-cultural factors within organisations, such as support from senior managers, commitment, trust, power and knowledge, will determine the success of how this is captured as well as socialisation between employees and the systems of support that facilitate transmission and sharing of tacit and practice knowledge. Leung (2007) outlines the hierarchical knowledge management system in social work organisations and suggests that moving between more tangible sources of knowledge as well as valuing tacit sources leads to better usability and quality. As we saw in Chapter 8 on decision-making, the real use of knowledge will involve insight into its meaning and judgement when applying it within a specific context.

Nonaka's (1994) original knowledge creation theory identified four conversion modes:

1. conversion of tacit knowledge through socialisation amongst individuals as often happens in social care practice environments

2. internalisation through the use of tangible sources, i.e. using a policy to develop procedures which inform and let practitioners know what to do in practice

3. externalisation: the conversion of tacit knowledge into an external artefact such as a model of intervention

4. combination: developing new knowledge by combining or synthesising different pieces of explicit knowledge through processes such as sorting, adding and so on.

In summary, knowledge management is a dynamic process using dialectal and interactive processes of knowledge creation which can be implicit or explicit and use opportunities within the day-to-day working of an organisation. It involves reconstituting and reconstructing different types of knowledge during the process of its creation and exchange, in essence, to encourage a diversity and difference of perspectives and viewpoints that allows everyday assumptions to be questioned in a transparent way (Payne 2001). We know from what has been written about managerialism that some management theories suppose that knowledge can be managed in a very rational-technical way which bypasses the act of 'knowing' (Lawler and Bilson 2010). Power struggles around knowledge such as those illustrated by user perspectives on social care are being constantly challenged. The principle of co-production, for example, means that practitioners facing service users with different problems in different contexts have to adapt their knowledge to the here and now in a reflexive and reflective way.

Case study – Knowledge management in social work

Leung (2009) undertook a single case study using a conceptual framework of knowledge management in which he identified ten kinds of social work knowledge and their characteristics located along a continuum. His extended framework highlighted the types and characteristics of good social work knowledge that an organisation must take into account when practising knowledge management. He also differentiated between the different types of sharing activities and platforms and demonstrated that integration between the two dominant knowledge management approaches – technical and people-oriented – is useful. Both are essential to accessing and transferring enormous amounts of knowledge, incurring both benefits and losses. Leung's study reminds us of the deeply social nature of knowledge management and the importance of managers attending to social networks and knowledge that encourage practitioners to pool information and their tacit knowledge.

Chapter summary

There are a number of reasons why managers may need to evaluate services either directly or indirectly. There is certainly an ethical obligation to ensure that all interventions in social care practices are examined and reviewed regularly in terms of management accountability. Evaluation can have a valuable role in protecting the public from inappropriate or harmful practices, and in obtaining evidence on their unintended consequences, both negative and positive. Likewise, research and evaluation is useful to establish whether short-term gains may be outweighed by long-term losses and vice versa. Harmful impacts on groups indirectly affected by interventions and the way in which services are provided have been consistently documented in many areas of social care. Examples can be seen in the way that legislation is enacted in the mental health field (Beresford 2004) and with looked after children (Barn, Andrew and Mantovani 2005). An example of a broader evaluative approach was demonstrated earlier in Chapter 3 when we looked at the role of equality impact assessments within the business planning process. Outcomes from evaluation are an important source of information in decision-making when managing a programme of change or service development. The receipt of funding within both the statutory and independent sector more often than not carries with it an obligation to evaluate and provide evidence of success or value for money (Hafford-Letchfield 2007). Some aspects of evaluation may well be part of regulations and statutory requirements. Commissioners commonly use evaluation as a control measure by monitoring service activities against a specification to check that the required standards have been met (see Chapter 6).

There is likely to be a greater call for qualitative measures in current evaluation of social care as opposed to experimental ones, particularly when exploring which outcomes are most important to service users. Thus, complex interventions require complex evaluations. Good evaluation requires attention to planning in advance and the involvement of relevant people, for example statisticians or economists, service users and other stakeholders (Byford and Sefton 2003). There are a number of roles that practitioners and service users and carers can take on within an evaluation. It is desirable that managers and evaluators involve people who use services and carers in the commissioning of any evaluation, and this will be facilitated if they routinely work with people who use services that they can engage at short notice because they have established networks. Evaluation inevitably has a political dimension to it as policies and practices will have their sponsors and advocates with both positive and negative investment in the outcomes (Robson 1993). This indicates that evaluation is not an activity for managers sensitive to criticism or controversy which may be methodological or political. Evaluators should have strong conflict-resolution skills and diversity in perspective, using people management and good communication skills in order to make the best use of everyone involved. The main message here is that paying meticulous attention to the design and conduct of the study is crucial and to encourage an appreciation of the complexity and sensitivity of the evaluator's task (Robson 1993).

Perversely, whilst evaluation is perceived to be an important aspect of strategy and business planning, it can also take up valuable time and resources which might be better directed within highly pressurised care environments. In conclusion, evaluation is just one further tool for management and organisational decision-making. Values, ethical considerations and equality issues will always play a part. Opportunities for gaining skills in conducting inquiries and research design should be part and parcel of any management development programme. Despite the abundance of knowledge in social care, however, there is no guarantee that this will lead to quality services, and the critical reflective manager has a key role to play. Taking an interest in knowledge management can enable your staff, teams and service to make best use of the knowledge available by recognising the interplay between knowledge, experiential practice and critical reflection embedded in everyday practice and supported by the organisation's culture and infrastructure (Hafford-Letchfield *et al.* 2008).

Manager's comment

As anyone who attends a learning course will know, the evaluation form or survey is something that is either thrust into your hand just before you try to leave the room or that turns up in your post box or email folder very soon after. What is sadly a common experience is that the arrival of the questionnaire is often greeted with a sigh and many are thrown away, remain blank or are returned with minimal useful information. Some learners, including me, find the task of completing an evaluation onerous because they are tired and want to go home, relax or eat. More likely it is because we do not really believe anyone is going to read the survey and do not feel confident that our comments will really make a difference.

Sadly, many of us who regularly conduct evaluation are also probably the professionals who unintentionally undermine the practice. I remember working for an organisation where employees would often comment that they felt inundated with workforce consultations and evaluations, including, for example, one that went to every employee seeking their opinions about how many waste paper bins should be used in offices. Another common complaint in this organisation was that they were either never told about the outcome of evaluations or they could not really see what difference they made.

Herein lies the lesson I have learnt: in truth I believe that that reflection should be a natural and basic component of learning and is essential to effective social work and social care practice. Evaluation is something many of us fail to do well, use properly and, more often than not simply fail to demonstrate has actually made a difference. Now that we provide learning support to a very wide spectrum of learners including statutory and third sector professionals, volunteers, carers and users, my learning and development team has gone back to basics to try to ensure the widest participation possible.

We have responded to feedback about our use of evaluation and implemented changes. To mention only a few, we now make sure evaluations are timely by giving participants reflection time rather than thrusting it upon them during or immediately after a learning event. We reward all feedback by entering participants into a prize draw and every questionnaire returned to us is formally acknowledged. We make sure evaluations are relevant by linking them to the aims, objectives and outcomes of the event. We also ensure participants evidence their own learning and development and explore the next steps in their learning, thus ensuring the practice of evaluation is part of the planning cycle.

We give participants the opportunity to suggest how they would develop or improve a programme and we ensure they receive feedback about the outcome of the evaluation. We include following up negative responses to demonstrate how we responded to these to minimise negative outcomes in the future.

We are trying to minimise evaluation fatigue by varying our methodologies, for example online questionnaires, paper versions and focus groups, and ensure evaluations are simple, accessible and concise. We use a variation of multiple choice, Likert scales and options for extended commentary. Finally, our aim is also to promote evaluation and reflection as worthwhile and essential to our practice, and to the practice of social work and social care employees.

Neil Chick is an organisational learning and development manager for a local authority.

References

Adams, R. (2002) 'Quality Assurance.' In R. Adams, L. Dominelli and M. Payne (eds) *Critical Practice in Social Work*. Basingstoke: Palgrave.

Aldgate, J. and Dimmock, B. (2003) 'Managing to Care.' In J. Henderson and D. Atkinson (eds) *Managing Care in Context*. London: Routledge.

Armstrong, M. (1990) *How to Be a Better Manager* (3rd edn). London: Kogan Page.

Arnstein, S.R. (1969) 'A ladder of citizen participation.' *Journal of American Institute of Planners 35*, 4, 216–224.

Asadi-Lari, M., Packham, C. and Gray, D. (2003) 'Need for redefining needs.' *Health Quality of Life Outcomes 1*, 34, 1–34.

Audit Commission (1986) *Making a Reality of Community Care*. London: Audit Commission.

Audit Commission (1997) *Take Your Choice: A Commissioning Framework for Community Care*. London: Audit Commission.

Audit Commission (2008) *Don't Stop Me Now: Preparing for an Ageing Population*. London: Audit Commission.

Audit Commission (2009) *A Councillor's Guide to Performance Management: Second Edition – The Performance, Management, Measurement and Information Project*. London: Audit Commission.

Baines, D. (2004) 'Caring for nothing: Work, organization and unwaged labour in social services.' *Work, Employment and Society 18*, 2, 267–295.

Barn, R., Andrew, L. and Mantovani, N. (2005) *Findings Informing Change: The Experiences of Young Care Leavers from Different Ethnic Groups*. London: Joseph Rowntree Foundation.

Barr, J. and Dowding, L. (2008) *Leadership in Health Care*. London: Sage.

Bass, B.M. (1990) *Handbook of Leadership: A Survey of Theory and Research*. New York, NY: Free Press.

Beck, U. (1992) *Risk Society: Towards a New Modernity*. Sage: London.

Beecham, J. and Sinclair, I. (2007) *Costs and Outcomes in Children's Social Care*. London: Jessica Kingsley Publishers.

Beresford, P. (2004) 'Madness, Distress, Research and a Social Model.' In C. Barnes and G. Mercer (eds) *Implementing the Social Model of Disability: Theory and Research*. Leeds: The Disability Press.

Beresford, P. (2007) 'User involvement, research and health inequalities: Developing new directions.' *Health and Social Care in the Community 15*, 4, 306–312.

Beresford, P. and Branfield, F. (2006) 'Developing inclusive partnerships: User-defined outcomes, networking and knowledge – a case study.' *Health and Social Care in the Community 14*, 5, 436–444.

Beresford, P. and Croft, S. (2001) 'Service users' knowledges and the social construction of social work.' *Journal of Social Work 1*, 3, 295–316.

Beresford, P. and Croft, S. (2003) 'Involving Service Users in Management: Citizenship, Access and Support.' In J. Sedan and J. Reynolds (eds) *Managing Care in Practice*. London: Routledge in association with the University Press.

Beresford, P. and Croft, S. (2004) 'Service users and practitioners reunited: The key component for social work reform.' *British Journal of Social Work 34*, 1, 53–68.

Blyth, L. (2005) 'Not Behind Closed Doors.' In R. Carnwell and J. Buchanan (eds) *Effective Practice in Health and Social Care: A Partnership Approach*. Berkshire: Open University Press.

Bratton, J., Sawchuk, P., Forshaw, C., Corbett, M. and Callinan, M. (2007) *Work and Organisational Behaviour*. (2nd edn) Basingstoke: Palgrave Macmillan.

Boddy, D. and Buchanan, D. (1992) *Take the Lead: Interpersonal Skills for Project Managers*. London: Prentice Hall.

Bostock, L., Bairstow, S., Fish, S. and Macleod, F. (2005) *Managing Risk and Minimising Mistakes in Services to Children and Families. Report 6*. London: Social Care Institute for Excellence.

Bowcott, O. (2009) 'Government Should Scrap PFI, says Unison.' *The Guardian*, 15 June 2009.

Boyne, G. (2002) 'Public and private management: What's the difference?' *Journal of Management Studies 39*, 1, 97–122.

Bradshaw, J. (1994) 'The Contextualization and Measurement of Need: A Social Policy Perspective.' In J. Popay and G. Williams (eds) *Researching the People's Health*. London: Routledge.

Bruntland, G. (ed.) (1987*)* *Our Common Future: The World Commission on Environment and Development*. Oxford: Oxford University Press.

Burgess, H., Sieminski, S. and Arthur, L. (2006) *Achieving Your Doctorate in Education*. London: The Open University in association with Sage.

Burr, V. (1995) *An Introduction to Social Constructionism.* London: Routledge.

Burton, J. and Van den Broek, J. (2009) 'Accountable and countable: Information management systems and the bureaucratization of social work.' *British Journal of Social Work 39,* 4, 1326–1342.

Butcher, D. and Clarke, M. (1999) 'Organisational politics: The missing discipline of management?' *Industrial and Commercial Training 31,* 1, 9–12.

Byford, S. and Sefton, T. (2003) 'Economic evaluation of complex health and social care interventions.' *National Institute Economic Review 186,* 98–108.

Cabinet Office (2000) *Wiring It Up: Whitehall's Management of Cross-Cutting Policies.* London: Performance and Innovation Unit.

Campbell, S., Maynard, A. and Winchcombe, M. (2007) *Mapping the Capacity and Potential for User-led Organisations (ULO) in England.* London: Department of Health.

Care and Social Services Inspectorate Wales (2009) *Joint review. Cydadolygiad. Reviewing Social Services in Wales 1998–2008: Learning from the Journey.* Cardiff: Care and Social Services Inspectorate Wales.

Care Services Improvement Partnership (2009) *Bringing the NHS and Local Government Together: A Practical Guide to Integrated Working.* London: Care Services Improvement Partnership and Integrated Care Network. Available from www.icn.csip.org.uk/practicalguidetointegratedworking, accessed on 8 March 2010.

Care Services Improvement Partnership and Institute of Public Care (2006) *Joint Commissioning Model for Public Care.* London: Department of Health and Care Services Improvement Partnership.

Carlisle and Eden Crime and Disorder Reduction Strategy (2006) *Tackling Crime, Substance Misuse and Anti-Social Behaviour.* Cumbria: Carlisle City Council.

Carnwell, R. and Buchanan, J. (eds) (2005) *Effective Practice in Health and Social Care: A Partnership Approach.* Berkshire: Open University Press.

Carr, S. (2004) *Has Service User Participation Made a Difference to Social Care Services?* Position Paper No. 3. Social Care Institute for Excellence. Bristol: Policy Press.

Carr, S. (2007) 'Participation, power, conflict and change: Theorizing dynamics of service user participation in the social care system of England and Wales.' *Critical Social Policy 27,* 2, 266–276.

Ceeney, N. (2009) 'Information management headache or opportunity?: The challenges that the recent focus on information management is presenting to senior leaders in the public sector.' *Public Policy and Administration 24,* 3, 339–347.

Challis, D., Clarkson, P. and Warburton, R. (2006) *Performance Indicators in Social Care for Older People.* Personal Social Services Research Unit. Aldershot: Ashgate.

Charities Evaluation Services (2006) *Using an Outcomes Approach in the Voluntary and Community Sector: A Briefing for Funders, Commissioners and Policy Makers on the National Outcomes Programme.* London: Charities Evaluation Services.

Children's Workforce Development Council and Department of Health (2006) *Options for Excellence: Building the Social Care Workforce of the Future.* Leeds: Department for Children and Families.

Clarke, J. (2004) *Changing Welfare, Changing States: New Directions in Social Policy.* London: Sage.

Clarke, J. and Newman, J. (1997) *The Managerial State.* London: Sage.

Clarkson, P. (2010) 'Performance Measurement in Adult Social Care: Looking Backwards and Forwards.' *British Journal of Social Work 26,* 5, 520–533.

Clogg, D. (2006) *The Importance of Well Worded Contracts in Commissioning.* London: Care Services Improvement Partnerships.

Coates, D. and Passmore, E. (2008) *Public Value: The Next Steps in Public Service Reform.* London: The Work Foundation.

Cohen, L., Manion, L. and Morrison, K. (2007) *Research Methods in Education* (6th edn). London: Routledge.

Coleman, M. and Earley, P. (2005) *Leadership and Management in Education: Cultures, Change and Context.* Oxford: Oxford University Press.

Commission for Social Care Inspection (2006) *Support Brokerage: A Discussion Paper.* London: Commission for Social Care Inspection.

Commission for Social Care Inspection (2008) *The State of Social Care in England 2006–07.* London: Commission for Social Care Inspection.

Commission for Social Care Inspection and Healthcare Commission (2006) *Joint Investigation into the Provision of Services for People with Learning Disabilities at Cornwall Partnership NHS Trust.* London: Commission for Healthcare Audit and Inspection.

Community Care (2009) *Time to more with less: Special report on the recession and social care.* December 2009. www.communitycare.com

Connelly, N. and Seden, J. (2003) 'What Service Users Say about Services: The Implications for Managers.' In J. Henderson and D. Atkinson (eds) *Managing Care in Context.* London, Routledge.

Cooper, A. (2005) 'Surface and Depth.' *Child and Family Social Work 10,* 1, 1–9.

Cooperrider, D.L., Whitney, D. and Stavros, J.M. (2003) *Appreciative Inquiry Handbook: The First in a Series of AI Workbooks for Leaders of Change.* Toledo, OH: Lakeshore Communications.

Crampton, J. and Ricketts, S. (2007) *A Catalyst for Change: Tackling the Long Ascent of Improving Commissioning.* London: Department of Health with Care Services Improvement Partnership.

Crisp, B.R. and Green Lister, P. (2007) 'Using Critical Incident Analysis to Assess Students in Both Classroom and Fieldwork Settings.' In M. Haigh, E. Beddoe and D. Rose (eds) *Towards Excellence in PEPE: A Collaborative Endeavour.* Auckland: The University of Auckland. Proceedings of Practical Experience in Professional Education (conference) 1–3 February 2006, Auckland, New Zealand.

Culpit, I. (1999) *Social Policy and Risk.* London: Sage.

Darlington, Y. and Scott, D. (2002) *Qualitative Research in Practice: Stories from the Field.* Buckingham: Open University Press.

Davis, K. and Hinton, P. (1993) 'Managing quality in local government and the health services.' *Public Money and Management 13,* 1, 31–34.

Davis, H. and Martin, S. (2009) *Public Services Inspection in the UK: Research Highlights 50.* London and Philadelphia, PA: Jessica Kingsley Publishers.

De Bono, E. (1990) *Six Thinking Hats.* Harmondsworth: Penguin.

Delbridge, R., Gratton, L., Johnson, G. and The AIMS Fellows (2006) *The Exceptional Manager: Making the Difference.* Oxford: Oxford University Press.

Department for Children, Schools and Families (2005a) *Interim Findings from the Evaluation of the New Degree in Social Work,* Leeds: Department for Children, Schools and Families.

Department for Children, Schools and Families (2005b) *Youth Matters.* London: The Stationery Office.

Department for Children, Schools and Families and Department of Health (2009a) *Building a Safe, Confident Future: The Interim Report of the Social Work Task Force, July.* London: Department for Children, Schools and Families.

Department for Children, Schools and Families and Department of Health (2009b) *Building a Safe, Confident Future: The Final Report of the Social Work Task Force, November.* London: Department for Children, Schools and Families.

Department for Education and Skills (2005) *Integrated Children's System: A Statement of Business Requirements.* London: The Stationery Office

Department for Education and Skills (2006) *Options for Excellence: Building the Social Care Workforce of the Future.* Leeds: Department for Education and Skills and Department of Health.

Department of Health (1998) *Modernising Social Services.* London: The Stationery Office.

Department of Health (1999) *Social Services Performance in 1998–99. The Personal Social Services Performance Assessment Framework.* London: Department of Health.

Department of Health (2000) *Framework for the Assessment of Children in Need and their Families.* London: the Stationery Office.

Department of Health (2001a) *Local Authority Circular 32: Fairer Charging Policies for Home Care and Other Non-Residential Social Services – Guidance for Councils with Social Services Responsibilities.* London: Department of Health.

Department of Health (2001b) *Valuing People: A new Strategy for Learning Disability for the 21st Century.* White Paper (Cm 5086). London: The Stationery Office.

Department of Health (2002) *Learning from Past Experience: A Review of Serious Case Reviews.* London: Department of Health.

Department of Health (2003) *Fair Access to Care Services: Guidance on Eligibility Criteria for Adult Social Care.* London: Department of Health.

Department of Health (2005a) *Independence, Wellbeing and Choice: The Vision for the Future of Social Care in England.* Green Paper (CM 6499). London: Department of Health.

Department of Health (2005b) *Research Governance Framework for Health and Social Care: Second Edition.* Available from www.dh.gov.uk/en/Publicationsandstatistics/Publications/PublicationsPolicyAndGuidance/DH_4108962, accessed on 8 March 2010.

Department of Health (2006a) *Our Health, Our Care, Our Say.* (White Paper) London: The Stationery Office.

Department of Health (2006b) *Welcoming Social Enterprise into Health and Social Care: A Resource Pack for Social Care Contractors and Commissioners.* London: Department of Health. Available from www.dh.gov.uk/en/Publicationsandstatistics/Publications/PublicationsPolicyAndGuidance/Browsable/DH_074302, accessed on 8 March 2010.

Department of Health (2007a) *Guidance on Joint Strategic Needs Assessment.* London: Department of Health.

Department of Health (2007b) *Commissioning Framework for Health and Wellbeing.* London: Department of Health.

Department of Health (2007c) *Welcoming Social Enterprise into Health and Social Care.* Available from www.dh.gov.uk/en/Publicationsandstatistics/Publications/PublicationsPolicyAndGuidance/DH_072928, accessed on 30 March 2010.

Department of Health (2008a) *Transforming Social Care.* (LAC (2008:1) London: The Stationery Office.

Department of Health (2008b) *Putting People First: A Shared Vision and Commitment to the Transformation of Adult Social Care.* London: The Stationery Office.

Department of Health (2009a) *Report on the Consultation: The Review of No Secrets Guidance.* London: Department of Health.

Department of Health (2009c) *Working to Put People First: The Strategy for the Adult Social Care Workforce in England Social Care*. Leeds: Department of Health.

Department of Health (2009b) *Use of Resources in Adult Social Care: A Guide for Local Authorities*. Leeds: Department of Health.

Department of Trade and Industry (2002) *Social Enterprise: A Strategy for Success*. London: Department of Trade and Industry. Available from www.cabinetoffice.gov.uk/media/cabinetoffice/third_sector/assets/se_strategy_2002.pdf, accessed on 8 March 2010.

Department of Trade and Industry (undated) *The Original Quality Gurus*. Available from http://webarchive.nationalarchives.gov.uk/+http://www.dti.gov.uk/mbp/bpgt/m9ja00001/m9ja000014.html, accessed on 30 June 2010.

Doel, M., Carroll, C., Chambers, E., Cooke, J. *et al.* (2007) *Participation: Finding Out What Difference It Makes*. Stakeholder Participation Resource guide 07. London: Social Care Institute for Excellence.

Dominelli, L. (2002) *Anti-oppressive Social Work Theory and Practice*. Basingstoke: Palgrave Macmillan.

Donabedian, A. (1980) *The Definition of Quality and Approaches to Its Assessment*, Vol. 1. Ann Arbor, MI: Health Administration Press.

Dowler, J. (2008) 'A framework for performance management of children's services partnerships.' *Journal of Care Services Management 3*, 1, 64–82.

Dummer, J. (2007) 'Health care performance and accountability.' *International Journal of Health Care Quality Assurance 20*, 1, 34–39.

Eden, E. and Huxham, H. (1996) 'Action research for management research'. *British Journal of Management, 7,* 1, 68–75.

Elmore, R. (1979–1980) 'Backward mapping: Implementation research and policy decisions.' *Political Science Quarterly 94*, Winter, 601–616.

Eraut, M. (1994) *Developing Professional Knowledge and Competence*. London: Routledge Falmer.

Farjoun, J. (2005) 'Towards an Organic Perspective on Strategy.' In J. Mahoney (ed.) *Economic Foundation of Strategy*. Thousand Oaks, CA: Sage.

Farnham, D. (2005) *Managing in a Strategic Business Context*. London: Chartered Institute of Personnel Development.

Ferguson, I. (2007) 'Increasing user choice or privatizing risk? The Antinomies of Personalization.' *British Journal of Social Work 37*, 3, 387–403.

Ferris, G.R., Treadway, D.C., Kolodinsky, R.W., Hochwater, W.A. *et al.* (2005) 'Development and validation of the political skill inventory.' *Journal of Management 31*, 1, 126–152.

Field, J. (2007) *Managing with Plans and Budgets in Health and Social Care*. Exeter: Learning Matters.

Finance Hub (2008) *Full Cost Recovery*. London: Charities Age Foundation.

Fletcher, P. (2008) 'Strategic commissioning for older people: Connecting up social care, healthcare and housing with a wider wellbeing approach.' *Journal of Care Services Management 2*, 2, 154–166.

Flynn, R. (1999) 'Managerialism, Professionalism and Quasi-Markets.' In M. Exworthy and S. Halford (eds) *Professionals and the New Managerialism in the Public Sector*. Buckingham: Open University Press.

Fook, J. and Askeland, G. (2007) 'Challenges of critical reflection: Nothing ventured, nothing gained.' *Social Work Education 16*, 2, 15–28.

Foster, N. (2005) 'Control, Citizenship and "Risk" in Mental Health: Perspectives from UK, USA and Australia.' In S. Ramon and J. Williams (eds) *Mental Health at the Crossroads: The Promise of the Psychosocial Approach*. Aldershot: Ashgate.

Foucault, M. (1982) *Power/Knowledge: Selected Interviews and Other Writings, 1972–1977*. New York, NY: Pantheon.

Garrett, P.M. (2009) 'The case of "Baby P": Opening up spaces for debate on the "transformation" of children's services?' *Critical Social Policy 29*, 3, 533–547.

General Social Care Council (2002) *Codes of Practice for Social Care*. London: General Social Care Council. Available at www.gscc.org.uk/codes, accessed on 8 March 2010.

Giddens, A. (1990) *The Consequences of Modernity*. Polity Press: Cambridge.

Giddens, A. (1998) 'Risk Society: The Context of British Politics.' In J. Franklin (ed.) *The Politics of Risk Society*. Polity Press: Cambridge.

Gilbert, T. (2005) 'Trust and Managerialism: Exploring Discourses of Care.' *Nursing and Health Care Management and Policy 52*, 4, 454–463.

Glasby, J. and Littlechild, R. (2009) *Direct Payments and Personal Budgets: Putting Personalisation into Practice*. Bristol: The Policy Press.

Glasby, J. and Peck, E. (2004) *Integrated Working and Governance: A Discussion Paper*. London: Department of Health.

Glasby, J., Smith, J. and Dickinson, H. (2006) *Creating 'NHS Local': A New Relationship between PCTs and Local Government*. Birmingham: Health Services Management Centre.

Glendinning, C. (2009) 'The Consumer in Health Care.' In R. Simmons, M. Powell, and I. Greener (eds) *The Consumer in Public Services: Choice, Values and Difference*. Bristol: The Policy Press.

Glendinning, C., Clarke, S., Hare, P., Maddison, J. and Newbronner, L. (2008) 'Progress and problems in developing outcomes-focused social care services for older people in England.' *Health and Social Care in the Community 6*, 1, 54–63.

Godwin, N. (2007) 'Developing effective joint commissioning between health and social care: Prospects for the future based on lessons from the past.' *Journal of Care Services Management 1*, 3, 279–293.

Grandy, G. and Mills, A.J. (2004) 'Strategy as simulacra? A radical reflexive look at the discipline and practice of strategy.' *Journal of Management Studies 41*, 7, 1153–1170.

Greater Manchester Public Health Practice Unit (2007) *Evaluation: Top Tips for Commissioners and Practitioners.* Available from www.gmpublichealthpracticeunit.nhs.uk/wp-content/uploads/2009/12/P005-PHPU-Evaluation-toolkit-2009.pdf, accessed on 31 March 2010.

Greener, I. (2009) *Public Management: A Critical Text.* London: Palgrave Macmillan.

Griffiths, R. (1988) *Community Care: Agenda for Action.* London: Her Majesty's Stationery Office.

Gunn, R. (2008) 'The power to shape decisions? An exploration of young people's power in participation.' *Health and Social Care in the Community 16*, 3, 253–261.

Habermas, J. (1973) *Knowledge and Human Interests.* London: Heinemann.

Hafford-Letchfield, T. (2007) *Practising Quality: Quality Assurance and Performance Management in Social Care.* Exeter: Learning Matters.

Hafford-Letchfield, T., Chick, N.F., Leonard, K. and Begum, N. (2008) *Leadership and Management in Social Care.* Thousand Oaks, CA, New Delhi, London: Sage.

Hafford-Letchfield, T. (2009) *Management and Organisations in Social Work* (2nd edn). Exeter: Learning Matters.

Hales, C. (1997) 'Power, Authority and Influence.' In A. Harris, N. Bennet and M. Preedy (eds) *Organizational Effectiveness and Improvement in Education.* Buckingham: Open University Press.

Hall, C. and Slembrouck, S. (2009) 'Professional categorization, risk management and inter-agency communication in public inquiries into disastrous outcomes.' *British Journal of Social Work 39*, 2, 280–298.

Hammersley, M. (2003) 'Conversation analysis and discourse analysis: Methods or paradigms?' *Discourse & Society 14*, 6, 751–781.

Harris, J. (2003) *The Social Work Business: The State of Welfare.* London: Routledge.

Harris, J. and White, V. (eds) (2009) *Modernising Social Work: Critical Considerations.* Bristol: The Policy Press.

Hartley, J. and Branicki, L. (2006) *Managing with Political Awareness: A Summary Review of the Literature.* London: Warwick Business School with the Chartered Management Institute.

Hartley, J. and Skelcher, C. (2008) 'The Agenda for Public Service Improvement.' In J. Hartley, C., Donaldson, C. Skelcher and M. Wallis (eds) Managing to Improve Public Services. Cambridge: Cambridge University Press.

Hernandez, L., Robson, P. and Sampson, A. (2010) 'Towards integrated participation: Involving seldom heard users of social care services.' *British Journal of Social Work, 40*, 3, 714–436. Advance access published on 9 September 2008, doi:10.1093/bjsw/bcn118.

HM Government (2003) *Every Child Matters.* Green Paper (CM 5860). London: The Stationery Office.

HM Government (2006) *Strong and Prosperous Communities.* (Cm 6939-I) Department of Communities and Local Government. London: The Stationery Office.

HM Government (2007a) *Strong and Prosperous Communities: The Local Government White Paper.* Department for Communities and Local Government. London: The Stationery Office.

HM Government (2009a) *Shaping the Future of Care Together.* Green Paper (CM 7673). London: The Stationery Office.

HM Government (2009b) *The Protection of Children in England: Action Plan. The Government's Response to Lord Laming.* London: The Stationery Office.

HM Treasury (2007) *Meeting the Aspirations of the British people: 2007 Pre-Budget Report and Comprehensive Spending Review.* Summary Leaflet. London: HM Treasury. Available from http://prebudget.treasury.gov.uk/pbrcsr07/docs/pbr07_leaflet.pdf, accessed on 8 March 2010.

HM Treasury (2009) *Securing the recovery: Growth and Opportunity.* Pre-budget report (CM7747), December. London: The Stationery Office.

Holmes, L., McDermid, S., Jones, A. and Ward, H. (2009) *How Social Workers Spend their Time: An Analysis of the Key Issues that Impact on Practice Pre- and Post Implementation of the Integrated Children's System.* Research Report DCSF-RR087. Loughborough: Loughborough University and Centre for Child and Family Research.

Hudson, B. (2005a) '"Not a cigarette paper between us": Integrated inspection of children's services in England.' *Social Policy and Administration 39*, 5, 513–522.

Hudson, B. (2005b) 'Will reforms suit users?' *Community Care* 28 July 2005–3 August 2005, 30–31.

Hughes, M. and Wearing, M. (2007) *Organisations and Management in Social Work.* London: Sage.

Hoyle, E. (1986) *The Politics of School Management,* London: Hodder and Stoughton.

Iles, V. and Sutherland, K. (2000) *Organisational Change: A Review for Health Care Managers, Professionals and Researchers.* London: NHS Service Delivery and Organisation R & D Programme.

Improvement and Development Agency (2006) *Ensuring Budgets Are Set to Reflect Operational Realities. Making Ends Meet.* London: Improvement and Development Agency. Available at www.makingendsmeet.idea.gov.uk/ idk/core/page.do?pageId=5127502, accessed on 8 March 2010.

Improvement and Development Agency (2008) *Making Successful Change Happen: Council Organisational Development in Action.* London: Improvement and Development Agency.

Institute of Public Policy Research (2001) *Building Better Partnerships: The Final Report of the Commission on Public Private Partnerships.* London: Institute of Public Policy Research.

Jackson, L. (2008) 'Food for Thought. Public Services Awards, Winners Special Report.' *Society Guardian* 26 November 2008. Available from www.SocietyGuardian.co.uk/publicservicesawards, accessed on 8 March 2010.

Jacobs, T., Shepherd, J. and Johnson, G. (1998) 'Strengths, Weaknesses, Opportunities and Threats (SWOT) Analysis.' In V. Ambrosini with G. Johnson and K. Scholes (eds) *Exploring Techniques of Analysis and Evaluation in Strategic Management.* London: Prentice Hall.

Janis, I.L. (1982) *Groupthink* (2nd edn). Boston, MA: Houghton Mifflin.

Jones, R. (2007) *Project Management Survival: A Practical Guide to Leading, Managing and Delivering Challenging Projects.* London and Philadelphia, PA: Kogan Page.

Jones, C. and Novak, T. (1999) *Poverty Welfare and the Disciplinary State.* London: Routledge.

Kelly, M.P., McDaid, D., Ludbrook, A. and Powell, J. (2005) *Economic Appraisal of Health Interventions.* London: Health Development Agency.

Kelly, M.P., McDaid, D., Ludbrook, A., Powell, J. and Kerslake, A. (2006) *An Approach to Outcome Based Commissioning and Contracting.* Care Services Improvement Partnership, Briefing Paper. London: Health Development Agency.

Kerslake, A. (2006) 'The Purchasing Process: An Approach to Outcome Based Commissioning and Contracting.' In Care Services Improvement Partnership and Health and Social Care Change Agent Team *Commissioning e-Book.* London: Department of Health. Available from www.dhcarenetworks.org.uk/_library/Resources/ BetterCommissioning/BetterCommissioning_advice/Chap9AKerslake.pdf, accessed on 8 March 2010.

Kings Fund (1992) *Living Options in Practice, Achieving User Participation: Planning Services for People with Severe Physical and Sensory Disabilities. Project Paper No. 3.* London: Kings Fund Centre.

Kirkpatrick, I. (2006) 'Taking stock of the new managerialism in English social services.' Social Work & Society 4, 1. Available (online only) from www.socwork.net/2006/1/series/professionalism/kirkpatrick/index_ html/?searchterm=Kirkpatrick, accessed on 31 March 2010.

Kirkpatrick, I., Ackroyd, S. and Walker, R. (2005) *The New Managerialism and Public Service Professions: Change in Health, Social Services, and Housing.* Hampshire: Palgrave Macmillan.

Kitson, A. (1988) *Quality and Standard Setting Workshop.* Birmingham: Directorate of Nursing and Quality.

Knapp, M. (1983) 'The outputs of older people's homes in the post-war period.' *International Journal of Sociology and Social Policy 3,* 30, 55–85.

Kramer, R. and Stafford, J. (2008) 'Involving people in the design and delivery of services.' *Journal of Care Services Management 2,* 4, 368–377.

Laing, W. (2008) *Calculating a Fair Market Price for Care: A Toolkit for Residential and Nursing Homes.* Bristol: The Policy Press with the Joseph Rowntree Foundation.

Lord Laming (2003) *The Victoria Climbié Inquiry: Report of an Inquiry by Lord Laming.* (Cm 5730). London: The Stationery Office.

Lord Laming (2009) *The Protection of Children in England: A Progress Report.* London: The Stationery Office.

Lawler, J. (2007) 'Leadership in social work: A case of caveat emptor?' *British Journal of Social Work 37,* 1, 123–141.

Lawler, J. and Bilson, A. (2010) *Social Work Management and Leadership: Managing Complexity with Creativity.* London and New York, NY: Routledge.

Leung, Z.C.S. (2007) 'Knowledge management in social work: Towards a conceptual framework.' *Journal of Technology in Human Services 25,* 1, 181–198.

Leung, Z.C.S. (2009) 'Knowledge management in social work: Types and processes of knowledge sharing in social service organizations.' *British Journal of Social Work 39,* 4, 693–709.

Levin, P. (1997) *Making Social Policy.* Buckingham: University Press.

Lewin, K. (1947) 'Frontiers in group dynamics: Channels of group life; social planning and action research.' *Human Relations 1,* 2, 143–153.

Lewis, J. (2007) 'Design Issues.' In J. Ritchie and J. Lewis (eds) *Qualitative Research Practice: A Guide for Social Science Students and Researchers.* London: Sage.

Mäkitalo, A. and Säljö, R. (2002) 'Invisible people: Institutional reasoning and reflexivity in the production of services and "social facts" in public employment agencies.' *Mind, Culture and Activity 9,* 3, 160–178.

Martin, V. and Henderson, E. (2001) *Managing in Health and Social Care.* London: Routledge with the Open University.

Martin, G.P. (2008) '"Ordinary people only": Knowledge, representativeness, and the publics of public participation in healthcare.' *Sociology of Health & Illness 30,* 1, 35–54.

Mauthner, N.S. and Doucet, A. (2003) 'Reflexive accounts and accounts of reflexivity in qualitative data analysis.' *Sociology 37*, 3, 413–431.

Mayo, E. (2009) 'Foreword.' In R. Simmons, M. Powell and I. Greener (eds) *The Consumer in Public Services: Choice, Values and Difference.* Bristol: The Policy Press.

McKimm, J. (2009) 'Professional Roles and Workforce Development.' In J. McKimm and K. Phillips (eds) *Leadership and Management in Integrated Services.* Exeter: Learning Matters.

McKimm, J. and Phillips, K. (2009) *Leadership and Management in Integrated Services.* Exeter: Learning Matters.

McLaughlin, K. (2010) 'The social worker versus the General Social Care Council: An analysis of care standards, tribunal hearings and decisions.' *British Journal of Social Work 40*, 1, 311–327.

McLaughlin, M. (2009) 'What's in a name: "Client", "patient", "customer", "consumer", "expert by experience", "service user" – what's next?' *British Journal of Social Work 39*, 6, 1101–1117.

Means, R., Richards, S. and Smith, R. (2008) *Community Care* (4th edn). Basingstoke: Palgrave MacMillan.

Mezirow, J. (1981) 'A critical theory of adult learning and education.' *Adult Education 32*, 1, 3–24.

Miles, M. and Huberman, A. (1994) *Qualitative Data Analysis: An Expanded Sourcebook.* London: Sage.

Mintzberg, H. (1985) 'The organisation as political arena.' *Journal of Management Studies 22*, 2, 133–154.

Moullin, M. (2003) *Delivering Excellence in Health and Social Care.* Maidenhead: Open University Press.

Munro, E. (2004) 'The impact of audit on social work practice.' *British Journal of Social Work 34*, 8, 1075–1095.

Nassehi, A., von der Hagen-Demszky, A. and Mayr, K. (2007) *The Structures of Knowledge and of Knowledge Production: Knowledge and Policy in Education and Health Sectors.* Project Report No. 0288848-2. Co-funded by the European Commission within the Sixth Framework Program. Available from www.knowandpol. eu/fileadmin/KaP/content/Scientific_reports/Literature_review/Nassehi_et_al_EN.pdf, accessed on 8 March 2010.

National Audit Office (2007) *Office of the Third Sector – Full Implementation of Full Cost Recovery: A Review by the National Audit Office.* London: National Audit Office.

National Council for Voluntary Organisations (undated) *A Little Bit of Give and Take: Voluntary Sector Accountability within Cross-Sectoral Partnerships.* London: National Council for Voluntary Organisations.

National Skills Academy for Social Care (2009) *Leadership and Management Prospectus.* London: National Skills Academy.

Needham, C. (2007) 'Realising the potential of co-production: Negotiating improvements in public services'. *Social Policy & Society 7*, 2, 221–231.

Needham, C. (2009) 'Narratives of Public Service Delivery in the UK: Comparing Central and Local Government.' In R. Simmons, M. Powell and I. Greener (eds) *The Consumer in Public Services: Choice, Values and Difference.* Bristol: The Policy Press.

Needham, C. and Carr, S. (2009) 'Co-production: An Emerging Evidence Base for Adult Social Care Transformation.' Research Briefing No. 31. London: Social Care Institute for Excellence.

Nelson, E.C., Splaine, M.E., Batalden, P.B. and Plume, S.K. (1998) 'Building measurement and data collection into medical practice.' *Annals of Internal Medicine 128*, 6, 460–466.

Newman, J. (2001) *Modernising Governance: New Labour, Policy and Society.* London: Sage.

Nonaka, I. (1994) 'A dynamic theory of organizational knowledge creation.' *Organization Science 5*, 1, 14–37.

Open University (undated) *Managing Projects through People.* Open Learn. Milton Keynes: The Open University. Available from http://openlearn.open.ac.uk/course/view.php?id=3549, accessed on 8 March 2010.

Parrott, L. (2005) 'The Political Drivers of Working in Partnership.' In R. Carnwell and J. Buchanan (eds) *Effective Practice in Health and Social Care: A Partnership Approach.* Berkshire: Open University Press.

Payne, M. (2001) *Modern Social Work Theory.* Basingstoke: Palgrave Macmillan.

Peck, E. and Dickinson, H. (2008) *Managing and Leading in Inter-Agency Settings.* Bristol: The Policy Press.

Pemberton, S. and Mason, J. (2008) 'Co-production and Sure Start children's centres: Reflecting upon users' perspectives and implications for service delivery, planning and evaluation.' *Social Policy & Society 8*, 1, 13–24.

Pettinger, R. (2001) *Mastering Management Skills.* Basingstoke: Palgrave.

Postle, K. and Beresford, P. (2007) 'Capacity building and the reconception of political participation.' *British Journal of Social Work 37*, 1, 143–158.

Poynter, K. (2008) 'Data Security is not Just a Matter of Technology.' *Financial Times*, 16 July 2008. Available from www.ft.com/cms/s/0/525bc6ec-526d-11dd-9ba7-000077b07658.html?nclick_check=1, accessed on 8 March 2010.

President of the Family Division (2009) *The President's interim guidance for England: agreement between the President of the Family Division, Ministry of Justice, HMCS, Department for Children, Schools and Families and CAFCASS.* High Court of Justice in England and Wales.

Preston-Shoot, M. (2009) 'Observations on the Development of Law and Policy for Integrated Practice.' In J. McKimm and K. Phillips (2003) *Leadership and Management in Integrated Services.* Exeter: Learning Matters.

Qureshi, H., Patmore, C., Nicholas, E. and Bamford, C. (1998) *Outcomes in Community Care Practice. Overview: Outcomes of Social Care for Older People and Carers.* Report No. 5. York: Social Policy Research Unit, University of York.

Ramsay, A. and Fulop, N. (2008) *Integrated Care Pilot Programme: The Evidence Base for Integrated Care.* London: Department of Health.

Reason, J. (2000) 'Human error: Models and management.' *British Medical Journal 320,* 7237, 768–770.

Rees, W.D. and Porter, C. (2003) *Skills of Management* (5th edn). London: Thompson Learning.

Research in Practice for Adults (RIPFA) (2008) *Support Brokerage, Key Issues 02.* Totnes: Research in Practice for Adults.

Rezania, D. and Lingham, T. (2009) 'Towards a method to disseminate knowledge from the post project review.' *Knowledge Management Research & Practice 7,* 2, 172–177.

Richardson, F. (2006) *The Commissioning Context: Introduction.* London: Department of Health with Care Services Improvement Partnership.

Robson, C. (1993) *Real World Research: A Resource for Social Scientists and Practitioner Researchers.* Oxford and Cambridge: Blackwell.

Rosenau, M.D, Jr. (1992) *Successful Project Management. A Step-by-Step Approach with Practical Examples.* New York, NY: Van Nostrand Reinhold.

Rose, N. (2000) 'Government control.' *British Journal of Criminology 40,* 2, 321–339.

Ruch, G. (2000) 'Self and social work: Towards an integrate model of learning.' *Journal of Social Work Practice 14,* 2, 99–112.

Saario, S. and Stepney, P. (2009) 'Managerial audit and community mental health: A study of rationalizing practices in Finnish psychiatric outpatient clinics.' *European Journal of Social Work 12,* 1, 41–56.

Sawyer, L. (2008) 'The personalisation agenda: Threats and opportunities for domiciliary care providers.' *Journal of Care Services Management 3,* 1, 41–63.

Schmidt, S., Bateman, I., Breinlinger-O'Reilly, J. and Smith, P. (2006) 'A management approach that drives actions strategically: Balanced scorecard in a mental health trust case study.' *International Journal of Health Care Quality Assurance 19,* 2, 119–136.

Schoech, D. and Toole, S. (1988) 'An Approach to Cross-Cultural Knowledge Engineering in the Domain of Child Welfare.' In B. Glastonbury, W. Lamendola and S. Toole (eds) *Information Technology and the Human Services.* Chichester: John Wiley & Sons.

Schön, D. (1983) *The Reflective Practitioner.* New York, NY: Basic Books.

Scott, J., Moore, T. and Ward, H. (2005) 'Evaluating Interventions and Monitoring Outcomes.' In J. Scott and H. Ward (eds) *Safeguarding and Promoting the Well-Being of Children, Families and Communities.* London: Jessica Kingsley Publishers.

Scottish Community Development Centre (2005) *National Standards for Community Engagement.* Edinburgh: Communities Scotland. Available from www.scdc.org.uk/uploads/standards_booklet.pdf, accessed on 8 March 2010.

Scourfield, P. (2007) 'Social Care and the Modern Citizen: Client, Consumer, Service user, Manager and Entrepreneur.' *British Journal of Social Work 37,* 1, 107–122.

Scourfield, P. (2010) 'Going for brokerage: A task of "independent support" or social work?' *British Journal of Social Work, 40,* 3, 858–877. Advance access published on 21 October 2008, doi:10.1093/bjsw/bcn141.

Seden, J. (2003) 'Managers and their Organisations.' In J. Henderson and D. Atkinson (eds) *Managing Care in Context.* London: Routledge.

Sefton, T. (2000) 'Getting Less for More: Economic Evaluation in the Social Welfare Field.' LSE STICERD Research Paper No. Case 044. London: Centre for the Analysis of Social Exclusion. Available from http://sticerd.lse.ac.uk/dps/case/cp/CASEpaper44.pdf, accessed on 8 March 2010.

Semple Piggot, C. (2002) *Business Planning for Healthcare Management* (2nd edn). Buckingham and Philadelphia, PA: Open University Press.

Sennet, R. (2006) *The Culture of the New Capitalism.* London and New Haven, CT: Yale University Press.

Shaw, I. and Norton, M. (2007) *The Kinds and Quality of Social Work Research in UK Universities.* London: Social Care Institute for Excellence.

Sheafor, B.W. and Horejsi, C.R. (2005) *Techniques and Guidelines for Social Work Practice* (4th edn). Boston, MA: Allyn & Bacon.

Simmons, L. (2007) *Social Care Governance: A Practice Workbook.* Produced by the Department of Health, Social Services and Public Safety. London: Social Care Institute for Excellence.

Simmons, R., Powell, M. and Greener, I. (eds) (2009) *The Consumer in Public Services: Choice, Values and Difference.* Bristol: The Policy Press.

Skills for Care (2007) *National Minimum Data Set for Social Care.* Leeds: Skills for Care.

Skills for Care (2008) *Leadership and Management Strategy Update 2008: Transforming Adult Social Care.* Leeds: Skills for Care. www.skillsforcare.org.uk/developingskills/leadership-and-management/, accessed 30 November 2008.

Snape, D. and Spencer, L. (2007) 'The Foundations of Qualitative Research.' In J. Ritchie and J. Lewis (eds) *Qualitative Research Practice: A Guide for Social Science Students and Researchers.* London: Sage.

Social Care Institute for Excellence (2009) *At a Glance 06: Personalisation Briefing, Implications for Commissioners.* London: Social Care Institute for Excellence.

Social Care Workforce Research Unit (2009) *Annual Report 2008–2009.* London: Kings College, University of London.

Social Services Inspectorate and Audit Commission (undated) *Making Ends Meet: Financial Planning and Management. A Joint Reviews Initiative.* London: The Audit Commission.

Spicker, P. (2007) 'The ethics of policy research.' *Evidence and Policy 3,* 1, 99–118.

Staley, K. (2009) *Exploring Impact: Public Involvement in NHS, Public Health and Social Care Research.* Eastleigh: INVOLVE.

Stanford, S. (2008) 'Taking a stand or playing it safe?: Resisting the moral conservatism of risk social work practice.' *European Journal of Social Work 11,* 3, 209–220.

Stanley, N. and Manthorpe, J. (eds) (2004) *The Age of Inquiry: Learning and Blaming in Health and Social Care.* London: Routledge.

Stonewall (2010) *Stonewall Top 100 Employers 2010: The Workplace Equality Index.* London: Stonewall.

Taylor, G. (2009) 'The reconfiguration of risk in the British state.' *Public Policy and Administration 24,* 4, 379–398.

Taylor, S. (2001) 'Locating and Conducting Discourse Analytic Research.' In M. Wetherall, S. Taylor and S.J. Yates (eds) *Discourse as Data: A Guide for Analysis.* London, Thousand Oaks, CA, New Delhi: Sage in association with The Open University.

Taylor, C. and White, S. (2006) 'Knowledge and reasoning in social work: Educating for humane judgement.' *British Journal of Social Work 36,* 6, 937–954.

Thompson, N. (2003) *Promoting Equality: Challenging Discrimination and Oppression* (2nd edn). Basingstoke: Palgrave Macmillan.

Tilbury, C. (2004) 'The influence of performance measurement on child welfare policy and practice.' *British Journal of Social Work 34,* 2,224–241.

Training and Development Agency for Schools (2006) *Extended Schools: An Overview.* London: Teachers Development Agency.

Tsui, M.S. and Cheung, F.C.H. (2004) 'Gone with the wind: The impacts of managerialism in human services.' *British Journal of Social Work 34,* 3, 437–442.

Turner, M., Brough, P. and Findlay-Williams, R.B. (2003) *Our Voice in Our Future: Service Users Debate the Future of the Welfare State.* York: Joseph Rowntree Foundation.

University of East Anglia and National Children's Bureau (2006) *National Evaluation of Children's Trusts: Realising Children's Trust Arrangements,* Cambridge: Institute of Technology.

Waine, B. and Henderson, J. (2003) 'Managers, Managing and Managerialism.' In J. Henderson and D. Atkinson (eds) *Managing Care in Context.* London: Routledge.

Walker, N. (2007) *Key Activities in Commissioning Social Care: Lessons from the Care Services Improvement Partnership Commissioning Exemplar Project, Second Edition.* London: Department of Health.

Waters, D. (2007) *Personal Budgets: A Guide for Local Authorities on Creating a Local System on Self-Directed Support.* Guide 1, Version 4. Wythall: In Control.

Watson, D. (2004) 'Managing quality enhancement in the personal social services: A front-line assessment of its impact on service provision with residential childcare.' *The International Journal of Public Sector Management 17,* 2, 153–165.

Webb, A. (1991) 'Co-ordination: A problem in public sector management.' *Policy and Politics 19,* 4, 229–242.

Webb, S.A. (2006) *Social Work in a Risk Society: Social and Political Perspectives.* Houndsmills: Palgrave Macmillan.

Weber, M. (1972) *Essays in Sociology.* New York, NY: Oxford University Press. Trans. from Weber, M. ([1921] 1972) *Wirtschaft und Gesellschaft, 1. Halbband. 4. Auflage.* Tübingen: Mohr.

Weindling, D. (1977) 'Strategic Planning in Schools: Some Practical Techniques.' In M. Preedy, R. Glatter and R. Levacici (eds) *Educational Management Strategy: Quality and Resources.* Buckingham: Open University Press.

Weiner, M.E. (1994) *Human Services Management: Analysis and Applications* (2nd edn). Storrs, CT: University of Connecticut.

Weiner, M.E. and Petrella, P. (2007) 'The Impact of New Technology: Implications for Social Work and Social Care Managers.' In J. Aldgate, L. Healy, B. Malcolm, B. Pine, W. Rose and J. Seden (eds) *Enhancing Social Work Management.* London: Jessica Kingsley Publishers.

Weiss, J.W. and Wysocki, R.K. (1992) *5-phase Project Management: A Practical Planning and Implementation Guide.* Reading, MA: Addison-Wesley.

White, V. (2009) 'Quiet Challenges? Professional Practice in Modernised Social Work.' In J. Harris and V. White (eds) *Modernising Social Work: Critical Considerations.* Bristol: Policy Press.

Willke, H. (2002) *Dystopia: Studien zur Krisis des Wissens in der modernen Gesellschaft.* Frankfurt: Suhrkamp.

Wistow, G. and Barnes, M. (1993) 'User involvement and community care.' *Public Administration 71,* 1, 279–299.

Yip, K.-S. (2006) 'Self-reflection in reflective practice: A note of caution.' *British Journal of Social Work 36,* 5, 777–788.

Zarb, G. and Nadash, P. (1994) *Cashing in on Independence: Comparing the Costs and Benefits of Cash and Services.* London: British Council of Organisations of Disabled People.

Contributors to Manager's Comments

Neil Chick has worked for nearly 30 years in social care, initially with children and then with adults and older people. He now works in organisation development and learning in housing and adult social care, with a particularly strong interest in coach mentoring, diversity and equality of opportunity and the impact of workplace learning on widening participation in adult learning and self-esteem.

Angie Lymer-Cox is a manager with Leicestershire County Council where she has worked for the last 15 years. Angie manages a team of staff that work with young people who are in care or are care leavers. She holds a profound belief that we all have skills and that with the right support and guidance they will appear.

Ann Flynn is a service manager in Cafcass (Child and Family Court Advisory and Support Service), and she manages an early intervention team which ensures children's representation by a social work professional at all first hearings in the family court. Ann has worked as a social worker and manager for 22 years, mainly with children and their families, and as an academic in social work education.

John MacDonough is a founder member of Richmond Care, a social enterprise run by and for people with learning disabilities. John is also a senior lecturer in social work at London South Bank University, and has a background in social work and service provision for people with learning disabilities.

Gwynn Raynes is an experienced child and family social worker and has been working in the National Society for the Prevention of Cruelty to Children (NSPCC) since the late 1990s. She manages a multi-agency team and holds a number of specialist and advanced awards in both child care and leadership and management. Gwynn has a special interest in domestic violence and children's participation.

Ali Burrow-Smith is a senior manager and registered social worker at National Health Service (NHS) Peterborough. She has been studying for an MSc in leadership and management at Leicester University. Ali's research interests include access to health and social care information, language and bureaucracy.

Lucy Titmuss is a service manager in a children and families social care organisation and has over 15 years' social work experience of specialising in working with children and families.

Subject Index

Author Index